THE CHOSEN HIGHWAY

THE CHOSEN HIGHWAY

By
LADY BLOMFIELD
(Sitárih <u>Kh</u>ánum)

"I am walking my chosen highway.
I know the destination."—*'Abdu'l-Bahá.*

LONDON
THE BAHÁ'Í PUBLISHING TRUST
46 Bloomsbury Street, W.C.1

George Ronald, *Publisher*
Oxford
www.grbooks.com

© National Spiritual Assembly of the
Bahá'ís of the United Kingdom

All Rights Reserved

First published by
the Bahá'í Publishing Trust, London 1940

Reprinted by
the Bahá'í Publishing Trust, Wilmette, Illinois
1956, 1966, 1970, 1975

Reprinted by George Ronald 2007, 2015

ISBN 978–0–85398–509–9

Cover photographs: Copyright © Denny Allen
Cover design by Steiner Graphics

PREFACE

Shortly before her passing on the last day of the year 1939, Lady Blomfield asked me to write this preface. To my infinite regret, it was not prepared in time to obtain her approval. And now I feel that I cannot let this opportunity go without paying my share of humble tribute to the shining memory of a gracious lady who served the Cause of Bahá'u'lláh with never-failing vigour and devotion. It is indeed hard to believe that Sitárih Khánum is no longer with us in her earthly temple. The contagion of her enthusiasm and the brilliance of her talk and description, her close association with the Master and His family, her unique privileges in the service of the Cause, the intense light of her faith and the captivating charm of her presence, to enumerate some of her qualities and qualifications, made her loved and revered by all. It is a great joy that she was permitted to bring this book to its conclusion before her departure to realms beyond.

The Chosen Highway will forever remain the greatest monument to the achievements of its author. Those who have met Sitárih Khánum in person will cherish this book in the tenderness of her remembrance. To others who know of her work, it will convey a vivid portrait of her gifts of the spirit. And to generations unborn it will hand a message rich in enlightenment.

The avowed adherent of Bahá'u'lláh cannot be alone in feeling incalculable gratitude to Sitárih Khánum. Every earnest student of the Bahá'í Faith will find in *The Chosen Highway* a wealth of material essential to the study of history. In my possession are two letters written by Professor Edward Granville Browne, of Pembroke College, Cambridge, to my father, in which he makes enquiries regarding the life and the origins of the Báb. Urging his correspondent to help him in his research, he states: "I am very anxious to get as accurate an account of all the details connected with the Bábí Movement as possible, for in my eyes the whole seems one of the most interesting and important events that has occurred since the rise of Christianity and Muḥammadanism, and I feel it my duty, as well as pleasure, to try as far as in me lies to bring the matter to the notice of my countrymen, that they may consider it . . . for suppose anyone could tell us more about the childhood and early life and appearance of Christ, for instance, how glad we should be to know it. Now it is impossible to find out much . . . but in the case of the Báb it *is* possible. . . . So let us earn the thanks of posterity, and provide against that day now."

Sitárih Khánum's work provides the intimate detail, which Edward Browne meant to seek and record, within the limits set by the author herself. *The Chosen Highway* offers every seeker a real feast of knowledge. It cannot but eternally merit the esteem of the historian.

But the true greatness of this work does not lie in its compendium of narrative and chronicle. It is the spiritual purport of *The Chosen Highway*, the pattern of love, justice, charity, and sacrifice that it weaves and depicts, the chord of harmony that it strikes, which place it in prominent relief. To a world shaken to its depths, it brings the assurance that evil can never achieve the final, the abiding victory.

H. M. BALYUZI.

LONDON, *March* 1940.

EDITOR'S NOTE

It was my privilege, not only to know Lady Blomfield, but to discuss with her, in company with Mr. Balyuzi, the publication of *The Chosen Highway*, and I was present when she asked him to write a preface. As a representative of the Bahá'í Publishing Trust, she authorized me to publish the book and to attend to the final arrangement of the manuscript.

An examination of her notes shows that at one time she had visualized the book as an historical outline of the Bahá'í Faith. This is disclosed in the rough draft of a letter to Lord Lamington, dated 14th March, 1939. "The book I am writing begins in Persia, before the proclamation of the Báb." The notes outline a continuous narrative down to the time when 'Abdu'l-Bahá returned to the shelter of heaven. "To this story is added some narrative of the progress of the Faith down to the present day, including the immense work of the Guardian, Shoghi Effendi, in administering the affairs of the Cause in forty countries, embracing eight hundred Assemblies, the members of which are quietly proceeding to awaken mankind to the necessity for a spiritual outlook on the problems of this great day."

Her desire to write the story of the Faith of Bahá'u'lláh in later times was not fulfilled. But we may be exceedingly thankful that the early history received the full measure of her attention and ardent devotion. During her two visits to the Holy Land she listened to the stories of Bahá'u'lláh's daughter, 'Abdu'l-Bahá's wife, His four daughters, and of several people who played a part in the Heroic Age of the Faith. In addition to this she received 'Abdu'l-Bahá when He came to London. Her qualifications for writing of the early days were thus unique.

The editing and preparing for press was greatly simplified by the amount of work which Sitárih Khánum herself had done, and by the many discussions I had had with her. I wish to express sincere thanks to Mrs. Basil Hall, her daughter, who gave the manuscript into my hands, for all the help which she has given. I am also deeply grateful to Mr. Balyuzi, both for his knowledge and his work. The uniform accuracy of the transliteration of Oriental words is due entirely to him, and his knowledge of the events described and the persons and places mentioned has been invaluable.

The system of transliteration used throughout is one adopted by a conference of Orientalists at Oxford, and recommended by Shoghi Effendi, Guardian of the Bahá'í Faith.

In that part of the book which contains the "Spoken Chronicles" (mainly Part II) it has been necessary to indicate where the actual narrative has been amplified and explained by Lady Blomfield. The simplest way to do this seemed to be by the use of stars to separate the spoken word from Lady Blomfield's own writing. Thus the reader will find, during the "Spoken Chronicles," that the story often ends thus   *   *   * . The following passage is Lady Blomfield's own, and is ended in the same way, after which the spoken narrative begins again.

In the original manuscript, the "Spoken Chronicles" are written down in a series of single sentences. This is understood when we realize that, as the speaker related the story, it was translated sentence by sentence, and written in that way. These sentences have been connected into paragraphs, thereby making a more flowing story, but no other alterations have been made.

Except in a few instances the old name of Persia has been used for Írán, since at the time the events recorded took place it was called Persia, and the chief characters always used the older name.

The pleasure and profit which I derived from many visits to Lady Blomfield "to talk about the book" remain with me. She asked for the cover to be in Irish blue, and this in itself will bring her to mind, but, in addition, now that she has returned to the presence of 'Abdu'l-Bahá, she will not object to the inclusion of a photograph of her beautiful and saintly face.

DAVID HOFMAN.

LONDON, *May* 1940.

PUBLISHER'S NOTE, 2007

Eighty-five years have passed since Lady Blomfield began to take written notes of the "spoken chronicles" of the ladies of the Family of Bahá'u'lláh. It was during her first visit to Haifa in 1922, "in the first days of mourning for the beloved Master's passing" that she listened to the Greatest Holy Leaf telling the story of her childhood and youth during the terrible imprisonment and exiles of Bahá'u'lláh, and began what she describes in her immortal book as "an attempt to indicate some phases of a great historic moment in the life of Spiritual Civilization, which have not been elsewhere recorded".

"I shall never forget the day news came of the passing of the Master," wrote Lady Blomfield's daughter Mary Basil Hall. "The Guardian was in London at the time, and his grief was heartbreaking to witness. My mother travelled with him to Haifa, and, I believe, her companionship and help were of service to him, stricken with overwhelming sorrow as he was."

No reader of *The Chosen Highway* or of the description of its author in the Preface by H. M. Balyuzi can fail to appreciate the qualities of warmth, spirit and faith that enabled her first to elicit and then to faithfully chronicle the stories told to her by Bahíyyih Khánum and by 'Abdu'l-Bahá's wife and daughters. No professional historian would have been taken into their confidence in the same way. "Her presence gives us much joy," wrote Munírih Khánum. "We look upon her, not only as a friend, but as one of our own dear family."

These accounts, together with Lady Blomfield's own description of 'Abdu'l-Bahá's visit to London when she welcomed him as a guest in her home, have ensured the lasting interest of *The Chosen Highway*. It gives us great pleasure to republish her book, photographed from the original edition published in 1940 for the British Bahá'í Publishing Trust by George Ronald's founder, David Hofman.

MAY HOFMAN

OXFORD *January* 2007

CONTENTS

	PAGE
PREFACE	v
EDITOR'S NOTE	vii
CONTENTS	xi
INTRODUCTION	1

PART I
THE BÁB

The Báb	11
Tablet of His Holiness the Báb	25
The Waiting Servants	26
The Body of the Báb	30

PART II
BAHÁ'U'LLÁH

The Spoken Chronicle of Bahíyyih Khánum

CHAPTER I.	Írán	39
CHAPTER II.	The Intrigues of Ṣubḥ-i-Azal	48
CHAPTER III.	Baghdád	53
CHAPTER IV.	Constantinople and Adrianople	59
CHAPTER V.	'Akká	65

The Spoken Chronicle of Muníríh Khánum

CHAPTER I.	Visit to Shíráz	75
CHAPTER II.	'Abdu'l-Bahá	80
CHAPTER III.	The Bride of 'Abdu'l-Bahá	84

The Spoken Chronicle of Ṭúbá Khánum

CHAPTER I.	Ásíyih Khánum	93
CHAPTER II.	Bahá'u'lláh in 'Akká	95
CHAPTER III.	'Abdu'l-Bahá in 'Akká	99
CHAPTER IV.	The Passing of Bahá'u'lláh	105
CHAPTER V.	The Marriage of Ḍíyáíyyih Khánum	112

The Spoken Chronicles of:
 Mírzá Asadu'lláh Ká<u>sh</u>ání . . 119
 Sakínih-Sultán <u>Kh</u>ánum . . . 129
 Siyyid 'Alí Yazdí 131

PART III
'ABDU'L-BAHÁ

CHAPTER I. 1892 to 1908 135
CHAPTER II. 'Abdu'l-Bahá in London . . . 147
CHAPTER III. 'Abdu'l-Bahá in Paris . . . 179
CHAPTER IV. 'Abdu'l-Bahá in War-time . . . 188
 Abú-Sinán 189
 First Visit of Rúhá <u>Kh</u>ánum to
  Abú-Sinán 198
 The Story of Mírzá Jalál Isfahání . 202
 Hájí Ramadán 206
 Bahá'í Villages 209
 The Master 211
CHAPTER V. Danger to 'Abdu'l-Bahá, His Family and
 Friends, and How it was Averted . 219

PART IV
VARIOUS DOCUMENTS

Letter from Lady Blomfield to Her Daughter . . 230
Letter from Mrs. Thornburgh-Cropper . . . 234
Story of Mírzá Ahmad told to Sitárih <u>Kh</u>ánum . . 237
The Story of <u>Sh</u>ay<u>kh</u> Mahmúd 239
The Famous Red Robe "Tradition" . . . 242
Notes on the Ba<u>gh</u>dád Period 243
The "Kitáb-i-Íqán" 245
From Memories of Nabíl 247
The Azalís in 'Akká 250
Bahá'u'lláh: A Discourse by 'Abdu'l-Bahá . . 256

INTRODUCTION

One day at a reception in Paris, at the house of Madame Lucien Monod, my daughter Mary and I heard these words from Miss Bertha Herbert:

"If I *look* happy, it is because I *am* happy. I have found the desire of my heart!"

The speaker, a tall, graceful girl with shining dark eyes, came across the room and seated herself between us.

"I should like to tell you why I am so happy. May I?"

"Yes," we answered.

"It is true! True!"

We fixed questioning eyes upon her glowing face.

"We have been taught to believe that a great Messenger would again be sent to the world: He would set forth to gather together all the peoples of good will in every race, nation, and religion on the earth. Now is the appointed time! He has come! He has come!"

These amazing words struck a chord to which my inner consciousness instantly responded, and I felt convinced that the portentous announcement they conveyed was indeed the truth. Great awe and intense exaltation possessed me with an overpowering force as I listened.

Miss Herbert continued:

"The Bearer of the Message suffered much persecution, and left an uncomprehending world in 1892. But His Son is still a captive in the fortress prison of 'Akká in Palestine."

"For the Cause of God I am a prisoner," said 'Abdu'l-Bahá.

"You *are* interested?" she asked.

"Indeed, yes, how could we fail to be interested?"

The news of the momentous event, long prayed for, steadfastly awaited in the "Faith, which is the substance of things hoped for," had come.

How should we not be *interested*?

"There is a lady in Paris," continued Miss Herbert, "who has just returned from a visit to 'Akká (St. Jean d'Acre). She had the privilege of speaking with 'Abbás Effendi, the name by which He is known in Palestine.

"Would you care to meet this lady? Shall I make an appointment?"

"Please, if you will be so kind."

Miss Herbert rose to go—but before she reached the door she came back.

"I do not know where you live, or even your name!"

These were outer, but necessary details!

The appointment was made. We were introduced to Miss Ethel Rosenberg and Monsieur Hippolyte Dreyfus. These two friends of 'Abbás Effendi told me much concerning the sacred task of the Great One, Bahá'u'lláh.

On our return to London we attended some meetings held at the Higher Thought Centre. There we learned that Mrs. Thornburgh-Cropper had been the first to bring the marvellous news to England. She and Miss Rosenberg welcomed all who were eager to investigate everything connected with the Event. Under the guidance of these two devoted ladies we met to make plans for spreading the glad tidings.

At this time we had the pleasure of hearing Mr. Wellesley Tudor-Pole, who explained to us the deeper significance of what afterwards became known as the Great Event of the Bahá'í Cause. The term "Bahá'í" may be rendered "Dweller in the City of God," "Follower of the Light," "Believer in Bahá'u'lláh."

I have given the title of *The Chosen Highway* to this work. It is not intended to be a connected history of the momentous events which took place as the New Cycle of Human Consciousness dawned upon the world. It is an attempt to indicate some phases of a great historic moment in the life of Spiritual Civilization, which have not been elsewhere recorded, but are supplementary to existing literature on the subject.

My desire is that this series of Spoken Narratives may serve to show the steps which marked the way towards the recognition of the "Glorious Day of God," and how some of the "Waiting Servants" arose to take the place destined for them; of how they became so preoccupied with things of the Spirit that

INTRODUCTION

material things lost their value in those early days of the New Dispensation.

Bahá'u'lláh's command restores the purity of religion to the religions of the world.

This Chronicle also seeks to show how the celestial power, when held fast by Faith and Works, is able to accomplish what we have been accustomed to regard as the miraculous.

Having been privileged to enjoy opportunities of intimate association with the family of Bahá'u'lláh and of 'Abdu'l-Bahá, during my visits to Their home in Haifa, I made notes at those times, and am now prompted to use them in the belief that they will be of wide interest. Many of these opportunities occurred whilst our roof in London had the honour of sheltering 'Abdu'l-Bahá, Who had brought the very words of His Father to us in Britain.

Bahá'u'lláh spoke with the power of the Great Ether*; its operation becomes manifest in the "Awakening." His Words of Power were heard, not only by the scribes, who wrote them down, but the sound of them went forth into all the world, and reached the inner hearing of the Waiting Servants. These devoted ones, born in every religion, every race, and every nation, were standing well-prepared on every hand to arise and set about their Father's business, when they should hear the Awakening Call.

The divine powers are focussed in the Spirit of the Messenger, Who ushers in the New Dispensation. This Messenger was described as "a glorious Sun, which burst upon a dark and dreary world; that world which is sick unto death. None but the Divine Physician has the power to heal."

Hearers, who were attuned, received the Word; to others it was as foolishness, to be "despised and rejected."

Ever since these days, when this call to awakening was heard in Britain, it gradually became the foremost desire of my heart to spread the message which I had myself received; so it was that this volume took shape, and it is at this present moment of world crisis that the reassuring words of 'Abdu'l-Bahá are uppermost in my mind. "This is a radiant century." In spite

---
* See page 134.

of the encircling gloom, that radiance is to be found abundantly in Bahá'u'lláh's teaching.

There are many notable signs of the awakening now in progress. Men and women everywhere, and the youth of both sexes in particular, are devoting their energies to the service of great ideals.

National service in itself is a training for the reconstruction which must take place in the world before the Will of God can be done upon Earth as it is in Heaven. National service is great, but world service is greater.

"Let not a man glory in this that he loves his country," said Bahá'u'lláh. "Let him rather glory in this that he loves his kind."

It is borne in on our minds that we may gather not only hope but certainty that the reconstruction we look for has begun; men and women in all parts of the world are working for it either consciously or unconsciously. The scheme of a Great Century enfolds us. It is for us to realize this truth, and make the fullest response that is in our power to meet the demands which Destiny makes upon us to bring the Divine purpose to fruition.

The keynote of the Bahá'í message is *Unity*. "Be united, be united," said 'Abdu'l-Bahá, addressing representatives of many humanitarian and religious bodies.

"Those of you who are working separately are as ants, but working together you will be as eagles; when working separately you will be as drops or little rivulets of water, but when working in union you will be a mighty river carrying the Water of Life into the barren desert places of the world; and," He added, "it is rather dangerous to be an isolated drop; you might be spilt or blown away."

In presenting, however inadequately, this Chronicle to the world, I am deeply conscious of the vital import of the Message it conveys to humanity, and of the reality of the truth it expresses. These are the latter days that herald the glorious day of God, in fulfilment of the prophecies which have come to us down the ages, through prophets, poets, and seers. In the great Indian classic, the Bhagavad Gita, we are reminded of the coming of this glorious day:

INTRODUCTION

"When there is decay of righteousness and there is exaltation of unrighteousness then I myself come forth for the protection of the good, for the destruction of the evildoer. I am born from age to age. The foolish regard me not when clad in human semblance, being ignorant of my true nature, the Great Lord of Being."

With that coming forth we listen with uplifted hearts to-day to the clarion voice of Bahá'u'lláh:

"*These ruinous wars shall cease and the Most Great Peace shall come.*"

LONDON, 1939.

PART I

THE BÁB

"No sooner had mankind attained the stage of maturity, than the Word revealed to men's eyes the latent energies with which it had been endowed, energies which manifested themselves in the plenitude of their glory when the Ancient Beauty appeared in the year sixty* in the person of 'Alí Muḥammad, the Báb."
Bahá'u'lláh.

"All created things have their degree or stage of maturity. . . . In the human kingdom, man reaches his maturity when the light of his intelligence attains the greatest power and development. . . . There are periods and stages in the collective life of humanity. At one time . . . the stage of childhood, at another . . . the period of youth, but now it has entered upon its long-predicted phase of maturity. . . . Humanity has emerged from its former state of limitation and preliminary training. New powers, new moral standards, new capacities are awaiting and already descending upon him. The gifts and blessings of the period of youth, although timely and sufficient during the adolescence of mankind, are now incapable of meeting the requirements of maturity."
'Abdu'l-Bahá.

---

* 1260 A.H.

PART I

The Báb

In order better to understand the extraordinary character of the great events which took place, as recorded in this Chronicle, it might be well briefly to consider a certain aspect of the religious world of Persia in the first decades of the nineteenth century.

Numerous Muslim thinkers are known to have been expecting the coming of the Twelfth Imám.* Many of the prophecies pointed to the year A.H. 1260 corresponding to A.D. 1844.

Each of the divisions of these religious people was looking for One, who should fulfil all prophecy, according to their own particular explanation.

This "Coming" was to them an event of the very greatest importance—nobody was apathetic, everybody cared. The enthusiasm was real, and became fanatical whenever an interpretation of any particular prophecy was suggested, differing from that which they accepted as "Orthodox."

At this time there were two learned, highly honoured, and saintly men, Shaykh Ahmad-i-Ahsá'í and Siyyid Kázim-i-Rashtí. These two were the only men of the large number of Mullás and scholars in Persia who, at that time, had any vision of the near approach of the Holy One, the Forerunner. They set themselves to the work of preparation for the Great Day, ignoring personal risk of persecution or death.

They taught to their followers, the Shaykhís, as they were called, three chief articles of faith:

FIRST:

The Spiritual interpretation of the Qur'án, which had become obscured in the superficial reading; the rescue of it, so to speak,

---

* It is good to remember that these Muslim Mystics were acquainted with the Christian Scriptures, and acknowledged "His Holiness Christ," as the "Spirit of God."

from the strictly literal, which they held to be stultifying to the souls and minds of the people, veiling the Truth from them. "The letter killeth, but the Spirit giveth Life."

SECOND:
That the "ascent" of Muḥammad to Heaven was a spiritual event, not a literal journey.

THIRD:
They believed, not in the resurrection of the material body, but in the resurrection of the soul, the spiritual body.

Now the Shaykhí sect was much hated and reviled by the Mullás, although the ordinary person knew very little of the teaching, which was given in close secrecy, and their written leaflets were most carefully guarded by the initiated.

Their interpretation of the prophecies led them to look for the Coming of that Imám, the Qá'im, who should be their Divine Leader; this "Coming" they held to be imminent, indeed they became more and more convinced that He was already on earth.

Therefore it naturally came about that the members of the Shaykhí sect were standing well prepared to hail the Imám, when He should proclaim Himself.

Siyyid Káẓim, who succeeded Shaykh Aḥmad, gave directions to his followers that, as soon as he should have passed into the invisible world, they were to go into every part of the country separately, and search for the Imám, who, he assured them, *was already on earth waiting to call the people.*

He directed them to prepare themselves by prayer, and by purifying their hearts, to recognize that Promised One, to announce whose appearance it was the mission of himself and of his friend, Shaykh Aḥmad.

He gave them certain signs, by which they should know this divinely-sent Herald.

These signs were written down in the form of a five-pointed star, following the chief lines of the human body—filled with Persian and Arabic writing.

"He would be young—neither tall nor short—large, kind, dark eyes, finely pencilled brows.

He would not smoke, nor drink alcohol.

He would be uninstructed in the learning of the world, His knowledge would be immanent.
He would be of the 'pure lineage,' that is a Siyyid, a descendant of the prophet Muḥammad."

Siyyid 'Alí Muḥammad was born at Shíráz in the year 1819. His father, having died when He was still a child, His mother took Him to live with herself and her brother, Hájí Siyyid 'Alí. His devoted mother and uncle brought Him up with loving care.
Many are the stories told of His childhood.
He showed that His knowledge was innate.
His schoolmaster came to His uncle and said: "If you pay school fees to me, it is a present! I can teach him nothing! His explanations of difficult passages in the Qur'án are marvellous! His answers to complex problems are amazing!"
His mother one day rebuked a servitor after the ablution in preparation for the sunset prayer.
"Beloved Mother," said Siyyid 'Alí Muḥammad, then a child of six, "would it not be well to repeat the purifying ablution before praying—that the rebuke may not tarnish thy prayer?"
So gentle and loving was His character that all who knew Him loved Him. The beauty of His mind was reflected in His person. He passed all His time, when He was not dutifully helping His uncle in his work, in meditating upon the Holy books.
"Surely," said the people, "He is a heavenly soul, this youth who walks with the dignified and serene step, who is of so shining a countenance, and withal so beautiful, and, moreover, greatly learned in the Sacred Writings."
Now there was a sweet and lovely cousin of Siyyid 'Alí Muḥammad named Khadíjih-Sultán-Bagum; these two had played together as little children, and had been great friends.
According to the custom of the country they did not meet as they began to grow up.
One night Khadíjih-Sultán-Bagum had a vision, which many years afterwards she related to Muníríh Khánum, wife of 'Abdu'l-Bahá, who was destined to play a great rôle in this amazing tale:
"I dreamed a dream in which Fátimih, the daughter of Muḥammad, came to me and said: 'Arise! I desire that you

become the wife of my son.' So majestic she looked, as she stood, tall, slender, and graceful, so wonderful was the beautiful mien, so marvellous her loveliness of expression, so glorious her countenance, that I could no longer gaze upon her, but looked down, feeling overcome with awe, and all unworthy of so high an honour.

"I did not speak of this vision to my sisters; they would have thought me to be filled with pride and self-assertion! But the vision filled my thoughts day and night; it seemed to enfold me in a kind of sacred atmosphere of joy indescribable!

"A few days after this vision, the mother of my playmate of years agone, Siyyid 'Alí Muḥammad, came to me, and standing in the self-same attitude, and in the very same spot as the visitant of my dream, spoke words to me, which I understood as conveying her wish that I should be the wife of her son.

"By this I became aware that her son, afterwards my glorious husband, was a Chosen One!"

Accordingly this lovely girl became the wife of Siyyid 'Alí Muḥammad. All the people wondered at the sublime beauty of the bridal pair.

Alas, that their happiness should be of so brief duration, should be cut short by one of the great world tragedies!

Theirs was a marriage of pure love; they both came of a family who took but one wife; this was remarkable, as the custom of the country was to marry two if not more, and it was often made very difficult to evade this custom!

In many ways the family was held in an almost sacred veneration by the friends and neighbours, both of high and of low degree.

One evening He, Siyyid 'Alí Muḥammad, said to His bride, as the newly wedded pair sat together:

"To-night there will come a very particularly dear friend, whom I am earnestly expecting; go to your rest; do not wait up for me, he may be quite late."

She saw a grave expression of determination on His face, as she rose to obey His wish; her intuitive soul at once understood that the guest for whom He waited must be of no ordinary kind.

As she went she turned to look at her Husband, the beautiful youth with the serene, earnest face, who then, as though in answer to the call of an invisible command, took His seat exactly facing the door, upon which He fixed His eyes.

There she left Him seated, waiting! Waiting!

At length a step was heard, and the awaited one came. The young wife, wondering too much for sleep, heard what caused even greater wonder.

This visitor was he who afterwards became known as the Bábu'l-Báb, his name being Mullá Ḥusayn-i-Bushrú'í. He was one of the foremost disciples of Siyyid Káẓim, and had now come to Shíráz in fulfilment of the charge laid upon his students, that after his death, "they should first spend forty days in retreat in the Mosque at Kúfih, fasting and praying, being thus prepared to become capable of recognizing the Imám, they were to disperse, travelling far and wide in search of Him, and having found Him, to let all the world know."

On his arrival the awaited visitor announced that he was seeking for his Master, and took from his wallet the Tablet before mentioned, the five-pointed star, following the chief lines of the form of the human body—filled with writing containing the description of the signs by which he should know Him whom he sought.

As this was recounted by the guest, the young host listened gravely, and then, taking off his green turban, said: "Look well at me, do I not show these signs?" His calm face was illumined by a smile full of meaning.

"That is a very high claim," wonderingly said the visitor.

Siyyid 'Alí Muḥammad then reminded him of a day long ago at the table of Siyyid Káẓim, who, speaking of the chapter in the Qur'án describing the story of Joseph, impressively told them to remember the discussion of that evening on the "Mystery of Joseph," adding that one day, in the future, the reason for this solemn injunction would be made clear to them.

Then and there Siyyid 'Alí Muḥammad wrote a detailed commentary on the "Mystery of Joseph," revealing the hidden meaning of the story; this He handed to His visitor.

As Mullá Ḥusayn-i-Bushrú'í read, his eyes were opened, and he became greatly perturbed and overcome, and excited. He wished to rush forth proclaiming the wondrous tidings to the world!

He had found the Herald! Him whom he sought, the Imám the Qá'im.

"Restrain thine enthusiasm for awhile, my friend, it is not yet the time to give forth the tidings. Be patient! Wait! Wait until eighteen persons of insight shall of themselves separately, through inner guidance, have recognized me."

The Báb himself was the "Primal Point" and, with the eighteen to be by Him appointed as they should come to Him, constituted "The Nineteen Letters of the Living."

This declaration was made on the twenty-third day of the month of May, in the year 1844.

What a day in the history of the world!

The Báb, the Herald of Bahá'u'lláh, the Promised One, opened the new age of mankind. On this day was born 'Abbás Effendi, 'Abdu'l-Bahá, Son of Bahá'u'lláh and Centre of His Covenant.

On this day the first telegraphic message was flashed along the wires in these remarkable words:

"Behold what God hath wrought!"

Mullá Ḥusayn-i-Bushrú'í was straightway named the Bábu'l-Báb, i.e., "The-gate-leading-to-the-Gate," and took his place as the first one of the sacred band of illuminated disciples who became known as "The Nineteen Letters of the Living."

When certain others had come to the Báb, and had been added to this band, He sent them forth far and wide into the length and breadth of the land, to give the glad tidings of the appearance of the Promised Herald, who had come to be their Divine Leader. In these words He addressed them:

"O My beloved friends! You are the bearers of the name of God in this Day. You have been chosen as the repositories of His mystery. It behoves each one of you to manifest the attributes of God, and to exemplify by your deeds and words the signs of His righteousness, His power and glory. The very members of your body must bear witness to the loftiness of your purpose, the integrity of your life, the reality of your faith, and the exalted character of your devotion. For verily I say, this is the Day spoken of by God in His Book:* 'On that day will We set a seal upon their mouths; yet shall their hands speak

---
* The Qur'án.

unto Us, and their feet shall bear witness to that which they shall have done.' Ponder the words of Jesus addressed to His disciples, as He sent them forth to propagate the Cause of God. In words such as these, He bade them arise and fulfil their mission: 'Ye are even as the fire which in the darkness of the night has been kindled upon the mountain-top. Let your light shine before the eyes of men. Such must be the purity of your character and the degree of your renunciation, that the people of the earth may through you recognize and be drawn closer to the heavenly Father who is the Source of purity and grace. For none has seen the Father who is in heaven. You who are His spiritual children must by your deeds exemplify His virtues, and witness to His glory. You are the salt of the earth, but if the salt have lost its savour, wherewith shall it be salted? Such must be the degree of your detachment, that into whatever city you enter to proclaim and teach the Cause of God, you should in no wise expect either meat or reward from its people. Nay, when you depart out of that city, you should shake the dust from off your feet. As you have entered it pure and undefiled, so must you depart from that city. For verily I say, the heavenly Father is ever with you and keeps watch over you. If you be faithful to Him, He will assuredly deliver into your hands all the treasures of the earth, and will exalt you above all the rulers and kings of the world.' O My Letters! Verily I say, immensely exalted is this Day above the days of the Apostles of old. Nay, immeasurable is the difference! You are the witnesses of the Dawn of the promised Day of God. You are the partakers of the mystic chalice of His Revelation. Gird up the loins of endeavour, and be mindful of the words of God as revealed in His Book:* 'Lo, the Lord thy God is come, and with Him is the company of His angels arrayed before Him!' Purge your hearts of worldly desires, and let angelic virtues be your adorning. Strive that by your deeds you may bear witness to the truth of these words of God, and beware lest, by 'turning back,' He may 'change you for another people,' who 'shall not be your like,' and who shall take from you the Kingdom of God. The days when idle worship was deemed sufficient are ended. The time is come when naught but the purest motive, supported by

---
* The Qur'án.

deeds of stainless purity, can ascend to the throne of the Most High and be acceptable unto Him. 'The good word riseth up unto Him, and the righteous deed will cause it to be exalted before Him.' You are the lowly, of whom God has thus spoken in His Book:* 'And we desire to show favour to those who were brought low in the land, and to make them spiritual leaders among men, and to make them Our heirs.' You have been called to this station; you will attain to it, only if you arise to trample beneath your feet every earthly desire, and endeavour to become those 'honoured servants of His who speak not till He hath spoken, and who do His bidding.' You are the first Letters that have been generated from the Primal Point,† the first Springs that have welled out from the Source of this Revelation. Beseech the Lord your God to grant that no earthly entanglements, no worldly affections, no ephemeral pursuits, may tarnish the purity, or embitter the sweetness, of that grace which flows through you. I am preparing you for the advent of a mighty Day. Exert your utmost endeavour that, in the world to come, I, who am now instructing you, may, before the mercy-seat of God, rejoice in your deeds and glory in your achievements. The secret of the Day that is to come is now concealed. It can neither be divulged nor estimated. The newly born babe of that Day excels the wisest and most venerable men of this time, and the lowliest and most unlearned of that period shall surpass in understanding the most erudite and accomplished divines of this age. Scatter throughout the length and breadth of this land, and, with steadfast feet and sanctified hearts, prepare the way for His coming. Heed not your weaknesses and frailty; fix your gaze upon the invincible power of the Lord, your God, the Almighty. Has He not, in past days, caused Abraham, in spite of His seeming helplessness, to triumph over the forces of Nimrod? Has He not enabled Moses, whose staff was His only companion, to vanquish Pharaoh and his hosts? Has He not established the ascendancy of Jesus, poor and lowly as He was in the eyes of men, over the combined forces of the Jewish people? Has He not subjected the barbarous and militant tribes of Arabia to the holy and transforming

---

* The Qur'án.
† One of the Báb's titles.

discipline of Muḥammad, His Prophet? Arise in His name, put your trust wholly in Him, and be assured of ultimate victory."

Having sent forth these messengers, the Báb set out for Mecca, where the great public proclamation of His Message took place. The mullás of Shíráz, alarmed by the sensational reports of the pilgrims returning from Mecca, fearing the influence of His pure teaching, and most of them entirely failing to comprehend the significance of the event, went in a body to the Governor of the town, Ḥusayn Khán, imploring him to take the Báb prisoner, and to keep Him in his own house in absolute solitude, that He might trouble the land no longer with His teaching.

Accordingly Ḥusayn Khán sent ten of his own soldier guards to make the Báb prisoner as He was returning to Shíráz. They met Him at night.

"Friends, where are you going?" asked the Báb.

"For a particular purpose," the soldiers replied, hesitating to tell Him what that purpose was.

"That purpose I know, you have orders to take me as prisoner to Shíráz. Here am I! I am He whom you seek."

The soldiers were amazed at the courage of the gentle-voiced and beautiful Youth, Who willingly gave Himself up to be a prisoner in the hands of so cruel a Governor.

They treated this calm and dignified young descendant of Muḥammad with great respect, their demeanour being rather that of retainers of a Prince, than of soldiers in charge of a prisoner.

Arrived at Shíráz, Ḥusayn Khán thought it wise to allow the Báb to be confined in the house of His uncle, requiring Him to undertake to teach no more in Shíráz. The uncle was also called upon to become surety for Him, that the promises should be kept.

Meanwhile "the Letters of the Living" were journeying throughout the land of Írán, carrying the good news of the Appearing of the Qá'im, the "Awaited One," for whose coming the prayers of the faithful had been offered up to the Court of the Invisible for so many centuries.

Despite the terrible danger to life and property, which overshadowed all who professed the new faith, numbers of these fearless souls continued to offer allegiance to the Báb, and wrote many letters to Him, questioning Him and assuring Him of their devotion, even unto death!

These followers were now called Bábís, and their numbers grew and increased—albeit few were able to come into touch with the young Prophet, whom they accepted as a Divine Messenger, because He was so frequently undergoing mock trial succeeding mock trial, being taken from one remote stronghold to a yet more distant fastness. His friends and His family were often unable to discover His whereabouts, all communication with them being forbidden. It was also very difficult to carry out any plan for letters to reach Him, or for receiving His Tablets in reply, such grave risks did any messenger run who attempted to reach Him.

To the fact that so many intrepid souls gallantly made these attempts, and that some were successful, we are indebted for such of His writings as remain to us.

These Tablets, as a rule, contain no name of those persons for whom they were written, and many of those which ultimately arrived at their destination were promptly buried under the earth or otherwise hidden, so as to escape destruction by their ever-watchful enemies.

Others again were destroyed by their owners who, when arrested, often made a sign to the wife, or some member of their family, to burn them (these priceless treasures!), in case they might incriminate any others of the friends, if found through treacherous spies; for by such persons were the brave Bábís constantly surrounded.

An old Persian Baha'í, Mírzá Asadu'lláh Ká_sh_ání, told me that when he was a boy, about nine years old, he was passing by an inn in his native town of Ká_sh_án, where many soldiers were gathered together.

"The Báb is here. He is being taken to Tihrán," someone whispered.

"I remember being told that a gentleman of the town, Hájí Muḥammad Ismá'íl, gave a sum of between fifty and sixty túmáns* to the soldier guards to allow the Blessed One to spend that one night at his house."

---
* A túmán was at that time equal to a pound sterling.

THE BÁB

This friend was afterwards denounced as a Bábí, taken prisoner, chained with Bahá'u'lláh at Tihrán, and, with his brother, Mírzá Jání, one of the first historians of the Cause, eventually gained the crown of martyrdom.

"My eldest brother heard some prophecies interpreted by a Mullá in our Mosque—he became convinced and embraced the Bábí faith; afterwards we three others also became Bábís; later on, when 'He, Whom God should make Manifest,' Bahá'u'lláh, had made His proclamation, we accepted Him, and then we became Bahá'ís."*

Meanwhile, the Sháh of Írán, having been in much perplexity concerning the Báb, of Whose teaching he had heard varying accounts, each contradicting the other, had sent for Siyyid Yahyáy-i-Dárábí, one of the most learned scholars of his time, and a highly esteemed divine. Preparations were made for his welcome, beautiful rugs and embroidered shawls were laid down before him, to show with what honour this guest was received.

The Sháh directed him to go to Shíráz, see this Prophet, Whom all were discussing, seek out the truth of the reports, and return to inform him of all he should be able to discover.

Siyyid Yahyáy-i-Dárábí went to Shíráz, saw the Báb, had long talks with Him, going into the fulfilment of prophecies, their explanations and interpretations! As he himself knew much of the Qur'án by heart, and nearly thirty thousand traditions foretelling the Promised One, and being withal of a character described as "Holy," he was well chosen for this mission, being suitably equipped, mentally and spiritually, to investigate so important a matter.

The result was that he, Siyyid Yahyáy-i-Dárábí, became convinced of the truth, embraced the faith, and was sent forth by the Báb to proclaim the New Day.

He was destined in the future to attain the crown of martyrdom, in the town of Nayríz.

Arrived again at Tihrán, he went to ask many questions of Mírzá Husayn-'Alí Núrí (afterwards Bahá'u'lláh).

* His story, as told to me, I will give in its own period further on.

On this day 'Abbás Effendi told us that He, being a little boy, was sitting on the knee of Qurratu'l-'Ayn, who was in the private parlour of His mother, Ásíyih Khánum, the door of this room being open, they could hear, from behind the curtain, the voice of Siyyid Yahyáy-i-Dárábí, who was talking and "arguing with my Father."

Qurratu'l-'Ayn, that beautiful, fearless poetess, addressing the Siyyid with her musical, yet penetrating voice, said:

"O Siyyid this is not the time for arguments, for discussions, for idle repetitions of prophecies or traditions! It is the time for deeds! The day for words has passed!

"If you have courage, now is the appointed hour for manifesting it; if you are a man of deeds, show a proof of your manhood by proclaiming day and night:

"The Promised Herald has come!

"He has come, the Qá'im, the Imám, the Awaited One has come! He has come!"

'Abbás Effendi told us that He remembered this episode very distinctly, the expression of enthusiasm on her lovely, radiant face as she spoke those inspiriting words from behind the curtain, which hung before the door, was wonderfully impressive.

'Abbás Effendi added:

"She used often, during her short visit, to take me on to her knee, caress me, and talk to me. I admired her most deeply."

Siyyid Ja'far-i-Kashfí foretold that his son, Siyyid Yahyáy-i-Dárábí, would be martyred as an infidel; this tragic prophecy was eventually fulfilled in the town of Nayríz.

Qurratu'l-'Ayn heard of the Herald who was the "Awaited One" through the disciples of Siyyid Kázim, and soon after the death of this beloved teacher she wrote to the Báb.

The Báb made her one of the "Nineteen Letters of the Living." He said of this marvellous woman:

"Lo! She answered my call, even before I had called her."

Mullá Ḥusayn, the first believer in the Báb, was one day summoned to the presence of his Master.

"I have a very important mission for you," said the Báb. "Take this tablet, it is for a great and holy person."

While Mullá Ḥusayn listened in wonder and awe, the Báb

continued. "Go to Tihrán, seek out one, who is a very highly placed personage and who is well known to be, above all things, spiritual, showing forth loving kindness and charity."

The disciple journeyed to Tihrán, filled with the thought of the sacred importance of his secret mission.

Having arrived, he prepared to inquire carefully, day after day, knowing by the faith of intuition that the Great One* was in reality on earth, moreover, that he should find Him, though as yet veiled, in that very town of Tihrán.

After some days had passed in fruitless seeking, he met one of the 'ulamás,† to whom the errand was confided, though not, of course, in its entire sacredness.

"There is but one personage in all this place who could possibly be the one you seek," he said.

"Tell me of him," said the Bábu'l-Báb.

"He is one of the noble class, but above all ostentation, seldom attending stately functions. Extremely wealthy, but caring naught for luxury and sumptuous faring. Full of a marvellous wisdom is he, yet he has never been instructed of men, even when a young boy, not consenting to receive lessons from the usual teachers of youth. He is the helper of all in need of succour. A refuge for those in sorrowful weariness; a comfort to the afflicted. A strong champion of those who suffer wrong. To the shelter of his house all who hunger or thirst are warmly welcomed. His hospitality is given freely to every comer. His doors are always opened to the friendless, and his heart to every tale of grief.

"The people say:

" 'He refuses all the lucrative posts which are offered to him; surely even his wealth must diminish, if he despises all means of adding to it, whilst he continues to bestow his goods so lavishly on these worthless poor creatures.'

"It is very difficult to understand his conduct, so differing from that of our other friends. What can be the meaning or the good of it all? Well, it certainly is not the way to fill his coffers with túmáns.

---

* The Báb declared His own message to be preparatory to that of "He whom God shall make Manifest," the Promised One of all peoples.—ED.

† "Learned ones"; applied generally to the clergy.

"But the poor of the people, the forsaken, the sick and the miserable, revere and love him with a kind of worshipful adoration; they speak of him as the 'Father of the Poor.'

"Moreover, it is whispered by many of his friends, both rich and poor, that there is something about him of the other world, the world of holiness.

"Say, my friend, think you this is he whom you seek?"

The Bábu'l-Báb, as he heard these things, knew that he had found Him whom he sought.

"Without doubt this is He. Now how can the precious Tablet be delivered to this unique personage?"

"I can do this, for I am frequently at his house, where I give teaching to some of his brethren."

So this tutor was entrusted to deliver the Tablet of the Báb to Mírzá Ḥusayn-'Alí Núrí, who, when He had read the wonderful, inspired words, called His brother, Mírzá Músá, saying: "Read this—if there be any truth in this mortal world, it is to be found in the words of the writer of this Tablet."

Mírzá Ḥusayn-'Alí sent back to S͟híráz by the messenger a present of tea to the Báb.

The contents of this Tablet being noised abroad amongst certain persons, the tidings of the appearance of the Forerunner of a new Manifestation caused great agitation in Tihrán.

The following extract from the Tablet of the Báb was translated for me by Mírzá Munír, son of one of the most devoted Bahá'í's, known as Zaynu'l-Muqarrabín, i.e., "the adorning of the favoured."

As was the Báb's custom, no name is given of him to whom the Tablet was written, nor of the friends mentioned; it seems to speak eloquently of the danger, which was the atmosphere in which the Writer and His disciples lived.

The Báb, having been told that the 'ulamás wished for a sign, a sort of trial by ordeal, consented to gratify their desire, thereby giving them proof of His willingness to meet them upon their own ground. He left it, moreover, to them to select the sign.

This Tablet refers to the time appointed for the ordeal.

Tablet of His Holiness the Báb

"In the Name of God the Most Merciful!

"Praise be unto God, Who hath bestowed upon me the Grace to thank Him for His ordeals.

"I thank Him for the calamities which have descended upon me, and for the hardships which have bestrewn my path.

"These misfortunes have come to me through those who believe not in the One True God, and are of the rebellious.

"I bring my sorrows and my griefs unto God.

"Ere long the unjust shall see their punishment.

"What thou hast written to me I have received, and I became aware of that which hath come through thy love.

"May God reward thee for that which thou hast wrought in His Religion, and for that which thou wilt achieve in His Path.

"I swear by Him, in whose hand is my soul, that those who quaff of the Chalice of Love are saved, and that those who reject me and my Mission shall perish.

"How can I describe that which befell me in that land?

"Verily, all the ink of the world, and all the parchments of the earth would fall short.

"By a sign it shall be made known unto thee, what are some of the calamities which overwhelmed me, when I journeyed from that land to present myself to one whom God had appointed to be ruler over it.

"I arrived at this place and tarried a space by the permission of His Honour Mu'tamidu'd-Dawlih; may God preserve and increase his good fortune and reward him with His bounties according to his merits. In truth he did not fail to care for us, and to take trouble on our behalf.

"One night a promise was made in Mu'tamidu'd-Dawlih's presence, and that of many nobles, concerning that which God had ordained and desired.

"This will in truth take place, should the 'ulamás present themselves, on the day of the Great Feast as appointed for that 'Trial by Ordeal.'

"This was agreed upon between me and the 'ulamás.

"Soon shall God establish the Truth by His Word, and make manifest the deeds of the people.

"Ere long I shall make a journey to the presence of Maliku'l-

Faḍl (the lord of grace); shouldst thou hear of this visit, present thyself in that place, and relate whatsoever thou hast seen of the actions of the ignorant.

"Verily, we are from God, and unto God shall we return.

"Peace be upon thee, and upon Aḥmad, and upon that one whom thou didst mention in thy letter—and upon those who shall join them.

"To-day is the appointed day,* and this day shall be fulfilled that which I promised thee—at five minutes before noontide shall this take place—should the 'ulamás present themselves!"

The 'ulamás failed to keep the appointment, thereby showing that they did not wish to know the Truth, which it was clearly their duty to investigate.

They were afraid of suffering defeat, and thus bringing about the humiliation of their religion.

Their refusal betrayed their lack of faith in the justice of their opposition.

They feared that the Truth of the Báb's Mission would, at the projected Ordeal, be proclaimed to the world.

Thus the spectres of grief and sorrow, and woe, and disappointment, stalked beside this Chosen One at all times.

This Tablet was written in 1846, two years after His proclamation.

The persecution of this "Awaited Qá'im," during the whole six years of His Mission, seems incredible—very difficult to understand, knowing as we do that prayers were constantly offered up for his Coming by those very mullás, who showed themselves to be His most cruel and bitter enemies, and that He showed forth all the requisite signs, mentioned in the prophecies. But this rejection was accepted by those who believed in the Báb, as in itself, one of the proofs of His Truth, being also a fulfilling of prophecy.

THE WAITING SERVANTS

It has been said that in the "Latter Days," "The Great Day of God," which is understood to be the Day of the Universal Manifestation, He Who should link all the religions and races

---

* 7th of Dhi'l-Hijjih, A.H. 1262, last month of the Muḥammadan year (Lunar).

THE BÁB

of the world together in a vast bond of honour and love, free from self-seeking, hatred, and prejudice, would appear.

It has been said, and by many believed, that in His Day the Lord God would send to the earth ten thousand thousand of His Saints.

These Saints, referred to as "the Waiting Servants," would be manifested in every religion, in every race, every tongue, every colour, and every nation in the world.

These "Waiting Servants" would, many of them, gather round the Forerunner, and in due time would hasten to that One "Whom God shall make Manifest," to be Their Apostles and Their Disciples. They would, wherever their abode, be the first to recognise the lessons of the Divine Educator, would be as leaven in the lethargic mass of the people, and, arising to set about their Father's work, would be as pure "life blood in the arteries of the sick body of the world."

It is believed that a number of these "Waiting Servants" were already manifested in Persia, and therefore were ready to recognise the Báb as the Promised One, the Imám, their Expected Leader, Whose ultimate mission was to herald the Great Universal Manifestation.

One of the most devoted of these "Waiting Servants" was the beautiful poetess of Qazvín, Zarrín-Táj (Crown of Gold), Fátimih Khánum, to whom the revered Siyyid Kázim gave the name of Qurratu'l-'Ayn (Consolation of the Eyes), so rare was her loveliness of body and soul.* The story of her fearless devotion and cruel martyrdom is elsewhere told.†

Many others, in defiance of torture and death, arose to serve the Cause of the Báb. Shaykh Sálih, Siyyid Yahyáy-i-Dárábí, Mullá Husayn, Quddús, Mírzá Jání, and Mírzá Ismá'íl, the brothers of Káshán, and many, many others. Not only were they steadfast unto death, but some of them even prayed to be permitted the honour of shedding their life blood for the watering of the Tree of Life. In their high devotion they counted the greatest gift of God to be that of martyrdom, which to them was the Crown of Life.

---

* She received the title of Tahirih, the Pure One, from the Báb.

† By practically all historians of *The Episode of the Báb*, but notably Nabíl and Professor E. G. Browne. Lady Blomfield, too, has written an account.—ED.

Mírzá Jání and Mírzá Ismá'íl went with Bahá'u'lláh to carry help to the Bábís who were defending themselves in Shaykh Tabarsí. On the way they were arrested. Bahá'u'lláh was set free through some friends of the royal circle, and the two brothers were bought as slaves by a fellow-townsman and promptly set free.

Trial after trial of the Báb took place, for the most part in the strictest secrecy, no friend being present, none but implacable, cruel enemies surrounding Him.

At these mock trials, with their false accusations, He is said to have either spoken so wisely that He could not be condemned, or again to have answered not one word to their subtle questions, holding His peace.

When it became known that the friends of the Báb had succeeded in finding out the castle in which He was imprisoned, and that large numbers of them were flocking to the prison gate, the enemies caused Him to be taken to some other more remote fastness; these changes usually took place in the darkness of night, so that the brave followers should not deliver Him from their hands.

Persistently the "Waiting Servants" gathered round Him, gallant and fearless, increasing in numbers, and in disregard of the danger of bonds, imprisonments, torture, and death, of which the shadow was always near these devoted ones, who refused to forsake Him, Whom they recognised as their Lord.

Thus the amazing six years passed (1844 to 1850).

The authorities, instigated by the religious enemies, who feared the increasing numbers of His adherents and their determined steadfastness, which threatened their own influence and power, decided upon the bold step of putting the Báb to death, hoping thereby to end His "troubling of the land."

"Let us kill this man, then see where his followers will be."

Accordingly, the Báb and His devoted disciple, Áqá Muḥammad-'Alí Zunúzí, were taken to Tabríz, there to be done to death.

The night before this took place, the Báb said to him who so loved Him:

"Wilt thou not send me to the other world? It is surely better to go by the hand of a friend than of a foe."

This He said to test the love and faith of him.

The answer came:

"Thy body is human, but Thy word is the word of God, I am ready to obey."

"It is well, thou shalt not be required to do this thing, O My companion, but I say unto thee, that never shalt thou be separated from me, thou shalt be for ever with me."

On the next day the Báb was brought out from His prison into the public square. His green turban was taken off, so that He should not be recognized as a descendant of Muḥammad; the people would not have permitted the sacrilege of putting a Siyyid to death. As to the mark on His forehead, the sacred sign, only the learned would be likely to see that, knowing its significance, and it was these very learned ones who had encompassed His death, in spite of this sign.*

The Báb and His friend were bound with ropes, and hung upon a wall, with their arms extended in the form of a cross. A company of soldiers stood ready, and the word of command was given to fire!

When the smoke had cleared, the Báb was seen to be seated in an adjoining room unharmed. Only the ropes, by which He was suspended, were severed. He was calmly writing. He looked up as officials rushed in, then continued His work. Soon He laid down His pen, saying:

"It is finished. I am ready."

He was then conducted to the place of martyrdom.

The officials, in terror and amazement, gave the word to fire once more.

The soldiers laid down their arms saying: "This thing is of God, we refuse to obey."

Another company was hastily brought, and the heroic young Herald allowed Himself to be sent forth into the other world by the bullets of His enemies.

The Martyrdom of the Báb and of His friend took place on 9th July in the year A.D. 1850.

His Holiness the Báb had accomplished His Mission, under

---

* The above details were told to the writer by Ḥájí 'Alí Yazdí.

difficulties inexpressible, in bonds and imprisonment, steadfastly facing scorn, contempt, revilings. He had succeeded in establishing the conditions of purity of heart in many "Waiting Servants," who had become His devoted followers; this condition of heart being necessary in order to be able to recognize "Him Whom God shall make Manifest."

"Blessed are they whose hearts are pure, for they shall see God."

As His Holiness the Spirit (the Lord Christ) hath said aforetime.

So the Báb said to the believers:

"The pure of heart shall see, that is with eyes of the spirit they shall recognize God, in His Great Manifestation now about to arise, as the glorious Sun on a dark and weary world."

And the "Gate" was thrown wide open into the Kingdom of Heaven.

Through this "Gate" the "Waiting Servants" should pass, drawing with them the despairing, the humble and lowly of heart, those whose heads are adorned with the Crown of Severance from all things of earth, and those pure and holy ones, whose lives are made perfect through love.

For of such are the dwellers in the new Heaven, and the new earth.

The Body of the Báb

The bodies of the Báb and of His faithful disciple, Áqá Muḥammad-'Alí, were taken in the dead of night, wrapped in one 'abá, to the house of Raḥím Khán-i-Kalántar.

The devoted Bábí, who achieved this task with the wonderful courage and promptitude necessary to its success, Mírzá Sulaymán Khán, was afterwards martyred in the most cruel manner—lighted candles were inserted into the skin of various parts of his body; whilst they burned, and his torturers gloated over his sufferings, he sang praises to God, and chanted prayers with his last breath.

From the house of the Kalántar, the two bodies being put into one wooden case, were taken and hidden in the warehouse of one Mírzá Aḥmad-i-Mílání, a place of concealment little likely to be discovered. Here they remained until Bahá'u'lláh requested Mírzá Sulaymán Khán to undertake again the dangerous guardianship of the revered bodies, and to bring them to Tihrán.

This was done, and they were successfully placed with great secrecy in the tomb of a descendant of an Imám. In this appropriate resting-place they were hidden for some years.

At length 'Abdu'l-Bahá arranged for the precious remains to be brought to Mount Carmel, near Haifa.

Those who were charged with the transportation had many obstacles to encounter on their way. To have taken it on board a ship, or on to any train, would have led to the disaster of discovery. Accordingly, they hired mules, and riding in a "Takht-i-Raván" (similar to a howdah), with the box, they brought it all the way by land from Tihrán through Baghdád, and at length arrived in safety at Haifa.

Here it remained in secret, first in one house, then being taken for greater security to another hiding-place.

After some years it was placed in the mausoleum (tomb shrine), which had been especially built by 'Abdu'l-Bahá on Mount Carmel.

The body of the faithful "companion," Áqá Muḥammad-'Alí, was now mingled with that of the Báb, his head resting on the breast of his beloved Master. Thus even in the earthly bodies, the promise, given the night before their martyrdom, was fulfilled.

"I say unto thee that never shalt thou be separated from me; thou shalt be for ever with me."

Immediately upon His release from the prison of 'Akká, 'Abdu'l-Bahá began to build a shrine for the body of the Báb, which had been kept so long in a secret place. Having with much difficulty, self-sacrifice, and great trouble accomplished this, He proceeded to have the sacred remains of the martyred Herald, and the beloved disciple, laid in a marble casket, which was placed in the shrine with great and solemn reverence.

Several persons who were present on the moving occasion of that sacred ceremony have tried to describe to the writer what they saw, and above all, what they felt.

"But it is impossible to find the words with which to tell you of the event of that great day. Perhaps you may touch the spirit of it with your spirit. The Master, bare-headed, with His hair like a halo of silver, His white robe falling round Him, His feet bare, descended into the tomb. His beautiful voice rose and fell in the cadence of the funeral chant, His face all shining and glorious, as though it were lighted from within.

"He Himself placed the earthly body of His Holiness the Báb, with that of His beloved and faithful disciple, in the marble sarcophagus.

"And when He spoke to us of the meaning of that day's event—of sacrifice, of love, of steadfastness, of heroism, shown all down the ages by those Great Messengers of God—our hearts, you can imagine, were too full for any utterance. We could but feel, Oh, the blindness of humanity! How it is unworthy of those whom it tortures and martyrs. And Oh, the stupendous love which came and endured for the sake of that same humanity!"

PART II

BAHÁ'U'LLÁH

A SPOKEN CHRONICLE

"The face of him on whom I gazed I can never forget, though I cannot describe it. Those piercing eyes seemed to read one's very soul; power and authority sat on that ample brow; while the deep lines on the forehead and face implied an age which the jet-black hair and beard flowing down in indistinguishable luxuriance almost to the waist seemed to belie. No need to ask in whose presence I stood, as I bowed myself before one who is the object of a devotion and love which kings might envy and emperors sigh for in vain!"

Professor Edward Granville Browne.

THE SPOKEN CHRONICLE

of

Bahíyyih Khánum, Daughter of Bahá'u'lláh,

known to the Persian friends

as

Varaqiyih 'Ulyá,

the Greatest Holy Leaf

of the

Tree of Life.

CHAPTER I

Írán

Most of the following details were given to me in conversations with Khánum (Bahíyyih Khánum) the daughter of Bahá'u'lláh, sister of 'Abdu'l-Bahá, called by the Persian Bahá'ís "Varaqiyih 'Ulyá (the Greatest Holy Leaf)":

I remember dimly very happy days with my beloved father and mother, and my brother 'Abbás, who was two years my senior.

My father was Mírzá Ḥusayn-'Alí of Núr, who married my beautiful mother, Ásíyih Khánum, when she was very young. She was the only daughter of a Persian Vizier, of high degree, Mírzá Ismá'íl. He, as well as Mírzá 'Abbás Buzurg, my paternal grandfather, possessed great wealth.

When the brother of my mother married my father's sister, the double alliance of the two noble families roused much interest throughout the land. "It is adding wealth to wealth," the people said. Ásíyih Khánum's wedding treasures were extensive, in accordance with the usual custom in families of their standing; forty mules were loaded with her possessions when she came to her husband's home.

For six months before the marriage a jeweller worked at her home, preparing jewellery—even the buttons of her garments were of gold, set with precious stones. (These buttons were destined to be exchanged for bread, on the terrible exile journey from Tihrán to Baghdád.)

I wish you could have seen her as I first remember her, tall, slender, graceful, eyes of dark blue—a pearl, a flower amongst women.

I have been told that even when very young, her wisdom and

intelligence were remarkable. I always think of her in those earliest days of my memory as queenly in her dignity and loveliness, full of consideration for everybody, gentle, of a marvellous unselfishness, no action of hers ever failed to show the loving-kindness of her pure heart; her very presence seemed to make an atmosphere of love and happiness wherever she came, enfolding all comers in the fragrance of gentle courtesy.

Even in the early years of their married life, they, my father and mother, took part as little as possible in State functions, social ceremonies, and the luxurious habits of ordinary highly-placed and wealthy families in the land of Persia; she, and her noble-hearted husband, counted these worldly pleasures meaningless, and preferred rather to occupy themselves in caring for the poor, and for all who were unhappy, or in trouble.

From our doors nobody was ever turned away; the hospitable board was spread for all comers.

Constantly the poor women came to my mother, to whom they poured out their various stories of woe, to be comforted and consoled by her loving helpfulness.

Whilst the people called my father "The Father of the Poor," they spoke of my mother as "The Mother of Consolation," though, naturally, only the women and little children ever looked upon her face unveiled.

So our peaceful days flowed on.

We used to go to our house in the country sometimes; my brother 'Abbás and I loved to play in the beautiful gardens, where grew many kinds of wonderful fruits and flowers and flowering trees; but this part of my early life is a very dim memory.

One day I remember very well, though I was only six years old at the time. It seemed that an attempt had been made on the life of the Sháh by a half-crazy young Bábí.

My father was away at his country house in the village of Níavirán, which was his property, the villagers of which were all and individually cared for by him.

Suddenly and hurriedly a servant came rushing in great distress to my mother.

"The master, the master, he is arrested—I have seen him!

He has walked many miles! Oh, they have beaten him! They say he has suffered the torture of the bastinado! His feet are bleeding! He has no shoes on! His turban has gone! His clothes are torn! There are chains upon his neck!"

My poor mother's face grew whiter and whiter.

We children were terribly frightened and could only weep bitterly.

Immediately everybody, all our relations, and friends, and servants fled from our house in terror, only one man-servant, Isfandíyár, remained, and one woman. Our palace, and the smaller houses belonging to it were very soon stripped of everything; furniture, treasures, all were stolen by the people.

Mírzá Músá, my father's brother, who was always very kind to us, helped my mother and her three children to escape into hiding. She succeeded in saving some few of the marriage treasures, which were all of our vast possessions left to us. These things were sold; with the money my mother was able to pay the gaolers to take food to my father in the prison, and to meet other expenses incurred later on.

We were now in a little house, not far from the prison. Mírzá Yáhyá (Ṣubḥ-i-Azal) had run away in terror to Mázindarán, where he remained in hiding.

Oh, the terrible anxiety my beloved mother suffered at that time! Surely greater than any woman, about to become a mother (as I afterwards knew), could possibly have strength to bear.

The prison into which my father had been cast was a terrible place, seven steps below the ground; it was ankle-deep in filth, infested with horrible vermin, and of an indescribable loathsomeness. Added to this, there was no glimmer of light in that noisome place. Within its walls forty Bábís were crowded; murderers and highway robbers were also imprisoned there.

My noble father was hurled into this black hole, loaded with heavy chains; five other Bábís were chained to him night and day, and here he remained for four months. Picture to yourself the horror of these conditions.

Any movement caused the chains to cut deeper and deeper not only into the flesh of one, but of all who were chained together; whilst sleep or rest of any kind was not possible. No food was provided, and it was with the utmost difficulty that my mother was able to arrange to get any food or drink taken into that ghastly prison.

Meanwhile, the spirit which upheld the Bábís never quailed for a moment, even under these conditions. To be tortured to a death, which would be the Martyr's Crown of Life, was their aim and great desire.

They chanted prayers night and day.

Every morning one or more of these brave and devoted friends would be taken out to be tortured and killed in various ways of horror.

When religious fanaticism was aroused against a person or persons, who were accused of being infidels, as was now the case with the Bábís, it was customary not simply to condemn them to death and have them executed by the State executioner, but to hand the victims over to various classes of the populace.

The butchers had their methods of torture; the bakers theirs; the shoemakers and blacksmiths yet others of their own. They were all given opportunities of carrying out their pitiless inventions on the Bábís.

The fanatics became more and more infuriated when they failed to quench the amazing spirit of these fearless, devoted ones, who remained unflinching, chanting prayers, asking God to pardon and bless their murderers, and praising Him, as long as they were able to breathe. The mob crowded to these fearful scenes, and yelled their execrations, whilst all through the fiendish work, a drum was loudly beaten.

These horrible sounds I well remember, as we three children clung to our mother, she not knowing whether the victim was her own adored husband. She could not find out whether he was still alive or not until late at night, or very early in the morning, when she determined to venture out, in defiance of the danger to herself and to us, for neither women or children were spared.

How well I remember cowering in the dark, with my little brother, Mírzá Mihdí, the Purest Branch, at that time two years old, in my arms, which were not very strong, as I was only six. I was shivering with terror, for I knew of some of the horrible things that were happening, and was aware that they might have seized even my mother.

So I waited and waited until she should come back. Then Mírzá Músá, my uncle, who was in hiding, would venture in to hear what tidings my mother had been able to gather.

My brother 'Abbás usually went with her on these sorrowful errands.

We listened eagerly to the accounts she gave to my uncle.

This information came through the kindness of a sister of my grandfather, who was married to Mírzá Yúsif, a Russian subject, and a friend of the Russian Consul in Tihrán. This gentleman, my great uncle by marriage, used to attend the courts to find out some particulars as to the victims chosen for execution day by day, and thus was able to relieve to some extent my mother's overwhelming anxiety as these appalling days passed over us.

It was Mírzá Yúsif who was able to help my mother about getting food taken to my father, and who brought us to the two little rooms near the prison, where we stayed in close hiding. He had to be very careful in thus defying the authorities, although the danger in this case was mitigated by the fact of his being under the protection of the Russian Consulate, as a Russian subject.

Nobody at all, of all our friends and relations, dared to come to see my mother during these days of death, but the wife of Mírzá Yúsif, the aunt of my father.

One day the discovery was made by Mírzá Yúsif that our untiring enemies, the most fanatical of the mullás, were plotting the death of Mírzá Ḥusayn 'Alí Núrí, my father.

Mírzá Yúsif consulted the Russian Consul; that powerful friend determined that this plan should be at once frustrated.

An amazing scene took place in the Court, where the sentences of death were passed. The Russian Consul rose and fearlessly addressed those in court:

"Hearken to me! I have words of importance to say to you" (his voice rang out, the president and officials were too amazed to reply).

"Have you not taken enough cruel revenge? Have you not already murdered a large enough number of harmless people, because of this accusation, of the absurd falseness of which you are quite aware? Has there not been sufficient of this orgy of brutal torture to satisfy you? How is it possible that you can even pretend to think that this august prisoner planned that silly attempt to shoot the S͟háh?

"It is not unknown to you that the stupid gun, used by that poor youth, could not have killed a bird. Moreover, the boy was obviously insane. You know very well that this charge is not only untrue, but palpably ridiculous.

"There must be an end to all this.

"I have determined to extend the protection of Russia to this innocent nobleman; therefore beware! For if one hair of his head be hurt from this moment, *rivers of blood shall flow in your town as punishment.*

"You will do well to heed my warning, my country is behind me in this matter."

An account of this scene was given to my mother by Mírzá Yúsif that night, and told by her to my uncle, Mírzá Músá, when he came for tidings.

Needless to say how eagerly my brother and I listened, and how we all wept for joy.

Very soon afterwards we heard that, fearing to disregard the stern warning of the Russian Consul, the Governor gave orders that my father should be permitted to come forth from that prison with his life. It was also decreed that he and his family were banished.

They were to leave Tihrán for Bag͟hdád. Ten days were allowed for preparation, as the beloved prisoner was very ill indeed.

And so he came to our two little rooms.

Oh, the joy of his presence!

Oh, the horror of that dungeon, where he had passed those four terrible months.

Jamál-i-Mubárak (a name given to my father, i.e., literally the Blessed Beauty) spoke very little of the terrible sufferings of that time! We, who saw the marks of what he had endured, where the chains had cut into the delicate skin, especially that of his neck, his wounded feet so long untended, evidence of the torture of the bastinado, how we wept with my dear mother.

He, on his part, told of the steadfast faith of the friends, who had gone forth to meet their death at the hands of their torturers, with joy and gladness, to attain the crown of martyrdom.

The glory had won so great a victory that the shame, and pain, and sorrow, and scorn were of comparatively no importance whatever!

Jamál-i-Mubárak had a marvellous divine experience whilst in that prison.

We saw a new radiance seeming to enfold him like a shining vesture, its significance we were to learn years later. At that time we were only aware of the wonder of it, without understanding, or even being told the details of the sacred event.

My mother did her best to nurse our beloved, that he might have some strength to set out upon that journey on which we were to start in ten days' time.

Now was a time of great difficulty.

How could she prepare?

The poor, dear lady sold almost all that remained of her marriage treasures, jewels, embroidered garments, and other belongings, for which she received about four hundred túmáns. With this money she was able to make some provision for the terrible journey. (The Government provided nothing for those whom they exiled.)

This journey was filled with indescribable difficulties. My mother had no experience, no servants, no provisions, and very little money left. My father was extremely ill, not having recovered from the ordeals of the torture and the prison. No one of all our friends and relations dared to come to our help, or even to say good-bye, but one old lady, the grandmother of Ásíyih Khánum.

Our faithful servant, Isfandíyár, and the one negro woman who did not fear to remain with us, did their best. But we three children were very young, my brother eight, and I six years old. Mírzá Mihdí, the "Purest Branch," was very delicate, and my mother allowed herself to be persuaded to leave the little fellow, only two years old, with her grandmother, though the parting with him was very sad.

At length we started on that fearful journey, which lasted

about four weeks; the weather was bitterly cold, snow was upon the ground.

On the way to Baghdád we sometimes encamped in wilderness places, but in that month of December, the cold was intense, and we were not well prepared!

My poor mother! How she suffered on this journey, riding in a takht-i-raván, borne on a jolting mule! And this took place only six weeks before her youngest son was born!

Never did she utter one word of complaint. She was always thinking of some kindness for somebody, and sympathy she gave unsparingly to all in their difficulties.

* * *

Seeing tears in my eyes while listening to this story, Khánum said:
"This time is very sad, Laydee, I shall make you grieve if I tell of it."

"Oh, I want to be with you in my heart through all your sadness, dearest Khánum," I said.

"Well, well! If I did not live in my thoughts all through the events of the sad days of our lives, I should have naught else in my life, for it has been all sorrow; but sorrow is really joy, when suffered in the path of God!"

* * *

When we came to a city, my dear mother would take the clothes and wash them at the public baths; we also were able to have baths at those places. She would carry the cold, wet clothes away in her arms—drying them was an almost impossible task; her lovely hands, being unused to such coarse work, became very painful.

We sometimes stayed at a caravanserai—a sort of rough inn. Only one room was allowed for one family, and for one night—no longer. No light was permitted at night, and there were no beds. Sometimes we were able to have tea, or again a few eggs, a little cheese, and some coarse bread.

My father was so ill that he could not eat the rough food—my mother was very distressed and tried to think of some way of getting different food, as he grew more weak through eating nothing.

ÍRÁN

One day she had been able to get a little flour, and at night, when we arrived at the caravanserai, she made a sweet cake for him. Alas!—the misfortune—being dark, she used salt instead of sugar. So the cake was uneatable! Quite a tragedy in its way.

The Governor of Tihrán sent soldiers with us to the frontier, where Turkish soldiers met us and escorted us to Baghdád.

When we first arrived there, we had a very little house, consisting of my father's room, and another one which was my mother's, and in which were also my eldest brother, the baby, and myself.

When Arab ladies came to see us, this was the only reception room. These ladies came because they had been taught by Táhirih, Qurratu'l-'Ayn, during her visit to Baghdád.

One day when an old lady was there, I was told to prepare the samovár—it was very heavy to carry upstairs, for my arms were not extremely strong. The old lady said: "One proof that the Bábí teaching is wonderful is that a very little girl served the samovár!"

My father was amused, he used to say, "Here is the lady converted by seeing your service at the samovár!"

Among the Arabians taught by Táhirih was Shaykh Sultán, whose daughter married Mírzá Músá, brother of Bahá'u'lláh. Their daughter eventually married Muḥammad-'Alí, half-brother of 'Abdu'l-Bahá.

Mírza Músá and his wife were always devoted to Bahá'u'lláh.

This uncle, Mírzá Músá, who came into exile with us, was a very kind helper in everything. At one time he did almost all the cooking, for which he had a talent; he would also help with the washing.

Ásíyih Khánum, my dear mother, was in delicate health, her strength was diminished by the hardships she had undergone, but she always worked beyond her force.

Sometimes my father himself helped in the cooking, as that hard work was too much for the dainty, refined, gentle lady. The hardships she had endured saddened the heart of her divine husband, who was also her beloved Lord. He gave this help both before his sojourn in the wilderness of Sulaymáníyyih, and after his return.

CHAPTER II

The Intrigues of Ṣubḥ-i-Azal

Meanwhile, Mírzá Yahyá (Ṣubḥ-i-Azal), a younger half-brother of Bahá'u'lláh, who was afterwards the cause of many of our troubles and difficulties, arrived in Baghdád.

He had fled into hiding at Mazíndarán, at the time of the episode of the mad youth shooting at the Sháh, and remained hidden for some time, then he thought that Baghdád might be a safer abode for him than any part of Persia, and for that reason he came.

Now Mírzá Yahyá was filled with pride, arrogance, and fierce jealousy of Bahá'u'lláh. When he arrived at Baghdád he much resented the attitude of reverence shown by all the friends to his majestic elder brother. He claimed the leadership of the Bábís, asserting that His Holiness the Báb had named him His successor.

This was manifestly an untruth.

* * *

Mírzá Ḥusayn-'Alí Núrí wrote on one occasion a letter to the Báb, at the request of His young half-brother, he being too illiterate to write it himself. The Báb, in His reply, referred to this youth as "*a* Mirror." Thereupon Ṣubḥ-i-Azal assumed the title of "*the* Mirror," as being particularly bestowed upon him; the fact being that the title, if not quite a general one, at least had been given to a number of the Bábís.

Now the Báb had thought out a plan of protecting Bahá'u'lláh by veiling Him from general recognition until the "appointed time." For, if it had been noised abroad prematurely that He was the "One Whom God should make Manifest," the opposing forces would undoubtedly have plotted to put Him to death, and the Great Design would, for that reason, have suffered delay. It was therefore above all things necessary to make sure and certain plans in two matters:

(1) Bahá'u'lláh must be known (eventually by all the world) to have been recognized by the Báb as "Him Whom God shall make Manifest," of Whom He was the Forerunner, the Herald! Of this recognition there must be no shadow of a doubt, no possibility of uncertainty—no ground for controversy in the future. This was the sublime meaning of the Mission, for which He, the Báb, endured scorn and persecution and imprisonment, and would in a short time sacrifice His life.

(2) The proclamation must not be made prematurely.

The "Great One" must, for obvious reasons, be veiled until the "appointed time."

In order that these two most important plans should be successful, the Báb confided in Mírzá 'Abdu'l-Karím Qazvíní.

The Báb gave into his custody His remaining papers, His last Tablets, in which Mírzá Ḥusayn-'Alí Núrí was referred to again and again as "Him Whom God shall make Manifest"—in which also the name of "Bahá'u'lláh" was given to Him.

The Báb also entrusted this devoted disciple with His seal and His qalam-dán (pencil-box), charging him to deliver all into the hands of Mírzá Ḥusayn-'Alí Núrí, Bahá'u'lláh, when "an event" should have happened to Himself.

This charge was faithfully carried out by Mírzá 'Abdu'l-Karím Qazvíní, and these precious things remained in the possession of Bahá'u'lláh until the days of Adrianople.

When Ṣubḥ-i-Azal asked to be permitted to see them Bahá'u'lláh consented—but they were never returned. Ṣubḥ-i-Azal kept them to support his claim to leadership, asserting that the Báb had given them to him!

To return to the arrangements made by the Báb for the protection of Bahá'u'lláh, by veiling His recognition until the "appointed time."

Ṣubḥ-i-Azal, not one of the nineteen Letters of the Living (he was one of the "Mirrors"—not *the* Mirror, as he afterwards declared), might well be thought by the uninitiated of these days of confusion, as well as by the uncomprehending open enemies of the Cause, to be a sort of leader of the Bábís after the death of the Herald, the Báb. He certainly could be counted upon to assume that position, so overwhelming was his vanity.

Ṣubḥ-i-Azal would thus, unconsciously, serve as a screen in attracting the attention of the people to himself, thus preventing the premature recognition of "Him Whom God should make Manifest" until His Own appointed time.

One point has been raised, i.e., the danger to Ṣubḥ-i-Azal himself of such a prominent position.

Now it was his own arrogance which prompted him to seize the leadership, for which he was ludicrously unfitted, both by nature and by training—his character being weak, his intelligence small, and his indolence great. Moreover, he could be relied upon to hide himself very effectively when danger threatened, till it should be overpast!

The Bábís, in general, concerned themselves very little with the pretensions of Ṣubḥ-i-Azal, and the true disciples looked upon him as an ignorant and presumptuous youth, whose claims were absurd, but they had the desired effect of diverting attention from the personality of Bahá'u'lláh.

When Ṣubḥ-i-Azal arrived in Baghdád he tried to get the friends to acknowledge him as their leader. They paid scant attention to him, and just laughed at his haughty airs.

He asserted that Jamál-i-Mubárak (Bahá'u'lláh) was preventing the acknowledgment of his position by the people.

* * *

At length my father decided to leave Baghdád for a time.

During his absence, Ṣubḥ-i-Azal could convince himself whether or no the Bábís desired to turn their faces to him as their leader, as he, in the petty conceit of a small mind and undisciplined nature, asserted, would, if given an opportunity, prove to be the case.

Before my father left for his retreat into the wilderness, he commanded the friends to treat Ṣubḥ-i-Azal with consideration. He offered him and his family the shelter and hospitality of our house.

THE INTRIGUES OF ṢUBḤ-I-AZAL

He asked Mírzá Músá, my mother and me, to care for them and to do everything in our power to make them comfortable.

Our grief was intense when my father left us. He told none of us either where he was going or when he would return. He took no luggage, only a little rice, and some coarse bread.

So we, my mother, my brother 'Abbás and I, clung together in our sorrow and anxiety.

Ṣubḥ-i-Azal rejoiced, hoping to gain his ends, now that Jamál-i-Mubárak was no longer present.

Meanwhile, he was a guest in our house. He gave us much trouble, complaining of the food. Though all the best and most dainty things were invariably given to him.

He became at this time more than ever terrified lest he should one day be arrested. He hid himself, keeping the door of our house locked, and stormed at anybody who opened it.

As for me, I led a very lonely life, and would have liked sometimes to make friends with other children. But Ṣubḥ-i-Azal would not permit any little friends to come to the house, neither would he let me go out!

Two little girls about my own age lived in the next house. I used to peep at them; but our guest always came and shouted at me for opening the door, which he promptly locked. He was always in fear of being arrested, and cared for nothing but his own safety.

We led a very difficult life at this time as well as a lonely one. He would not even allow us to go to the Hammám to take our baths. Nobody was permitted to come to the house to help us, and the work therefore was very hard.

For hours every day I had to stand drawing water from a deep well in the house; the ropes were hard and rough, and the bucket was heavy. My dear mother used to help, but she was not very strong, and my arms were rather weak. Our guest never helped.

My father having told us to respect and obey this tyrannical person, we tried to do so, but this respect was not easy, as our lives were made so unhappy by him.

During this time the darling baby brother, born after our arrival in Baghdád, became seriously ill. Our guest would not allow a doctor, or even any neighbour to come to our help.

My mother was heart-broken when the little one died; even then we were not allowed to have anybody to prepare him for burial.

The sweet body of our beautiful baby was given to a man, who took it away, and we never knew even where he was laid. I remember so clearly the sorrow of those days.

A little while after this, we moved into a larger house—fortunately Ṣubḥ-i-Azal was too terrified of being seen, if he came with us—so he preferred to occupy a little house behind ours. We still sent his food to him, also provided for his family, now increased, as he had married another wife, a girl from a neighbouring village.

His presence was thus happily removed from our daily life; we were relieved and much happier.

Lady Blomfield
(Sitárih Khánum)

Bahíyyih Khánum, *circa* 1895

'Abdu'l-Bahá

Lady Blomfield in the prison in 'Akká

Lady Blomfield in the Master's House in Haifa

CHAPTER III

Baghdád

Now our great anxiety was concerning the whereabouts of Jamál-i-Mubárak.

All this time my mother and Mírzá Músá made every possible inquiry. My brother's distress at the prolonged absence was pathetic. On one occasion he prayed the whole night a certain prayer with the one intention, that our father might be restored to us.

The very next day, he and our uncle, Mírzá Músá, overheard two people speaking of a marvellous one, living as a dervish in the wild mountain district of Sulaymáníyyih; they described him as "The Nameless One," who had magnetized the countryside with his love. And they immediately knew that this must be our Beloved.

Here at last was a clue!

Without delay, Shaykh Sultán, our faithful friend, with one of the other disciples, set forth on their quest. Needless to say how our hearts went with them, and that our prayers for their success were unceasing.

Hope now brought its brilliance into the dark shadow of our anxiety, which had saddened our lives for two years.

As these days of intensified waiting passed by, our faith as well as our hope increased and grew. We knew that in the days that were very near at hand, our wanderer, our father, would be once more with us.

My mother had made a coat for him out of some pieces of precious Persian stuff (Tirmih—red cloth),* which she had carefully kept for the purpose out of the remains of her marriage treasures. It was now ready for him to put on.

At last! At last! As my mother, my brother, and I sat in a

---
* See page 242.

breathless state of expectancy, we heard a step. It was a dervish. Through the disguise we saw the light of our beloved one's presence!

Our joy cannot be described as we clung to him.

I can see now my beloved mother, calm and gentle, and my brother holding his father's hand fast, as though never again could he let him go out of his sight, the lovely boy almost enfolded in the uncouth garment of the dervish disguise. I could never forget this scene, so touching and so happy.

Many were the incidents of that two years' sojourn in the wilderness, which were told to us; we were never tired of listening.

The food was easy to describe—coarse bread, a little cheese was the usual diet; sometimes, but very rarely, a cup of milk; into this would be put some rice, and a tiny bit of sugar. When boiled together, these scanty rations provided the great treat of a sort of rice pudding.

One day, near a village in the mountains, Bahá'u'lláh saw a young boy weeping bitterly.

My father, always compassionate for anyone in sorrow, especially if it were a child, said, "Little man, why art thou weeping?"

The boy looked up at the one who spoke, and saw a dervish!

"Oh Sir!" and he fell to weeping afresh. "The schoolmaster has punished me for writing so badly. I cannot write, and now I have no copy! I dare not go back to school!"

"Weep no longer. I will set a copy for thee, and show thee how to imitate it. And now thou canst take this; show it to thy schoolmaster."

When the schoolmaster saw the writing which the boy had brought, he was astonished, for he recognised it as of the royal penmanship, this amazing script.

"Who gave this to thee?" said the master.

"He wrote it for me, the dervish on the mountain."

"He is no dervish the writer of this, but a royal personage," said the schoolmaster.

BAGHDÁD

This story being noised abroad, caused certain of the people to set out to find this one, of whom many wonderful things were said. So great was the throng which pressed in upon him, that he had to go further away; again and again, he moved from place to place, hiding himself from the crowds, in the caves of the mountains, and in the desert places of that desolate land.

One evening the Súfís of that country-side, assembled together, were discussing a mystical poem, when a dervish arose in their midst and gave so wonderful an interpretation of its meaning that awe fell upon the gathering. All his hearers were silent for a while, and then they came together close round him and entreated him to come again to teach them.

But his time was not yet.

When one said sorrowfully, "Oh Master! Shall we then see thee no more?"

"In a time to come, but not yet, go to the city of Baghdád, ask for the house of Mírzá Músá Írání. There shalt thou hear tidings of me," the "Nameless One" replied.

He went out from their midst and again retreated into the desolate places.

* * *

Many were the events of importance to the progress of the Cause that took place during the sojourn at Baghdád.

The following was told by 'Abdu'l-Bahá to the friends at Abú-Sinán in 1915.

Whilst at Baghdád many learned mullás and others came into the Holy Presence, several of whom became His devoted friends; one of those was Kayván Mírzá, grandson of Fath-'Alí Sháh. This gentleman came and asked Mírzá Muhít to obtain permission for an audience at some midnight in secret.

The reply was:

"When I was in the wilderness of Kurdistán I composed this poem:

If thou hast in thine heart one desire for thy life, then come not hither!
But shouldst thou be prepared to sacrifice soul, and heart and life, come and bring others!
Such is the path if thou desire to enter the Kingdom of Light,
If thou art not of those able to walk this path—
Begone, and trouble us not!

Mírzá Muhít conveyed this reply to Kayván Mírzá. He chose to "Begone," his heart failed him!

Of another kind was Áqá Siyyid Mujtahid, who also desired to be admitted to the Holy Presence at the secret midnight hour.

He stayed until morning, and accepted the teaching.

"Well, what thinkest thou?" asked his friend.

Áqá Siyyid Mujtahid said: "I had been told that these Bábís were wine-bibbers, that there was much wine in the room of Bahá'u'lláh, that, moreover, they had no moral principles whatsoever!

I went to investigate for myself and found Purity within Purity. I was filled with amazement at the sanctity of that place, and bewildered to find the exact opposite of that which I had heard. I am firmly convinced that
    "THIS IS THE TRUTH."

* * *

Now followed a period when we might have had a little peace. The Governor had become a friend; the fanatics did not dare to show openly a very fierce hostility. Some of the proceeds of our property, which our friends had succeeded in rescuing and keeping for us, had begun to arrive from Persia. Several of the faithful Bábís, who had followed Bahá'u'lláh and his family into exile, had opened little shops, where their absolute honesty had begun to attract buyers.

Many learned and interesting people gathered round Bahá'u'lláh, appreciating his wisdom, and the helpful counsel he gave when different perplexing problems were laid before him: "Surely his knowledge must be from Heaven!" the people said. As he spoke to them of the "Most Great Peace"

BAGHDÁD

which will come to the world, and shewed his kindness to all who were in trouble and in want, and became known to the poor as "Our Father of Compassion," they understood how it was that for the teaching of true peace and brotherhood and loving-kindness he was driven into exile, and all his vast possessions taken from him. As the truth of the matter was gradually realized, more and yet more people came to him from all the surrounding country.

"There is something of another world in this Majestic Person," they said.

Accounts of what had taken place during his sojourn in the wilderness of Sulaymáníyyih were also told abroad.

As the people pondered on these things, many were amazed, and reverenced the mysterious and majestic guest who tarried in their midst.

When his ever-watchful enemies, the most fanatical and bigoted of the mullás, became aware of the influence of his mere presence on all who came to him, and of the profound impression he had made in the land, they again set themselves to work against him.

The authorities at Constantinople were approached with sundry plausible tales of the harm that was being done by him to the religion of the people, and requests that he might be driven from Baghdád.

At length the Governor came to Bahá'u'lláh in great distress, telling him that a decree had arrived from Constantinople. By this decree Bahá'u'lláh was commanded to leave Baghdád; He would be escorted by Turkish soldiers to an unknown destination.

Our peace was at an end!

When it became known that this departure was to take place, great was the consternation among the friends. We had to make preparation for a journey, we knew not how long, to a place we knew not where. The friends came weeping helplessly, "What shall we do? What is going to happen to our Beloved? What?"

There was such turmoil that we could not proceed with our preparations.

At this juncture Najíb Páshá, who had become a reverent

admirer of Bahá'u'lláh, invited him to bring some of the friends, and come to stay in his garden, a short distance outside Baghdád.

This relieved some of the turmoil, and we worked hard to make ready for the departure.

* * *

It was during Bahá'u'lláh's stay in this garden that the declaration was made to His eldest son, 'Abbás Effendi, and a few friends, that He was "Him Whom God shall make Manifest," and in commemoration of this event the Feast of Riḍván (meaning Feast of Paradise) was instituted, and continues to be observed annually by the Bahá'ís throughout the world.

The story of this Declaration is told by H. M. Balyuzi in his short biography *Bahá'u'lláh*. The following is an extract:

"Bahá'u'lláh moved to the garden of Riḍván, outside the gates of Baghdád. The Bábís thronged there to see the last of their Beloved so cruelly torn from their midst. It was the twenty-first day of April. With tears in their eyes they gathered around Him. He was calm, serene, and unruffled. The hour had struck. To that company Bahá'u'lláh revealed Himself—He was the Promised One in Whose path the Báb had sacrificed His life, 'Him Whom God will make Manifest,' the Sháh Bahrám, the Fifth Buddha, the Lord of Hosts, the Return of Christ, the Master of the Day of Judgment. A deep silence fell upon the audience. Heads were bent as the immensity of that Declaration touched the consciousness of men. Not a breath of dissent—one and all they threw themselves at His feet. Sadness had vanished; joy, celestial joy, prevailed."

CHAPTER IV

Constantinople and Adrianople

Ṣubḥ-i-Azal, always in fear for his own safety, left Baghdád about a fortnight before our departure, and joined our party on the way, having discovered our whereabouts.

He, therefore, had heard nothing of the Declaration in the Riḍván.

When we arrived at Constantinople, our band, being augmented by the way, numbered over seventy persons. We were taken by the Governor to an inn, where we were crowded together into the small space allotted to us. The Master asked the Governor to let Bahá'u'lláh and His family have a house apart. The house was given, but Ṣubḥ-i-Azal and his family were invited by my father to share this house with us.

Amongst the Bábís were members of all classes, simple tradesmen, mullás, and nobles. The latter, as disguise, described themselves as tailors, cooks, confectioners, bakers, etc., so that they might be permitted to remain near Him they revered.

The Persian Consul-General became a friend of Bahá'u'lláh, and was a great help to the Bahá'ís. He suggested to my father that He should pay a visit to the court officials.

The reply was: "I have no wish to ask favour from them. I have come here at the Sultán's command. Whatsoever additional commands he may issue, I am ready to obey. My work is not of their world; it is of another realm, far removed from their province. Why, therefore, should I seek these people?"

This Consul was full of respect for such a majestic mind, and described this occurrence on his return to Tihrán, saying:

"I was extremely proud of my august compatriot. Frequently I feel ashamed of my fellow-countrymen, with good reason, for their almost invariable custom is to pursue high officials, begging for favours. The dignified aloofness of Bahá'u'lláh was a very refreshing experience."

After the return to Tihrán of this Consul he met Mírzá Riḍá-Qulí, to whom he said, "Mírzá Ḥusayn-'Alí Núrí is a wonderful and great man; you are his brother I believe."

To which Mírzá Riḍá-Qulí replied: "No indeed, Oh no! I am not his brother!"

Such was the attitude of Bahá'u'lláh's kindred, and His own father's house; that is when they were not actively vindictive, like Ṣubḥ-i-Azal.

Whilst at Constantinople, the fame of the wisdom of Bahá'u'lláh had gone abroad, and many noble-minded people were anxious to come into His Presence. Such a profound impression was made on these visitors, that they spoke of the majesty of His person, and the holiness of His teaching to their friends. This made His enemies again uneasy, and they plotted on some pretext or another to get Him removed from Constantinople. This plan was successful, and our Beloved One was sent to Adrianople.

When we arrived at Adrianople we were at first in an inn, but we were permitted at length to abide in a hired house.

Bahá'u'lláh at this time made a fuller Declaration of Himself as the expected "Him Whom God shall make Manifest," and Who had been heralded by the Báb. He wrote the Tablet of Declaration (Lawḥ-i-Amr), directing His amanuensis to take it to Ṣubḥ-i-Azal, who, when he had read this, became very angry and "jealous fire consumed him."

He invited Bahá'u'lláh to a feast and shared a dish with Him, one half of which he had mixed with poison. For twenty-one days Bahá'u'lláh was seriously ill from the effects of this attempt.

Incensed at this failure, Ṣubḥ-i-Azal tried another plan. He asked the bath attendant (for a bribe) to assassinate Bahá'u'lláh whilst he should be taking His bath, suggesting how easily it could be done without fear of detection.

This man was so shocked and horrified that he rushed out into the street unclothed.

* * *

Mírzá Asadu'lláh Káshání related to the writer, that when the friends brought the Tablet from Adrianople to Baghdád, they spoke of the nefarious conduct of Ṣubḥ-i-Azal, and that he had been forbidden all intercourse with the Holy Family.

The friends were so enraged with him, that only the express command of Bahá'u'lláh prevented them from ridding the world of "so perjured a traitor."

Siyyid 'Alí Yazdí narrated how Mírzá Ja'far brought the wonderful Tablet to Yazd, telling that Jamál-i-Mubárak (Bahá'u'lláh) had, at Adrianople, made the Great Public Declaration, that He was "Him Whom God shall make Manifest."

And so we, too, heard the soul-stirring news.

We had always known in our hearts that Ṣubḥ-i-Azal was not, could not be, the Promised One; he showed none of the signs; on the other hand, he had many faults, well known to the friends.

"But Mírzá Ḥusayn-'Alí Núrí," they said, "He shows forth the Heavenly Attributes."

Therefore it was that when the blessed Tablet came, we were ready and well prepared to recognize Him.

* * *

Ṣubḥ-i-Azal's high claims were proven to be absurd as well as false, and the friends, when not enraged at his teaching, laughed him to scorn.

At this time the trouble Ṣubḥ-i-Azal caused, and the mischief he made, was so constant that the authorities lost patience, and it was decided to exile the Beloved One and His family yet again.

Ṣubḥ-i-Azal's conduct was, however, not the only cause of this further exile. Our ever-watchful enemies, fearing the great influence of Bahá'u'lláh, made use of the persistent annoyance of the traitorous half-brother as a pretext to induce the Government to banish the august prisoner to a place where no learned and important people would have access to Him.

Ṣubḥ-i-Azal's libels were amplified, and the Government officials were induced to believe them—with this result:

We were sitting one day in our house, when we heard discordant music, loud, insistent! We wondered what could be causing this uproar. Looking from the windows we found that we were surrounded by many soldiers.

The Governor was reluctant to tell Bahá'u'lláh that the order had come for still another banishment. He explained this to Sarkár-i-Áqá* ('Abdu'l-Bahá), and we were told that we had three days to prepare for the journey to 'Akká. Then we learnt that we were all to be separated. Bahá'u'lláh to one place, the Master to another, and the friends to still another place.

I well remember, as though it were only yesterday, the fresh misery into which we were plunged; to be separated from our Beloved; and He, what new grief was in store for Him?

He accepted all vicissitudes with His calm, beautiful smile, cheering us with wonderful words.

One of the friends, Karbilá'í Ja'far, in despair at the threatened separation, attempted to kill himself; he was saved, but was too ill to travel. Bahá'u'lláh refused to leave him unless the Governor of Adrianople undertook to have him well cared for, and sent after us when he should be recovered. This was done, and forty days after we arrived at 'Akká, Karbilá'í Ja'far joined us.

During our sojourn in Adrianople, Bahá'u'lláh's custom was to walk only in the garden of the house, which was also His prison.

Here the friends crowded, weeping and wailing, refusing to be comforted. They determined to resist the separation; great was the tumult. Many telegrams were sent to the Government at Constantinople. At length we all started together on the journey to Gallipoli, and in three days we arrived, having travelled in carts and wagons.

Here the Governor announced that he had received orders for our separation. He came to see Bahá'u'lláh and the Master, and becoming friendly, he tried to help us in our distress. Again many telegrams were sent to Constantinople; we stayed for a week waiting for the replies.

At last permission was given for us all to embark together in

---

* A title given to 'Abdu'l-Bahá by Bahá'u'lláh. It is translated "His Highness the Master."

a Turkish boat. In this small boat we, seventy-two persons, were crowded together in unspeakable conditions, for eleven days of horror. Ten soldiers and two officers were our escort.

There was an appalling smell in the boat, and most of us were very ill indeed.

* * *

At Adrianople were written some of the Epistles to the Kings and Queens of the earth, in which Bahá'u'lláh called upon them as "Servants of the Most High God and Guardians under Him of the people entrusted to their guidance," to join with Him, Bahá'u'lláh, to form an International Arbitration Council, that humanity should never again suffer the disgrace and misery of war.

He proclaimed now more publicly that His authority was Divine, being directly given to Him by God—*that He was the Chosen One, Whom, under various names, all the religions of the earth were awaiting.*

The turmoil was great; the sacred influence radiating from Him reached a wider and still wider circle.

The fanatics, fearing anew this wonderful Personage, and foreseeing the loss of their prestige, and the end of their acquisition of worldly power and wealth if His teachings were accepted, that holy things were not to be sold to mankind, but must be given untarnished "without money and without price," decided to renew their attacks upon Him.

Of course this teaching appealed to the unself-seeking, the noble-minded and the pure in heart only; to all the rest the Message was as foolishness and a menace to every scheme in which figured the worship of the Golden Calf.

A material, greedy, and parochial-minded people turned away from such simple and pure counsel, uncomprehending, and with scornful derision.

These persons took counsel together, and aided by the treacherous half-brother, they agreed to bring new charges against Him.

The result was the further exile to 'Akká, that unhealthy town, the penal convict city, where Turkey sent the most hardened criminals. The idea was that Bahá'u'lláh's influence could not radiate from that pestilential city, where He would be closely guarded, also there was hope that He would not be able to live long in that place, where the air was so poisonous that "If a bird flies over 'Akká it dies!" became the proverb.

Therefore it was that the Great One, with the band of exiles who refused to be separated from Him, set forth on this fourth and last journey of banishment; they were, thanks to the traitor brother and bigoted religious enemies, labelled as malefactors, sowers of sedition, hardened criminals, enemies of the pure religion of God and of man. The faithful were commanded to shun these outcasts.

Such was the character which preceded Bahá'u'lláh and His disciples to 'Akká.

The list of false charges was, moreover, directed to be read to the worshippers in the Mosques, so that all who injured the captives might flatter themselves that they "did God service."

In this way was manufactured the atmosphere of hatred which awaited the "Followers of the Light" when they arrived at the prison fortress city of 'Akká "by way of the sea beyond Jordan—the valley of Achor, which should be given as a door of hope."

Thus, the world unknowing, were the prophecies being daily fulfilled.

Arriving at 'Akká, Bahá'u'lláh said to the Master: "Now I concentrate on My work of writing commands and counsels for the world of the future, to thee I leave the province of talking with and ministering to the people. Servitude is the essence of worship. I have finished with the outer world, henceforth I meet only the disciples."

CHAPTER V

'Akká

We had embarked so hurriedly that we had been unable to provide for the voyage—a few loaves and a little cheese, brought by one of the friends, was all the food we had for those indescribable days.

A dear friend of the family, Jináb-i-Muníb, was taken seriously ill. When the boat stopped at Smyrna, Sarkár-i-Áqá ('Abdu'l-Bahá) and Mírzá Músá carried him ashore, and took him to a hospital. The Master bought a melon and some grapes; returning with the refreshing fruit for him—He found that he had died. Arrangements were made with the director of the hospital for a simple funeral. The Master chanted some prayers, then, heartsore, came back to the boat.

Arrived at Alexandria, again came that spectre, the rumour of our immediate separation.

The friends, though prostrated by sickness, worn out by the wretchedness of the voyage, and crushed by this repeated blow, determined to refuse submission. One friend, in his dire distress, jumped into the sea, but was saved.

Bahá'u'lláh and the Master cheered us. "Why did you jump into the sea? Did you wish to give a banquet to the fishes?" asked Bahá'u'lláh.

Nabíl, the historian, and another of the Bahá'ís, were in the prison near the port at Alexandria. In their chains they stood, gazing out of the small windows. To their amazement they saw Bahá'u'lláh and the Master standing amongst the friends on the deck of our boat.

The prisoners succeeded in attracting the attention of one of our servants, who very cautiously went to them and heard them say: "We were brought here a week ago, we know not to what fate we are destined."

Thence we proceeded to Haifa.

There was no place in which we could lie down in that vessel. There were also some Tartar passengers in the boat. To be near them was very uncomfortable; they were dirty beyond description.

Our lack of food had reduced us to a seriously weak state of health.

At length we arrived at Haifa, where we had to be carried ashore in chairs. Here we remained for a few hours. Now we embarked again for the last bit of our sea journey. The heat of that month of July was overpowering. We were put into a sailing boat. There being no wind, and no shelter from the burning rays of the sun, we spent eight hours of positive misery, and at last we had reached 'Akká, the end of our journey.

The landing at this place was achieved with much difficulty; the ladies of our party were carried ashore.

All the townspeople had assembled to see the arrival of the prisoners. Having been told that we were infidels, criminals, and sowers of sedition, the attitude of the crowd was threatening. Their yelling of curses and execrations filled us with fresh misery. We were terrified of the unknown! We knew not what the fate of our party, the friends and ourselves would be.

We were taken to the old fortress of 'Akká, where we were crowded together. There was no air; a small quantity of very bad coarse bread was provided; we were unable to get fresh water to drink; our sufferings were not diminished. Then an epidemic of typhoid broke out. Nearly all became ill.

The Master appealed to the Governor, but he was at first very little inclined to relax the strict rules, which he had been directed to enforce.

The Muftí had read to the people in the Mosque a Farmán full of false accusations.

We were described as enemies of God, and as the worst kind of criminals. The people were exhorted to shun these vile malefactors; this naturally caused the attitude of intense hatred and bitter antagonism with which we were regarded.

After a while the Governor was persuaded by the Master to allow a little money instead of the uneatable rations which had been allotted to us; he also permitted one of the servitors, Mírzá Ja'far, to go into the town, accompanied by a soldier, to buy food. By this our condition was considerably bettered. Bahá'u'lláh and His family were imprisoned in three little rooms, up many steps, for two years.

During this time Dr. Petro, a Greek, became a friend, and having been able to make investigations, he assured the Governor that these prisoners, far from being vile criminals, were high-minded persons and innocent of all harm.

So closely were we watched that we had been in 'Akká six or seven months without being able to get into touch with Mírzá 'Abdu'l-Aḥad, a devoted Bábí disciple, who had been sent by 'Abdu'l-Bahá to 'Akká some time before our arrival, and had opened a shop.

So great would his danger have been, had his connexion with the Bahá'ís been suspected, that the strictest caution was absolutely necessary.

Having heard a rumour that the Beloved Ones had been sent to 'Akká, a friend, Abu'l-Qásim Khán, and his wife, made that long and dangerous journey from Persia in order to find out the truth. Arrived in 'Akká they met Mírzá 'Abdu'l-Aḥad. He, fearing lest his secret should be disclosed, hurriedly hid the pair behind stacks of boxes at the back of his shop.

The news of their arrival was, with much difficulty, conveyed to Bahá'u'lláh. He sent them back to Persia, after a stay of only three days, so grave was the risk. These friends accordingly left 'Akká. They had not even seen Bahá'u'lláh, but they were able to carry the news back to Persia that the Beloved Ones were really imprisoned in this desolate place.

The first Persian friends to telegraph to 'Akká were the "King of the Martyred" and his brother, "The Beloved of the Martyred." The help they succeeded in sending was much needed, as we were past the end of our resources. Little by little the news of our whereabouts filtered through to the other friends in Persia. Shaykh Salmán's self-constituted mission was to carry news from Bahá'u'lláh to Persia, and to bring back letters to Him.

Many were the difficult and dangerous journeys made, mostly on foot.

Shaykh Salmán it was who, when he was arrested at Aleppo, bearing a most important supplication from a friend in Persia to Bahá'u'lláh, wondering how he could prevent the enemy finding it, knowing the dire consequences of its falling into their hands, swallowed it.

It was this devoted and resourceful friend who was entrusted with the significant mission of bringing Muníríh Khánum from Isfahán to 'Akká, she who was to become the wife of Sarkár-i-Áqá ('Abdu'l-Bahá) the Master, and my much-loved sister.

When Nabíl, the historian, came to 'Akká he was unable to get into the city. He lived for some time in the cave of Elijah on Mount Carmel. Thence he used to walk (about ten miles) to a place beyond the wall of the fortress. From this point he could see the windows of those three little rooms of our prison; here he would wait and watch for the rare and much-coveted happiness of seeing the hand of Bahá'u'lláh waving from the small middle window.

Meanwhile the war between Russia and Turkey was in progress. More barrack room was required for the soldiers. Bahá'u'lláh protested against the friends being crowded in with the soldiers. By that time the Governor had become friendly and consented to allow the family to leave the fortress, and live in a little house which a Christian merchant had let to us.

How we rejoiced in our liberty, restricted though it was. Only three times had we been permitted to go out, for even an hour, from the prison barracks during the whole of that first two years.

How tired we were of those three little rooms!

* * *

During the period of the sojourn in Baghdád, Bahíyyíh Khánum, the Greatest Holy Leaf, was her mother's loving helper, working always beyond her strength, in the various household tasks. No childish pleasures or companions were hers. Always with eyes on her mother, alert to spare her any fatigue, she rejoiced beyond measure when she could minister in any way to her or her illustrious father.

"My mother," she said, "sometimes gave lessons to my brother 'Abbás; at other times Mírzá Músá would teach Him, and on some occasions he would be taught by His father."

"And *your* lessons?" I asked.

"But I never had any time for studies," she said, in a tone which spoke volumes of absolute self-effacement, and this is the keynote of her whole life, no thought of her unselfishness entered her mind.

Her thoughtfulness and consideration for all who came near her; the countless acts of never-failing kindness, were, in her eyes, all to be taken as a matter of course. Her one joy was to devote every moment of her existence to being of use to her mother and father, to whom she was passionately attached. This loving service was extended, as He grew older, to her brother 'Abbás, Sarkár-i-Áqá, and these three were her being's end and aim.

Her life was spent in prayer to God and service to her loved ones, from the time when, as a small child of six, she cowered in the dark house alone with the tiny Purest Branch, a baby of two, in her little arms, listening in terror to the yells of the infuriated, cruel mob, not knowing if they were murdering her father, or whether they had seized her mother and the little eight-year-old 'Abbás.

After those terrible days in Tihrán, and the not less terrible journey to Baghdád, during the sojourn in this city, she grew into a beautiful girl, very much like her lovely mother in grace of body and character, a gentle, slender maiden with large, grey-blue eyes, golden-brown hair, and warm, ivory-coloured skin. Her sense of humour was keen and her intelligence remarkable.

As she grew up, she implored her father to allow her to remain unmarried, that she might the better devote herself to her three dearly loved ones.

And so it was.

An old man, a friend of Bahá'u'lláh, told me that He once said to him: "I know no man worthy to marry such purity as my daughter."

I said, "Khánum *must* have been very lovely?"

"I have been told so; naturally, I never saw her."

THE SPOKEN CHRONICLE

of

Munírih Khánum,

wife of 'Abdu'l-Bahá,

the Greatest Branch

of the

Tree of Life.

One night during dinner, Mírzá Ibráhim turned to the Báb and said "My brother, Mírzá Muḥammad-'Alí, has had no children. Bless him, I entreat Thee, and grant unto him his heart's desire."
The Báb took a portion of the food with which He had been served, placed it in a platter, and handed it to His host, saying "Take this to Mírzá Muḥammad-'Alí and his wife. Let them partake of this food; their wish shall be fulfilled."
By virtue of that portion which the Báb had bestowed upon her, the wife of Mírzá Muḥammad-'Alí conceived, and in due time gave birth to a child, who eventually was joined in wedlock with the Most Great Branch, and therefore became the consummation of the highest hopes of her parents.

Nabíl: The Dawn-breakers.

* * *

"The next event in the order of time was the arrival of Munírih Khánum, who was destined to become the loving wife, the staunch helpmate, the adoring friend of the Master.
"She is a majestic woman, stately yet simple, with an innate dignity and strength of character."

Lady Blomfield.

Muním̓h K͟hánum, as the writer knew her, in the first days of mourning for the beloved Master's passing—wiping away the tears of the sorrow-stricken friends, which poured afresh as they came into her presence, comforting them with her love, whilst her own grief was infinitely greater than theirs.

The wonderful, the perfect wife!

The devoted, the Holy Mother, not only to her own daughters and their children, but to all the friends who came to Haifa!

She has a most beautiful voice, and her eyes are large, dark, still, with a serenity in their depths that holiness alone can give.

She lives in Heaven, whilst she is on earth, and, like Bahíyyih K͟hánum, the Greatest Holy Leaf, she takes upon herself the burden of everybody's trouble.

These two saints, who lived so near their sacred Beloved Ones, whilst they sojourned in this world, and whose whole happiness lay in ministering to them!

Muním̓h K͟hánum would sometimes, at my desire, tell me of the events of her marvellous life, which I will try to write down from the notes I made at the time.

First of all it is needful to understand that none of the ladies of the holy household, Ásíyih K͟hánum, the wife of Bahá'u'lláh, Bahíyyih K͟hánum, their lovely daughter, Muním̓h K͟hánum, the Holy Mother, and the four daughters of the Master, have ever bemoaned the difficulties of their daily lives. The conditions of suffering in all the prison period called forth a superhuman patience and self-sacrifice in trying to mitigate the misery of their fellow-exiles.

The fortitude of these gentle ladies never wavered in face of incredible hardships—endured for others' good—in that sorrow-laden time, when the days lengthened out into years of privation, where the simplest comforts of life were lacking.

Radiant acquiescence met all the incredible vicissitudes of the life in 'Akká, from their arrival in 1868 to the release of 'Abdu'l-Bahá forty years later.

None of these difficulties seemed to them worthy of being remembered; they were all a matter of course, even as the air they breathed; it never occurred to them to mention them; it is only by inference that we have a glimpse into the depths of the pain which has been theirs, which has made up their laborious days.

Upheld by that holy preoccupation of the spirit, its courage and its joy, they are calm and loving to all, yet aloof, dwelling consciously in that "Peace which passeth understanding" in the presence of God, in Whose path all the sufferings and persecutions, heaped upon them by uncomprehending persons, count as less than nothing.

It is this attitude of theirs, this spirit, which is more arresting, more amazing, than the mere events; this spirit it is that gives the great significance, which envelops all the episodes and incidents of their existence with its radiant atmosphere.

We stand, trying to absorb something of its all-pervading influence, and gaining an inkling of the inadequacy of every kind of worldly plan with which men think to accomplish the Coming of the Kingdom, without seeking first this spirit.

If we do not realize somewhat of this attitude of the beloved ladies, we cannot but fail to grasp the meaning of the following events as told by Munírih Khánum, the Holy Mother.

CHAPTER I

Visit to Shíráz

If I were to tell you all the vicissitudes of my journey from Isfahán to 'Akká, you would be able to fill a large book with them alone. Therefore I will limit the story to my visit to Shíráz.

Always before my mind is the evening of our arrival in Shíráz—the Dayspring of the Light of God—the birthplace of His Holiness the Báb.

My feelings of exaltation were indescribable. The whole air seemed to be full of the sweet songs of glad tidings, to which I listened with joy; all my soul and spirit vibrated to the voiceless sounds of the music I heard that day.

I was taken to the Khán (a sort of hotel), in which there is a part reserved for ladies.

Some of the Afnán* family came to welcome me, and cordially invited me to their houses. I went to the house of Siyyid Muḥammad, uncle of the Holy One. So dainty was the room, it seemed like a guest chamber in Paradise.

The ladies of the house consisted of the daughter of Siyyid Muḥammad and two daughters-in-law; they were not absolutely Bahá'ís, though interested in the Cause.

Therefore I thought it wise not to confide to them my destination.

After our ablutions, and when we had all joined in chanting the sunset prayer, they, being pleased that I had stood and prayed with them, questioned me.

"Where are you going? Is it to some far distant country?"

"I am going to the Holy Land."

"Because your love for God is so great, therefore are you journeying to the Holy Land?"

---

* The collateral relations of the Báb and their descendants are called "Afnán." It is a sort of surname.

Now the Holy Land was to them Mecca, the place of pilgrimage of Islám, and Bahá'u'lláh had directed us to journey through this Holy Place on our way to 'Akká.

When one of the ladies said to me: "The widow of the Báb will come to visit you in the morning," I was so moved that my tears flowed, and my heart was full.

Oh to see the wife of the Báb!

We greeted each other meaningly; I saw that she knew my journey's aim and end.

She took me to her home.

"I will first take thee to the room where He was born."

This room was kept sacred.

Here the dear Khadíjih Khánum embraced me, and gave way to her heart's sorrow. I wept with her; my soul seemed filled with her sorrow, yet this sorrow was mingled with the joyful songs of the Glad Tidings, those which I had heard at the sunset hour of my arrival.

Dear, dear lady, how beautiful she was, even then, with her dark hair and eyes, lovely still for all their weeping, and her soft, creamy skin.

She took me to the house of the martyred uncle of the Báb, he who had cared for Him, and brought Him up from the time when, His father having died, His widowed mother brought Him to live with her at her brother's house.

Khadíjih-Sultán-Bagum's eldest sister was the wife of this uncle. She was now growing old, and had suffered terribly; all the more terribly because she had not been able to share in the joy of the Glad Tidings of the Coming of the Herald of "Him Whom God shall make Manifest," nor to understand that the Great One also had come. She was firmly attached to the orthodox ordinary Muslim religion, notwithstanding the martyrdom of her husband and his holy nephew.

She moaned "Why should religion cause so much bloodshed? Surely it should be a cause of peace. I am perplexed and distressed, and my heart is full of sorrow."

I tried to help her, I longed to do so. Being a stranger, she listened to me. I chanted some prayers, and she wept, but understood not at all.

This condition of mind was very usual amongst those Persians who, far from being enemies, were kind and good, but whose eyes had not been opened.

Whilst she talked, Khadíjih-Bagum was silent. Then I said, "Please tell me of the childhood of the Báb, what thou rememberest of Him."

Gently she spoke: "The child came to us when He was four years old. From the first He was quite different from other children, so wise and gentle and serene. When He was seven years old He was taken to the school of Shaykh 'Ábid.

"The schoolmaster came to my husband and said:

" 'The fees thou givest for teaching 'Alí Muḥammad I can only accept as a present. He has no need of my teaching!

" 'For instance, I said to him "Repeat this verse of the Qur'án after me.

" ' "I wish first to know the meaning, then I will repeat it unto thee."

" 'I said to Him "No, Thou say it first, then its signification will be told unto Thee."

" 'He amazed me by saying, "I, then, will explain it to thee."

" 'The verse was "He is the All-knowing." His explanation of this was so marvellous that I was profoundly impressed.' "

(Shaykh 'Ábid became a believer in the Báb.)

"Now, Khadíjih-Bagum, tell me, I pray thee, some of the many things thou must remember of Him."

"We were three sisters; our father was the least prosperous of the great-uncles of my Beloved. We were far from being wealthy when we married, as the world counts wealth. Therefore there was little joy amongst our relations and friends at our union. But this was of no importance to us; the memory of my dream of two years before was always with me, and filled the time of my engagement with great happiness.

"I will tell of that dream, should you desire to hear it.*

"Whilst the Báb was at Búshihr, I again dreamed a dream: "I saw Him in an attitude of prayer, His vesture was marvellous and beautiful, embroidered with fine needlework, and round its borders were written, in gold and in silver, verses from the Qur'án. The radiance of a sacred light shone round Him.

---

* This dream is related on page 14, Part I.

"When I told my sisters of this dream, they also recognized the truth that "He must be the Chosen One!"

I tarried with Khadíjih-Bagum for twenty-one days of joy and wonderment.

* * *

She told me of those sad days, when He was in prison. How that she was full of anxiety, longing for news of Him. She was very closely watched—none of the friends were permitted to visit her. Very rarely would one of them, disguised as a beggar, succeed in reaching her door, bringing her such news as he had been able to gather. But this took place, oh! so seldom, and her lonely days dragged on, full of an anxious uncertainty as to His fate.

At length the devoted uncle, the father by adoption of the dear young husband, left Shíráz secretly to try if haply he could find out where they had imprisoned Him; perchance, with great care and trouble, he might even be able to discover some means of seeing Him.

Alas! never did he arrive, for he was arrested in Tihrán, and went to his cruel death, one of the "Seven Martyrs."

Such a spirit of ecstasy and devotion did they show, chanting prayers and smiling with joy in the faces of their torturers, that all were amazed.

But their praise to God never wavered, that they were counted worthy by Him to attain the Crown of Martyrdom.

When at length the terrible story of the martyrdom of her husband came, even her mother, who had been staying with her in her isolation, was taken away from her, so that Khadíjih-Bagum had no earthly comforter in this time of anguish.

* * *

During my visit to Shíráz, I seemed to be all ears, so eagerly did I listen to the stories of those days when agony and joy, the depths of earthly agony, and the height of sacred joy were the only companions of this dear, gentle lady, at that time little more than a girl, so young was she.

VISIT TO SHÍRÁZ

She gave me two supplications to convey to Bahá'u'lláh, for she knew that it was to Him I was journeying.

One was to pray that the two families, the Afnán (relations of herself and of her husband the Báb) and the family of Bahá'u'lláh should be united in marriage.

The other was that she might receive permission to make the pilgrimage to 'Akká.

Bahá'u'lláh granted both her wishes.

The first came to pass when my eldest daughter, Ḍíyá Khánum, married Áqá Mírzá Hádí, one of the Afnán, again when Ṭúbá Khánum married Áqá Mírzá Muḥsin, respectively grandson and son of the brothers-in-law of the Báb, therefore also one of the Afnán.

How I longed to take Khadíjih-Bagum with us, my brother and me, to 'Akká, but the journey, we knew, would have been too unsafe, as well as too wearisome for her.

So we left her with great sorrow and weeping, never were we to meet again on this sad earth.

Some time afterwards a party of pilgrims were starting from Yazd on a pilgrimage to 'Akká. They arranged to go by way of Shíráz, so that she might journey with them.

This plan gave her the utmost happiness, and she made ready for the great pilgrimage with much joyful looking forward.

Alas! the conditions at Shíráz became so increasingly dangerous that the Yazd pilgrims were obliged to give up their intention of passing through that town.

They managed with difficulty to get a letter taken to her saying:
"To our regret and sorrow, we are compelled to go to that place without thee, but we will send one of the Afnán as thine escort, to the place where it is thy desire to be."

Thus the bitter disappointment came to her; but in a life filled with all possible griefs, sorrows, and sufferings this was to be the last, for, when the letter arrived, she was so distressed that she fell ill, and, chanting:
"We are from God and to God do we return.
"Praise be unto Him for the Coming of His Great Day, and for all the glory of my life,"
her gentle spirit returned to its celestial shelter.

CHAPTER II

'Abdu'l-Bahá

The following is a paraphrase of what Munírih Khánum related to me about the early life of the Master.

* * *

'Abdu'l-Bahá, even in early childhood, shared in the woes of His family, upon whom the most terrible troubles descended.

The teaching of the Báb had caused a great turmoil in all the land of Persia. The Bábís, feeling forced to defend themselves and their families, took refuge in various towns and forts of Mázindarán, Zanján, and Nayríz. Being besieged, their supplies of food were diminished and they were in dire straits.

Bahá'u'lláh, Who had become a disciple of the Báb, led rescue parties, carrying food and money to the brave and sorely pressed garrisons.

He thereby incurred the hatred of the most fanatical of the mullás. These men were unscrupulous in their methods, employing spies to watch, so that some pretext might be found for the active persecutions which they were plotting.

When the insane youth shot at the Sháh, the fanatics rejoiced. Here was a grand opportunity!

'Abdu'l-Bahá, then only eight years old, was broken-hearted at the ruthless treatment of His adored Father. The child suffered agonies, as a description of the tortures was related in His hearing—the cruel scourging of the feet, the long miles Bahá'u'lláh had to walk afterwards, barefooted, heavy chains cutting into the delicate flesh, the loathsome prison; the excruciating anxiety lest His very life should be taken—made a load of suffering, piteous for so young and sensitive a child to endure.

All the former luxury of the family was at an end, deserted as they were by relations and friends. Homeless, utterly impoverished, engulfed in trouble, sorrow, and misery, suffering from sheer want and extraordinary privations—such were the conditions under which His childhood's life was spent.

These things counted not at all whilst He was with His Father; so that the exile and the earlier days in Baghdád were happy, in spite of outside miseries. But when Bahá'u'lláh retreated into the wilderness of Sulaymáníyyih the dear child was beside Himself with grief.

He occupied Himself with copying those Tablets of the Báb which had remained with them. He tried to help His dear mother, Ásíyih Khánum, in her arduous tasks.

During this time He was taken by His uncle, Mírzá Músá, to some of the meetings of the friends. There He spoke to them with a marvellous eloquence, even at that early age of eleven or twelve years. The friends wondered at His wisdom and the beauty of His person, which equalled that of His mind.

He prayed without ceasing for the return of Bahá'u'lláh. He would sometimes spend a whole night through praying a certain prayer. One day after a night so spent they found a clue! Very soon the Beloved One returned!

Now His joy was as great as His grief had been!

Many were the gatherings of the friends on the banks of the Tigris, to which the young boy was taken by His Father. These meetings, necessarily secret, were now His greatest pleasure. He drank in the teaching of divine things which were to educate the world, with an understanding of universal conceptions astounding in such a young child.

So life went on; He grew into a beautiful youth, beloved by all who knew Him.

And now came fresh sorrow!

The ever-active enemies, fearing the growing influence of Bahá'u'lláh, petitioned that He, with His disciples, should be again exiled.

The Governor of Baghdád requested Bahá'u'lláh to attend at the Court House, to hear a Farmán read, which had been sent by the Sultán. The Governor was loath to inform Bahá'u'lláh of the decree, being unwilling that any discourtesy should be shown to the kingly exile, for Whom he himself felt a profound reverence.

The reply came:

"My mission is not with the rulers of this world, neither with their statesmen, nor their officials. For what reason, therefore, should I enter their Court House?"

The Governor was bewildered, and knew not what to do in his perplexity. At length, he said within himself:

"If I invite Him to the mosque, He will surely come, for is it not the House of God? In the holy place the Farmán can be read to Him."

Bahá'u'lláh consented to go to the mosque, where the decree was announced to Him, that He and His family were to be exiled from Baghdád to an unknown destination.

The family and the friends were very sad at this new uprooting. The preparations for the journey were extremely difficult.

The Master, as He was now called, shielded His adored Father in all ways that lay in His power from undesirable intruders, from the world's insistence, and from those who merely wanted idly to see and to hear something new.

He made the arrangements for the Beloved One to go to the Riḍván, there to abide until the family should have been able to make preparations for the departure.

Whilst He tarried in the Riḍván, the appointed time had arrived for the momentous proclamation.

Bahá'u'lláh confided to the eldest son, 'Abbás, the Master, that He Himself was "He Whom God shall make Manifest," heralded by the Forerunner, the Báb.

As the Master heard the soul-stirring words, and realized that His own beloved Father was He Who should educate mankind in universal conceptions, abolish prejudices, bring unity and the most Great Peace into the distracted world, establish the Kingdom of God upon this sad earth, by making religion again a healing spring for all woes of the world, He understood why the Manifestation had once again become the cause of evil men's hatred and malignant persecution.

As these things were pondered by the Master, His mind, well-endowed with a peculiar receptiveness that was inborn, and strengthened by the education given to Him by His Father, saw, as in a radiant vision, the world of the future, when the divine Message, having become known and comprehended by "men of goodwill," would change the heart of the world, and the Kingdom where God's will shall be done *on earth*—for which we have been praying for nigh two thousand years—would be established.

Henceforth a new joy and increased devotion to His Father, Bahá'u'lláh (The Glory of God) took possession of Him. He consecrated Himself, body and soul and spirit, to the sacred work of the Bahá'í Cause, spreading abroad the new message of Love and Justice, that message which His Holiness the Lord Christ had brought to man, and which man had grown to disregard, forgetting his loyalty to the Lord of Compassion, and, as of old, worshipping the Golden Calf.

And now the preparations being completed, they set forth on their journey of exile to an unknown destination.

Bahá'u'lláh, the Master, and the ladies of the family rode horses and mules, and some were in Kajávihs, a sort of erection (of the most jolting description) on the back of a mule, and the rest rode horses and mules.

They were escorted by some Turkish soldiers, who behaved very respectfully to the exiles, although they were prisoners. So great was the influence of the majestic personality of Bahá'u'lláh, that it affected all who came within its lines of force. Discourtesy shrank abashed from His Presence.

At length the tedious journey by land from Baghdád to Constantinople was accomplished—that being the "unknown destination."

Many were attracted to Bahá'u'lláh at Constantinople, and again the enemy, fearing anew His influence, plotted the further exile to Adrianople.

The account of the sojourn in this place, and the intrigues of another type of enemy, Bahá'u'lláh's half-brother, Ṣubḥ-i-Azal, are written in another place.

Henceforth, His bitterest and most unscrupulous foe was "of His own kindred, and His own Father's house."

Consumed with the burning flame of jealousy, as soon as Bahá'u'lláh sent the Tablet of Declaration to this half-brother, acquainting him with the proclamation of His station as the Chosen One, every mischief which wounded vanity, joined with cunning and ruthless hatred, could devise was plotted and carried out.

CHAPTER III

The Bride of 'Abdu'l-Bahá

Munírih Khánum, having spoken of some of the incidents, aspects, and sufferings of the Master's life before she met Him, now said:

When I was a young girl, I loved to think over the lives of the Holy Ones, the Lord Christ, Muḥammad, and the other prophets of God. I used to weep and lament that I had not lived in their time.

My father went to Baghdád to visit Bahá'u'lláh when I was about nine years old.

I became aware that my parents were enthralled with their devotion to a new and secret religion. I used to meditate on what it could be, indeed I grew to have some suspicion in my mind regarding it, and to have even a little fear of its importance as I watched its effect upon my dear ones.

Once a dream came to me, of which, even now, I retain the impression.

In my dream, I carried many things in my arms; wearily I walked, dragging my feet across the endless desolation of desert sand. My strength seemed to be ebbing away, and my burden too heavy to hold. I was, oh! so tired, almost unable to walk one more step, when suddenly, to my surprise, I came to two rivers. A bridge connected these two rivers. Leaning against the wall of this bridge, I saw in my dream one of the disciples, an old Siyyid. He came forward to me and asked:

"What dost thou want? Where dost thou wish to go?"

I replied earnestly:

"I desire greatly to go to the blessed cities of Jerusalem—Love—and Bahá."

The Siyyid said solemnly:

"Carrying those things that burden thee, thou canst not journey to those cities, neither canst thou enter therein. First cast away thy burden, then shalt thou have strength and power to attain thy desire."

Instantly I let fall all the things of my burden.

The old Siyyid thereupon, looking approvingly, took me by the arm and plunged me into the rivers, first into the one, then into the other. When I emerged I suddenly found myself flying without effort, as it were floating, over amazingly beautiful country. I was awe-struck at its sacred loveliness, as of Paradise. During my flight, my joy was so overwhelming as to seem a celestial gladness.

I arrived at a radiant city of shining glory. On its walls were written in Arabic in letters of brilliant light:
"LOVE. BAHÁ. JERUSALEM.
JERUSALEM. LOVE. BAHÁ.
BAHÁ. JERUSALEM. LOVE."
In the great Temple of this city were all the Holy Ones, the Prophets of God, in Whose presence I had so ardently longed to stand—His Holiness the Lord Christ, Moses, Isaiah, and every other Prophet of Whom I knew.

At one altar was Muḥammad; He gave to me a radiant necklace of diamonds. This I handed to my mother, and, trying again to fly, I awoke!

It seemed that this golden dream had come in answer to my eager wishes and prayers.

I remember when I was a girl the news came to Iṣfáhán from Nabíl that Jamál-i-Mubárak was imprisoned in the fortress town of 'Akká, shut in behind iron doors, never going out!

As I thought of Him in that poisonous climate—He Who loved the seas, the hills, and the plains, gardens, flowers, and quick movement in the open air—my heart seemed broken, and I shut myself into my room alone, that I might weep rivers of tears.

And now came the never-to-be-forgotten day, when Shaykh Salmán arrived at Iṣfáhán, bringing word from Bahá'u'lláh that He wished me to come to Him.

I was beside myself with joy, that I should, whilst I lived, see my Lord! Even though the journey should be full of difficulty and danger, of suffering indescribable, of risks uncountable, none of these considerations weighed anything in the balance against the gladness of starting on a pilgrimage, with my face steadfastly set towards the presence of the Holy One.

Accordingly, I set forth with my brother and Shaykh Salmán on the journey from Isfahán to 'Akká.

Extreme caution was necessary—we refrained from intercourse with any of the friends—especially we took care that, not through any word or action of ours, should it become known that the two devoted brothers, Mírzá Ḥasan and Mírzá Ḥusayn of Isfahán, were Bábís. These two dear first cousins of mine were always of great help to any of the friends who were in trouble, but that aid was necessarily given in strict secrecy, so terrible was the danger to property, limb, and life incurred by any, upon whom the suspicion of being a Bábí might fall.

These two brothers were the first to send material help to the exiles at 'Akká, and the friends, sojourning at Mosul, were rescued from sheer starvation by supplies of corn and money, promptly despatched to them by these generous disciples.

The tragedy of their martyrdom in 1878, when they were given the glorious names of "King of the Martyrs" and "Beloved of the Martyrs," was indeed a work of evil, by base hands wrought; truly one of the "dark deeds without a name."

Shaykh Salmán had brought directions from Bahá'u'lláh for our journey.

We gave out that we were going to Mecca.

On our return from the holy shrine, we were directed to stay at Jiddah until all the twenty Bábís who had accompanied us had gone back to their homes, having accomplished the pilgrimage to Mecca; none of them being permitted, because of the perilous conditions, to proceed to 'Akká.

We waited at Jiddah, exercising the greatest circumspection; extreme danger surrounded all.

Bahá'u'lláh was in strictest confinement.

We had grown accustomed to looking into the face of sudden death and numberless other perils, with the fortitude inspired by our gladness and heart of grace; for were we not pilgrims, making our way to the presence of our beloved Lord at His own express command?

At length we left Jiddah; my brother and myself, Shaykh Salmán, and one servant, such was the little party of four who were permitted to make this pilgrimage to 'Akká.

To describe all the incidents of that memorable journey would be to fill a great book.

My wonderful stay at Shíráz—my precious friendship with Khadíjih Khánum, that gentle, sorrow-stricken lady, the widow of the Supreme Báb—all this you know.

Always exercising the greatest discretion we proceeded on our way. We embarked at Alexandria for 'Akká; a telegram came:

"Do not land until fetched."

Nobody came!

We thought that our boat would depart with us still on board. At the last moment we saw a small boat coming swiftly towards us. "Shaykh Salmán, Shaykh Salmán"! We heard the cry; our joyful hearts were singing glad songs as we climbed down into the tiny skiff.

And we had arrived at 'Akká.

Permission to enter the city was obtained in this way.

'Abbúd, a Christian merchant, landlord of the "little house," as it came to be called, where Bahá'u'lláh and His family were then living, had stated that he expected some friends to visit him. As his friends we entered 'Akká, and went straightway to his house.

The room prepared for me was that of which the door was eventually opened into the "little house." This room was to become my bridal chamber, my nursery night and day, my sitting-room, my all! Glorious was my happiness! I am living it all over again in telling it to you, dear Ladyee, now.

In a few days I went to stay at the house of Mírzá Músá, the brother of Bahá'u'lláh; here I remained for six months.

My brother and I used to stand at a window and watch 'Abbás Effendi swimming; such a strong and graceful swimmer. Every afternoon about five o'clock the wife of Mírzá Músá would go with me to visit Bahá'u'lláh. I cannot describe the wonder and gladness and happiness of being in His presence. My soul was wrapt in an ecstasy of utter joy, and seemed to float in a celestial atmosphere of peace and loving-kindness.

Many beautiful daughters were offered from time to time by parents anxious that their child should have the honour of becoming the wife of the Master. He refused to consider any of them, until I arrived; we met each other once, and our marriage was arranged.

There was a delay because there was no room available in the "little house."

Now 'Abbúd, the landlord of the "little house," and of the larger one next to it, had become devoted to the Master, in whom he recognized qualities like unto those of the Lord Christ.

One day he asked to be received by Bahá'u'lláh, to Whom he said:

"Wherefore the delay in the marriage?"

Being told the reason, he exclaimed:

"I can arrange about the room. I pray Thee, let me have the honour of preparing a place for the Master and His bride."

He hastened to have the door opened through into an extra room, which he furnished simply and comfortably.

"The room is now ready, O Master."

The next day, Bahá'u'lláh asked Khánum, His daughter, not to let their visitor (Munírih Khánum) return to her abode. Khánum brought a dainty white frock (which Ásíyih Khánum and she had made for me of white batiste) and put it on to me, with a fresh white niqáb (head-dress) on my head—and I was adorned for my wedding.

The guests were few, Ásíyih Khánum, Bahíyyih Khánum, the wife of 'Abbúd, her three daughters (one of these wished to dress my hair more elaborately than usual, but I preferred to leave it in its two plaits), and the wife of Mírzá Músá.

Bahá'u'lláh spoke wonderful words to me:

"Oh Munírih! Oh my Leaf! I have destined you for the wife of My Greatest Branch. This is the bounty of God to you. In earth or in heaven there is no greater gift. Many have come, but We have rejected them and chosen you. Oh Munírih! Be worthy of Him, and of Our generosity to you."

THE BRIDE OF 'ABDU'L-BAHÁ

If I were to try to describe my elation, my ecstasy of joy, "Mathnaví would become seventy volumes" (Persian proverb; "Mathnaví," a book of poems).

Oh that this hour had been everlasting!

Bahá'u'lláh had previously revealed a Tablet for us, which the guests wished me to chant to them.

"When the gates of the sacred garden are set open, and the holy youth issues forth, verily he hath come with a Message of great import.

"Glad tidings! Glad tidings!

"This is that holy youth who hath come, bringing the Message of great joy."

(In Persian this is remarkably beautiful, and the guests were deeply touched by the poetry of the language, chanted by the lovely voice of Munírih Khánum.)

Bahá'u'lláh had said to the Master:

"Come back early this afternoon, the wedding must take place to-day."

Bahá'u'lláh chanted the prayers.

Oh the spiritual happiness which enfolded us! It cannot be described in earthly words.

The chanting ended, the guests left us. I was the wife of my Beloved. How wonderful and noble He was in His beauty. I adored Him. I recognized His greatness, and thanked God for bringing me to Him.

It is impossible to put into words the delight of being with the Master; I seemed to be in a glorious realm of sacred happiness whilst in His company.

You have known Him in His later years, but then, in the youth of His beauty and manly vigour, with His unfailing love, His kindness, His cheerfulness, His sense of humour, His untiring consideration for everybody, He was marvellous, without equal, surely in all the earth!

At the wedding there was no cake, only cups of tea; there were no decorations, and no choir, but the blessing of Jamál-i-Mubárak; the glory and beauty of love and happiness were beyond and above all luxury and ceremony and circumstance.

For fifty years my Beloved and I were together. Never were

we separated, save during His visits to Egypt, Europe, and America.

O my Beloved husband and my Lord! How shall I speak of Him?

You, who have known Him, can imagine what my fifty years have been—how they fled by in an atmosphere of love and joy and the perfection of that Peace which passeth all understanding, in the radiant light of which I await the day when I shall be called to join Him, in the celestial garden of transfiguration.

Five of my children died in the poisonous climate of 'Akká.

The bad air was, in truth, only the outside material reason. The inner spiritual reason was that no son of the Master should grow into manhood.

When my darling little son Ḥusayn passed away, Bahá'u'lláh wrote the following:

"The knowledge of the reason why your sweet baby has been called back is in the mind of God, and will be manifested in His own good time. To the prophets of God the present and the future are as one."

Therefore I understand how that wisdom has ordained the uniting of the two families, that of Bahá'u'lláh and of the Báb, in the person of Shoghi Effendi, eldest son of our daughter, Ḍíyáíyyih Khánum, by her marriage with Áqá Mírzá Hádí Afnán.

I have been writing to the friends in Persia:

"You are longing to meet us, we are longing to meet you; what is the wisdom in our separation?"

Let us understand that if Bahá'u'lláh had not been exiled to Baghdád, Constantinople, Adrianople, and 'Akká, the Divine Message could not have been so quickly spread, and the prophecies in the Holy Books would not have been fulfilled.

THE SPOKEN CHRONICLE
of
Ṭúbá K͟hánum,
daughter of 'Abdu'l-Bahá.

CHAPTER I

Ásíyih Khánum

I remember our beloved grandmother, Ásíyih Khánum very well, though I was only seven years old when she passed from us.

Bahá'u'lláh used to address her as "Navváb," a title of great courtesy and respect, used by Persian noblemen to their wives. She was very beautiful, kind, and gentle. Everybody in trouble went to her for comfort. If any were ill, it was she who nursed them, and soothed and cared for them.

As no laundress was allowed to come whilst we were all in the barrack prison at 'Akká, she did much of the washing and cooking, helped always by my dear aunt Khánum.

The only servant they had, a negress, had neither time nor strength to do all that was needed. My grandmother and Khánum, then quite young, did much of the hard work, so that this servant should not be overtired.

They also made and mended the garments of the family, a formidable undertaking.

I was told how my grandmother and Khánum made a wonderful coat for Bahá'u'lláh, to be ready for Him when He should return from the retreat in the wilderness of Sulaymáníyyih. They worked at this labour of love, using small pieces of red tirmih, very precious stuff, which had survived, in some way, the loss of nearly all her extensive and rare wedding treasures. For six months they sewed and fitted these pieces together, and a beautiful coat was the result. Very acceptable indeed, for He came back in the coarse, rough coat of a dervish. And they had no money for buying coats at that time in Baghdád.

Ásíyih Khánum lived through the imprisonment time, and afterwards, in the little hired house in the town of 'Akká.

Her tiny room was simple and bare—the narrow, white bed, which was also the divan in the daytime; a very small table, on which was her prayer and other holy books, her "qalam-dán" (pen case), and leaflets for writing; there was also her rosary, sometimes a flower in a pot, and lastly an old painted box holding her other frock and her other under-garment.

Bahá'u'lláh had only two coats (made of Barak, a Persian woollen cloth); they were apt to wear out, and much of her time was spent, as I remember her, in patching and darning them and His stockings.

My eyes will always see her in her blue dress, with a white "niqáb" on her head, and little black slippers on her tiny feet. Her sweet, smiling face, and her wrapt expression, as she chanted prayers in her musical voice.

One sad day I came in from my lessons, finding many people gathered together in a troubled way. I asked "What is the matter?"

"Your grandmother is very ill."

I saw Bahá'u'lláh go into her room; after a time He came out; she had passed from the sadness and grief-filled days of her life on earth.

How we all wept! We missed her beautiful presence; her unfailing loving-kindness, and her perfect unselfishness had endeared her to us all.

Lovely and loving, refined and dainty, keenly intelligent, with more strength of character than of physique. A strong sense of humour was also one of her many gifts.

The terrible hardships and anxieties of her life had impaired her health; she had always exerted her strength, however failing, to its utmost.

CHAPTER II

Bahá'u'lláh in 'Akká

My first continuous memories began in 1892, when I was twelve years old.

Before that there were impressions of episodes, a sort of patchwork of mind-pictures, strung together on the thread of love for those, whose sacredness I very early began to realize, accepting this atmosphere as in the natural order of daily life; not analysing it, neither reasoning about it, but, childlike, breathing it in without question.

I remember that Bahá'u'lláh had suffered acutely from the close confinement in one room. He loved gardens, flowers, stretches of country, riding, walking, picnics under the trees, and all open-air simple pleasures.

As time went on, the Muftí of 'Akká and the Páshá, who was the Governor, became attached friends of the Master, mainly through witnessing the beauty of the life He led, in which ministering service to all was manifested before their eyes. They had begun to comprehend something of the holiness of the ideals of the exiles, and came to look upon Bahá'u'lláh with awe and respect and great honour.

The Governor, who had become friendly, would from time to time be recalled, and would be replaced by another who would take up his post in an attitude of unfriendliness to the exiles; his mind having been filled with false reports.

As these suspicions translated themselves into action, stricter rules would be made; our little freedom would be curtailed, and our lives become more and more restricted. As the days passed on, the enmity of the Governor would melt away under the warmth of the Master's invariable loving-kindness, rules would relax, and our lives become again happy, so that the friendship of the Governor made a marvellous difference to our comfort.

After Bahá'u'lláh had been imprisoned in one room for nine years, the Governor of that time consented to the Master's request that He might be at liberty to visit the Riḍván.

* * *

(The Riḍván is a beautiful garden, which the Master had planted in a plot of land which He had acquired. It is on the bank of a brook. There is a large mulberry tree with seats round its trunk. Many beautiful blossoming trees are now flourishing there, also flowers innumerable, and sweet-smelling herbs; it is a blaze of glorious colour and wonderful beauty. The scent of attar roses, of rosemary, bergamot, mint and thyme and balm, lemon-scented verbena, and musk makes the air sweet with their wealth of various fragrances. Scented white and scarlet and rose-coloured geraniums are there in wild luxuriance, and trees of pomegranate with their large, brilliant scarlet blossoms, also other lovely blooming shrubs. Each a symbol of devoted, loving service.

Most of the flowering plants have been brought from Persia by the pilgrims.

These wonderful pilgrims! How they came on that long, toilsome journey on foot, braving numberless dangers, malignant human enemies and bad weather, and through all the fatigue, carrying, as the greatest treasure, some plant for their adored one's garden. Often the only water, which the devoted pilgrims so urgently needed for themselves, was given to the plant.

Some of the gardeners who had been in the employ of Bahá'u'lláh in His glorious gardens at the beautiful country house, His former home in Persia, remembered that a particular white rose was a favourite flower of Bahá'u'lláh's. This rose, single with golden centre, brownish stalks, shiny leaves, and a peculiarly delightful scent, is now flourishing in the Riḍván. Many bushes of these beautiful roses are in full bloom; the waxen cream and gold of their blossoms, and their burnished leaves, make a pure and peaceful note in the love-laden harmony of the glory of that garden.

One seems to sense the atmosphere of devotion, which made this garden out of the desert.

The pilgrims who carried the plants through the difficulties of the pilgrimages tended them by the way, successfully and joyfully presenting their precious gift, alive and full of the power of growth, to their beloved Lord.

Friends from California and from Europe brought their offerings later on, so that the Riḍván is a veritable joining-together of the East and the West—symbolic of the great Mission of Bahá'u'lláh, which is to unite, in one great and vital unity, the members of the human family from every religion, race, and nation in the world.

All different colours, roses and trees, fruits and herbs gathered into God's Garden of joyful, harmonious, loving friendship.)

*   *   *

Oh the joy of the day when Bahá'u'lláh went to the beautiful Riḍván, which had been prepared for Him with such loving care by the Master, the friends, and the pilgrims!

The Master's heart was gladdened indeed to see the enjoyment of His beloved Father, resting under the big mulberry tree, by the side of the little river rippling by, the fountain which they had contrived splashing and gurgling in sounds refreshing indeed after the long years of confinement in the pestilential air of the penal fortress of 'Akká. Only those who were present there could realize in any degree what it meant to be surrounded by such profusion of flowers, their colours and their scents, after the dull walls and unfragrant odours of the prison city.

I remember well the greatest of our joys was to go with Bahá'u'lláh for the occasional picnics to the Riḍván.

How happy we were with Him. He was indeed the brightness of our lives in that time of difficulty.

Our days were then very monotonous. We saw little of our Father, so much was He occupied with the affairs of those who constantly came to beg for His help.

We loved our early morning tea, when He would chant prayers and tell us stories of the Lord Christ and His Mother, of Muḥammad, of Moses and other Prophets.

After that we were taken by a servant to the school at the K͟hán; it was rather dull to sit there from seven in the morning till five in the afternoon listening to readings of the Qur'án, of which no explanation was given. A little reading and writing—no pleasant breaks for play—rather tasteless and scanty midday dinner, which we took with us.

We children looked upon Bahá'u'lláh as another loving Father; to Him we carried all our little difficulties and troubles. He took an interest in everything which concerned us.

He used to send a servant to Beirut every year to buy stuff for our clothes. Bahá'u'lláh would then call for us to choose which we liked best for our frocks. My mother, my aunt, and the children would make this cotton material into garments.

He was always punctual, and loved daintiness and order.

He was very particular and refined in his personal arrangements, and liked to see everybody well groomed, and as neatly dressed as possible. Above all things, cleanliness was desirable to Him.

"Why not put on your prettiest frocks?" He would say to us.

All our holidays, all our treats and our happiness came from Him in those days; when boxes of sweets were brought to Him He would set some aside for us.

"Put that box of sweets over there, or Áqá will give it away to the people," He would say in fun.

"Let the dear children come in, and have some dessert," He often said, when we were being sent off to bed—my Father and my mother not wishing that we should disturb Him—but He always welcomed us with loving words.

How we adored Him!

"Now children, to-morrow you shall come with Me for a picnic to the Riḍván," He would say, and our night was so full of joy we could scarcely sleep.

The Master was not often able to come with us to these wonderful picnics, so much did the people take up all His days.

CHAPTER III

'Abdu'l-Bahá in 'Akká

The time came when Bahá'u'lláh went to live at Bahjí, and the Master, my mother, my aunt, and my three sisters lived in the larger house at 'Akká.

Bahá'u'lláh for some time had rarely received any but the Bahá'í friends, to whom He gave audience nearly every afternoon. His arrangements were very regular.

I remember that Nabíl, the historian, was received every Tuesday.

The Master, by making all arrangements, doing all the business, seeing applicants and pilgrims, planning interviews at stated hours, protected His Father from every troublesome detail, and made it possible for Him to lead a peaceful life, with leisure in which to write His Tablets and to formulate laws and instructions for the world of the future.

The Master occupied Himself with the affairs and interests of the people of the place, all outside news being brought to Him by the Governor and the Muftí.

Every week the Master went to Bahjí, carrying all the news which would be of interest to Bahá'u'lláh.

He would tell him particularly of the affairs of the Persian pilgrims, many of whom had settled in 'Akká, keeping shops of various kinds, carrying on their several trades and professions. A number of these devoted disciples, rich and great in their own land, had sacrificed everything, their property and their positions, barely escaping with their lives, and were now working humbly for their daily bread, joyful to be near Him Whom they looked upon as the Great Manifestation of God. And thus they lived their beautiful and happy lives.

The Master would tell Bahá'u'lláh how Christians came to ask explanation of difficult sayings in the Bible. Or again, how Muslims came with questions of Qur'án perplexities. He would tell how people in trouble would come for advice and help. Bahá'u'lláh always wished to know what answers were given by the Master.

"Khaylí Khúb, very good, Áqá," He would say.

The Master would also tell news from different countries far and near, related in the newspapers, which the Governor used to bring for discussion and explanation.

The life of the Master in 'Akká was full of work for others' good.

He would rise very early, take tea, then go forth to His self-imposed labours of love. Often He would return very late in the evening, having had no rest and no food.

He would go first to the Bírúní, a large reception room, which had been hired, on the opposite side of the street to our house. We often used to watch from our windows, the people crowding there to ask for help from the Master.

A man who wished to take a shop must ask advice from Him. Another would request a letter of introduction, or recommendation for some government post. Again, it would be a poor woman whose husband had been falsely accused, or had been taken for a soldier, whilst she and the children were left to starve. One would tell Him of children who were ill-treated, or of a woman beaten by husband or brother.

'Abbás Effendi would send a competent person with these poor people to state the case to the judge at the Court House, so that they might have justice.

The Bírúní also received other guests; it came to be looked upon as a centre of interest.

The Muftí, the Governor, Shaykhs, and officials of the Court came singly or in groups to call on the Master at the Bírúní. Here they would be offered a specially delicious make of "qahviyi-khánigí" (coffee). Sipping this, they would talk over all the news, appealing for explanations, advice, or comment, to the Master, Whom they grew to look upon as learned, wise, full of compassion, practical help, and counsel for all.

When the Court rose the judge invariably came to the Bírúní, where he would speak of any complicated case, sure that 'Abbás Effendi would solve the problem, however difficult. In this way He was often able to steer the course of law, preventing the triumph of the tyrant, and bringing comfort to the oppressed.

Some days He hardly saw His own family, so hard pressed was He by those who crowded to the Bírúní for some kind of help.

The many sick people, Bahá'í and others, were His constant care; whenever they wished to see Him, He went.

One poor old couple, who were ill in bed for a month, had twenty visits from the Master during that time.

To every sick person He sent each day a servant to ask "Did you sleep? How are you? Do you need anything?" All their needs He supplied.

Never did He neglect anything but His own rest, His own food; the poor were always His first care.

All sweets, fruits, and cakes which had been sent to Him He would take to the Bírúní for the friends, whom He made very happy.

The Arabs called Him the "Lord of Generosity."

To this day, if anybody be hospitable he is praised thus: "His house is like the Bírúní, the home of 'Abbás Effendi."

As there was no hospital in 'Akká, the Master paid a doctor, Nikolaki Bey, a regular salary to look after the very poor. This doctor was asked not to say who was responsible for this, "His right hand was not to know what His left wrought."

But for those other things the poor needed when they were ill, numberless, various, always to the Master did they turn their eyes.

One instance—a poor, crippled woman named Na'úm used to come every week for alms; one day a man came running: "Oh! Master, that poor Na'úm has measles. She is lying by the hot room of the Hammám; everybody is keeping away from her. What can be done about her?"

The Master immediately engaged a woman to care for her; took a room, put comfortable bedding (His own) into it, called the doctor, sent food and everything she needed. He went to see that she had every attention, and when she died in peace and comfort, He it was Who arranged her simple funeral, paying all charges.

Another instance out of many:

A notoriously bad man, calling himself a Christian, being about to die, sent to pray 'Abbás Effendi to come to him: "O Master, I have been a wicked man. Forgive me all my sins and mistakes and help me, I pray; my wife will be so alone, my family will oppress her, and if not prevented, will rob her of all her sustenance. I beg of you, Master, to protect her and guide her when I am gone."

The promise was given—the man died in peace, his mind at rest, knowing that his poor wife would be helped and protected.

Another call to 'Abbás Effendi came in this way:

'Abdu'lláh Páshá Dilí of San'á, a city in the province of Yemen, Arabia, had been banished to 'Akká, with only one old servant to attend him. He lived in one room in the Mosque. Now 'Abbás Effendi had a room near his, to which He would retire for quiet meditation and prayer, whenever He could spare any time from His multitudinous works of ministration.

The Master was very kind to the poor, lonely, exiled Páshá, who one day being struck with illness, felt his death drawing near, and prayed that the Master would come to him.

"O 'Abbás Effendi, I have a secret, I want your help. One daughter only is left to me of all my family; I know not where she is now; her husband is not kind to her. You, and you only, can I trust.

"I have here (my servant is out of hearing?) a bag of gold, 70,000 piastre (£700). This sum I wish my dear daughter to have, after deducting 500 piastres for my funeral. I do not wish this money to get into the hands of that cruel man, her husband."

The Master agreed to endeavour to find this lady, and to have the bag of gold given into her own hands.

The next day the Páshá died at peace.

A witness from the Court being sent for to count the gold, the receipt was signed.

The Master chose certain of the Páshá's few belongings for the daughter, and gave the rest to the old servant. He then arranged an honourable funeral, befitting the station of the Páshá, defraying all expenses Himself, so that the bag of gold might not be lessened.

The state allowance to the exiled Páshá was owing. This the

Governor paid, after much insistence, and it was added to the daughter's gold.

Then to arrange to get the gold safely taken to San'á. A difficult task in those lawless days!

Now there was a dervish, named Muḥammad-'Alí, a devoted disciple, whose joy it was to serve his Master in toilsome and dangerous journeys. This servant was entrusted with the mission of safely conveying the bag of gold and her father's belongings to the daughter of the exiled Páshá.

The dervish, Muḥammad-'Alí, set forth on his quest, being furnished with minute instructions for seeking the lady, and with sufficient money for his long, laborious journey.

In five months he returned to 'Akká. He had reached San'á and, though encompassed with difficulties and risk, had achieved his task, escaping the cruelty and avarice (which had been feared by the Páshá) of the husband. He had succeeded in delivering the bag of gold, and the little treasures of her father, into the beloved daughter's own hands. All was accomplished, and this faithful messenger returned, bringing a receipt from the lady, signed and witnessed by the Válí of San'á.

It would be impossible to write even a small part of the many compassionate acts of love and charity wrought by the Master; all His life was spent in ministering service to every unhappy creature who came to Him, and in being the devoted son to His Father.

When my little sister, Rúḥ-Angíz Ásíyih, arrived, there was some disappointment that she was not a boy.

Bahá'u'lláh said "I will love her more than all the rest; you must not wish that she had been a boy."

Little Rúḥ-Angíz loved Bahá'u'lláh very fervently. When He had passed from earth she was full of sadness:

"I want to go through that same door to Heaven; didn't He go through it?"

"No thank you," she would say, "I do not wish for anything. I would like best of all to go to Him."

So often she spoke of the other world, that she seemed to grow nearer and nearer to it. The next year she passed from earth to the Heaven where she wished to be.

The Master hardly saw the dear child in her illness. His time was so constantly taken up by the needs of the poor, that only His tired moments were spared to His own family from His incessant work for all in trouble. Indeed, my mother and sisters tried to conceal their difficulties and trials, not wishing to add to the heavy burden of others' griefs, which were so constantly borne by Him.

At this period the pilgrims who came to 'Akká were taken care of at the Khán (the inn). Mírzá Muḥammad cooked their food. They seldom had more than soup and rice, sometimes a "pulau" (stewed rice, with a little meat, and some herbs and vegetables) was provided as a great treat.

CHAPTER IV

The Passing of Bahá'u'lláh

And now a very sad day dawned for us all.
My mother, my Aunt K͟hánum, my three sisters, and I lived in the bigger house at 'Akká with our beloved Father; Bahá'u'lláh lived at Bahjí.
At this time the people of the place greatly respected and honoured Him and the Master, and we were as happy as was possible in the unhealthy atmosphere of 'Akká.
On this day of sadness a servant rode in from Bahjí with a tablet for the Master from Bahá'u'lláh: "I am not well, come to Me and bring K͟hánum."
The servant, having brought horses for them, my Father and my aunt set off immediately for Bahjí; we children stayed at home with my mother, full of anxiety. Each day the news came that our adored Bahá'u'lláh's fever had not abated. He had a kind of malaria.
After five days we all went to Bahjí; we were very distressed that the illness had become serious.
On the fifteenth day of the illness the Persian pilgrims and Bahá'í friends from 'Akká were admitted to His presence.
Mírzá 'Andalíb from S͟hiráz, Mírzá Bassár, the blind poet, were there. They, weeping, circled round and round His bed, praying and beseeching Bahá'u'lláh to permit them to be a sacrifice for the saving of His precious life for the world, if only for a short time longer.*
Bahá'u'lláh spoke loving words of peace and calm to them, exhorting them to be faithful to the Cause of God, to be loyal, true, and steadfast, letting their characters speak to the world.
"I am very pleased with you all. My hope is that your deeds

---

* It is a Persian custom that a lamb should be sacrificed to prolong a greatly beloved life—and these friends wished to take the place of the sacrificial lamb—for their Lord's life.

will be examples worthy of the Bahá'í Faith—that you may ever be true followers of the Light of God's Law."

Two lambs were brought into His room, then the Master went into 'Akká to arrange various matters, to see the friends, giving the good news that His Father was slightly better. He then superintended the distribution of the two sacrificial lambs amongst the poor prisoners of 'Akká.

In the evening He came back to Bahjí.

Bahá'u'lláh asked for us, the ladies and children, to go to Him. He told us that He had left in His will directions for our future guidance; that the Greatest Branch, 'Abbás Effendi, would arrange everything for the family, the friends, and the Cause.

"The loving devotion of 'Andalíb has touched me very much, also the love of them all. I hope they will every one be true and faithful servants."

On the nineteenth day of His illness He left us at dawn.

Immediately a horseman galloped into 'Akká to carry the news to the Muftí.

Forthwith from the seven minarets of the mosque the event was proclaimed:

"GOD IS GREAT.

HE GIVETH LIFE! HE TAKETH IT AGAIN!

HE DIETH NOT, BUT LIVETH FOR EVERMORE!"

This proclamation from the minarets is a custom of Islám at the passing of a very greatly honoured, learned, and holy man.

The tidings spread throughout the land, and were proclaimed from the minarets of every mosque. People from all the villages of the country-side crowded to Bahjí to show their respect, and to join in the mourning. Many Shaykhs brought lambs, rice, sugar and salt. This is an Arab custom: the idea is, that as these gifts are distributed to the poor, they will, in return, pray for the soul of the departed.

Muslim friends, the Muftí, mullás, Governor and officials, Christian priests, Latin and Greek, Druses from Abú-Sinán, and surrounding villages, and many other friends gathered together in great numbers in honour of the Beloved One.

Marthíyih, songs in His praise, were chanted by poets. Laments and prayers were chanted by Shaykhs. Funeral

THE PASSING OF BAHÁ'U'LLÁH

orations were spoken, describing His wonderful life of self-sacrifice.

Many of the guests encamped under the trees round the Palace of Bahjí, where more than five hundred were entertained for nine days.

This hospitality entailed much trouble on the Master, Who made all the arrangements and superintended every detail; money also was given by Him on each of the nine days to the poor.

At dawn on these days the "Call to Prayer" and some of the "Munáját" (prayers chanted) of Bahá'u'lláh were chanted from the balcony of the palace.

Very touching and impressive it was to hear the beautiful voice of our Arabian Bahá'í friend, chanting the call to prayer.

At its sound the Master arose, and we all followed Him to the tomb-shrine, where He chanted the funeral prayer and the

TABLET OF VISITATION

(The following is a translation by Shoghi Effendi, guardian of the Bahá'í Faith.)

The praise which hath dawned from Thy most august Self, and the glory which hath shone forth from Thy most effulgent Beauty, rest upon Thee, O Thou Who art the Manifestation of Grandeur, and the King of Eternity, and the Lord of all who are in Heaven and on earth. I testify that through Thee the sovereignty of God and His dominion, and the majesty of God and His grandeur, were revealed, and the Day-Stars of ancient splendour have shed their radiance in the Heaven of Thine irrevocable decree, and the Beauty of the Unseen hath shone forth above the horizon of creation. I testify, moreover, that with but a movement of Thy pen Thine injunction "Be Thou" hath been enforced, and God's hidden Secret hath been divulged, and all created things have been called into being, and all the Revelations have been sent down.

I bear witness, moreover, that through Thy beauty the beauty of the Adored One hath been unveiled, and through Thy face the face of the Desired One hath shone forth, and that through a word from Thee Thou hast decided between all created things, causing them who are devoted to Thee to ascend unto the summit of glory, and the infidels to fall into the lowest abyss.

I bear witness that he who hath known Thee hath known God, and he who hath attained Thy presence hath attained unto the presence of God. Great, therefore, is the blessedness of him who hath believed in Thee, and in Thy signs, and hath humbled himself before Thy sovereignty, and hath been honoured with meeting Thee, and hath attained the good pleasure of Thy will, and circled around Thee, and stood before Thy throne. Woe betide him that hath transgressed against Thee, and hath denied Thee, and repudiated Thy signs, and gainsaid Thy sovereignty, and risen up against Thee, and waxed proud before Thy face, and hath disputed Thy testimonies, and fled from Thy rule and Thy dominion, and been numbered with the infidels whose names have been inscribed by the fingers of Thy behest upon Thy holy Tablets.

Waft then, unto me, O my God and my Beloved, from the right hand of Thy mercy and Thy loving-kindness, the holy breaths of Thy favours, that they may draw me away from myself and from the world unto the courts of Thy nearness and Thy presence. Potent art Thou to do what pleaseth Thee. Thou, truly, hast been supreme over all things.

The remembrance of God and His praise, and the glory of God and His splendour, rest upon Thee, O Thou Who art His Beauty! I bear witness that the eye of creation hath never gazed upon one wronged like Thee. Thou wast immersed all the days of Thy life beneath an ocean of tribulations. At one time Thou wast in chains and fetters; at another Thou wast threatened by the sword of Thine enemies. Yet, despite all this, Thou didst enjoin upon all men to observe what hath been prescribed unto Thee by Him Who is the All-Knowing, the All-Wise.

May my spirit be a sacrifice to the wrongs Thou didst suffer, and my soul be a ransom for the adversities Thou didst sustain. I beseech God by Thee and by them whose faces have been illumined with the splendours of the light of Thy countenance, and who, for love of Thee, have observed all whereunto they were bidden, to remove the veils that have come between Thee and Thy creatures and to supply me with the good of this world and the world to come. Thou art, in truth, the Almighty, the Most Exalted, the All-Glorious, the Ever-Forgiving, the Most Compassionate.

Bless Thou, O Lord my God, the Divine Lote-Tree and its leaves, and its boughs, and its branches, and its stems, and its offshoots, as long as Thy most excellent titles will endure and Thy most august attributes will last. Protect it, then, from the mischief of the aggressor and the hosts of tyranny. Thou art, in truth, the Almighty, the Most Powerful. Bless Thou, also, O Lord my God, Thy servants and Thy handmaidens who have attained unto Thee. Thou, truly, art the All-Bountiful, Whose grace is infinite. No God is there save Thee, the Ever-Forgiving, the Most Generous.

* * *

The Master sent to 'Akká for the box in which the Will of Bahá'u'lláh had been locked up for two years. On the ninth day after the passing of Bahá'u'lláh the Will was read by Mírzá Majdi'd-Dín* to all the men friends, in the presence of the Master.

The friends showed great joy that their beloved Master had been appointed by Jamál-i-Mubárak to be their Protector, their Leader, their Guide.

The Master then came to see us, the ladies of the household. We called together the servitors, and, when we were all assembled, the Will was read to us by Majdi'd-Dín, at the request of the Master.

The mother of Muḥammad-'Alí expressed herself, at that time, as being pleased at the appointment of the eldest son.

Whilst we were all at Bahjí there was a serious outbreak of cholera in the town of 'Akká. Now it was the custom that members of the family should remain in the house of the departed one for a period of forty days. But the mother of Muḥammad-'Alí, and her other sons, showed us by many discourtesies that they did not wish us to remain.

---

* The son of Bahá'u'lláh's brother, Mírzá Músá.

Accordingly, in spite of the raging cholera, we all, Sarkár-i-Áqá, <u>Kh</u>ánum, my mother, my sisters, and I, left Bahjí and returned to our house at 'Akká, trusting in the protection of God.

We were almost the only family left in 'Akká. Most of the people had fled in fear of the terror; others had died in great numbers. We children were much frightened, the sight of the poor dead people being carried out for burial appalled us.

We heard that Sarkár-i-Áqá asked for those Tablets of Bahá'u'lláh which He had revealed for many of the friends, and for others, concerning the Cause. Muḥammad-'Alí replied: "There are no such papers."

After bringing us back to 'Akká, the Master went back to the shrine at Bahjí, returning to us next day very sad; the two younger half-brothers were with Him. My mother asked them to stay and help Sarkár-i-Áqá with the numberless matters needing to be done. They refused, saying that they were too busy. There was no man of the family to assist our beloved Father in all the work of that difficult time.

After nine days Sarkár-i-Áqá wrote a Tablet telling the sad news, directing that it be copied and sent to all the friends in Persia.

* * *

The first message of 'Abdu'l-Bahá to His friends throughout the world after the ascension of Bahá'u'lláh.*

He Is the All-Glorious

The world's great Light, once resplendent upon all mankind has set, to shine everlastingly from the Abhá Horizon, His Kingdom of fadeless glory, shedding splendour upon His loved ones from on high, and breathing into their hearts and souls the breath of eternal life.

O ye beloved of the Lord! Beware, beware lest ye hesitate and waver. Let not fear fall upon you, neither be troubled nor

---

* Translated by Shoghi Effendi, and sent for this book.

dismayed. Take ye good heed lest this calamitous day slacken the flames of your ardour, and quench your tender hopes. To-day is the day for steadfastness and constancy. Blessed are they that stand firm and immovable as the rock, and brave the storm and stress of this tempestuous hour. They, verily, shall be the recipients of God's grace, shall receive His divine assistance, and shall be truly victorious.

The Sun of Truth, that most great Light, has set upon the horizon of the world to rise with deathless splendour over the Realm of the Limitless. In His *Most Holy Book* He calleth the firm and steadfast of His friends: "O peoples of the world! Should the radiance of My beauty be veiled, and the temple of My body be hidden, feel not perturbed, nay arise and bestir yourselves, that My Cause may triumph, and My Word be heard by all mankind."

CHAPTER V

The Marriage of Ḍíyáíyyih Khánum

The ladies of the family were helpless, as according to the Muslim law, they were unable to speak to any man, even on business affairs; so that it was only within the house that we were able to do anything at all to lighten the burden of our beloved Master.

The time passed on until about three years after the passing of Bahá'u'lláh, when the conditions of our lives, owing to the ceaseless action of the enemy (cunningly devised false representations and accusations), became much more difficult.

Suddenly the Master went to Tiberias to spend some time in retreat. He was accompanied by one servant only.

We, the ladies of the family,* were much in despair; we had no man to do anything for us; none that we could trust; our veiling kept us, of necessity, almost prisoners.

There was a certain young man, of the family of the Báb (the members of which were given the name of "Afnán"), who had for some time been wishing to be accepted by the family of Bahá'u'lláh as husband of the eldest granddaughter.

Bahá'u'lláh had once asked His daughter, Bahíyyih Khánum, to tell Áqá (the Master) "that this young man, Áqá Mírzá Hádí Afnán, is very good indeed, I think most highly of him."

The mother of Áqá Mírzá Hádí was very fond of Ḍíyáíyyih Khánum.

After the Ascension of Bahá'u'lláh, Áqá Mírzá Hádí and his mother went back to their own country, Shíráz in Persia. They constantly wrote letters to the Master, my mother, and my aunt, in which frequent reference was made to their desire for the marriage.

---

* Khánum, the Greatest Holy Leaf; Munírih Khánum, wife of 'Abdu'l-Bahá; Ḍíyáíyyih Khánum, their eldest daughter; Túbá Khánum, Rúhá Khánum and Munavvar Khánum, the three younger daughters.

THE MARRIAGE OF ḌÍYÁÍYYIH KHÁNUM

The mother would speak of her great liking for Ḍíyáíyyih Khánum and add praises of her son.

Now, whilst the Master was in retreat at Tiberias, we, the ladies of the household, were in much distress because of being without any man in the family to make whatever necessary arrangements were required from time to time, to which we, because of being veiled, were unable to attend. Our difficulties grew and increased.

We therefore determined to write to the Master, asking Him to permit the marriage of Ḍíyáíyyih Khánum to that spiritually-minded young man, Áqá Mírzá Hádí Afnán, who was so anxious to be accepted as son-in-law by the Master, and who had been approved by Bahá'u'lláh.

At this time Áqá Mírzá Hádí Afnán was actually in 'Akká, as about two years after the Ascension of Bahá'u'lláh he had received permission to come back.

The tablet giving consent to the marriage arrived from the Master.

TABLET FROM THE MASTER

Every season hath its own condition.

Every place hath its own beauties.

In the time of spring the blossoming of the wilderness gives loving pleasure.

It is a joy to look upon the flowers blooming in the garden. Our ears are charmed by listening to the jocund voices of song birds.

Our nostrils delight in the fresh sweetness of thyme and mint, in the fragrance of flowering jasmine, and of hyacinth.

We enjoy the delicious fruits, as of the delectable paradise. All these are welcomed with love and joy in the season of spring.

But, in the season of falling leaves, it is well to seek shelter and rest within a house.

In the time of winter a small room in the simplest dwelling is desired.

To retreat into a peaceful cell is a longing.

Now, because it is the day of separation, and the time of mourning, the fire of anxiety is flaming; the heat of burning sorrow is, as it were, shrivelling up the universe!

The calamities of my family are beyond endurance, and the troubles of those sorrowful leaves (sister, wife, daughters) are without end.

From all directions the arrows of hardship are being showered upon them, like rain-drops in spring, and the spears of the unfaithful are being hurled upon them without ceasing.

The breezes of peace are being cut off in every direction, so that to breathe is impossible.

Eyes are weeping bitter tears.

Hearts are sore wounded. With hidden wounds are they smitten. Lamentations rend the soul, and the shaft of grief, piercing through all our hearts, joins them together.

This must needs be, for the Sun of the world has gone down below the horizon!

On the table of His departure is set out every kind of harmful viand, and every kind of death-dealing poison!

Verily the table of disaster is spread with every imaginable food!

Oh, family of this sorrowful one, all is sacrifice.

No pleasure is desired by you.

I know your sorrows.

The Muftí may be asked to chant the Marriage Chant at the Holy Shrine on Sunday.

* * *

My aunt invited the family of Muḥammad-'Alí to come in the evening. They came and jeered at the simplicity of the wedding with great ridicule.

None of our friends knew that it was a day of marriage.

My mother, my aunt, and we four girls were together.

Áqá Mírzá Hádí Afnán arrived.

We said "Bismi'l-láh!"

He kissed the hands of my aunt, my mother, and Ḍíyáíyyih Khánum.

The Muftí chanted the Marriage Chants, and the marriage ceremony was accomplished.

THE MARRIAGE OF ḌÍYÁÍYYIH KHÁNUM

We were all full of sorrow because of the Master's sufferings for the good of the Cause of God.

There was no ordinary marriage happiness. A sense of difficulty and danger oppressed us. We seemed to be under a dark cloud of grief and sorrow, but we all welcomed Áqá Mírzá Hádí as a great help and comfort in our distress.

THE SPOKEN CHRONICLES
of
Mírzá Asadu'lláh Káshání,
Sakínih Sultán Khánum,
and
Siyyid 'Alí Yazdí.

Some incidents illustrating certain aspects of the progress of the Bábí teaching during the Baghdád exile period, narrated by

MÍRZÁ ASADU'LLÁH KÁSHÁNÍ,

whose life had been linked with the Cause from his early youth:

I well remember the agitation amongst our family and friends when my eldest brother became a Bábí.
He had heard a mullá preach in a mosque, expounding the prophecies concerning the coming Imám, and had accepted the Truth. Now, being a Bábí, he no longer followed the mullá, to whom (according to the Muslim custom) he had been attached.
Therefore this man became a bitter enemy.
One day he obliged my brother to go to a barber, and have his head shaved; not content with having caused this indignity, the mullá broke a pitcher, from which "the infidel" had drunk, as to his mind it had thereby become unclean!
This was a well-known sign.
It being unsafe to remain, after this, in Káshán, my brother and a friend left for the holy shrine at M'asúmih.
They carried brass and copper vessels, the making of which was their trade; these they sold, using the money gained for the journey to Baghdád, which it was their secret intention to accomplish.
One night I dreamed a dream:
Flying through the air towards Baghdád, I arrived at the river separating the old and new towns. His Holiness Bahá'u'lláh dwelt in old Baghdád, in a part of the town called Karkh. In my dream I saw the thin "Dividing Line of the Day of God" above the river. I flew over that line and came to the house in which Jamál-i-Mubárak dwelt. I saw a window over the door; through this window I gazed, and saw a room

into which five or six steps led. I went down into that room, and there I saw Jamál-i-Mubárak.

After this dream I could not rest for the great desire I had to journey to Baghdád to serve the Blessed One.

At this time one of the friends came from Baghdád to Káshán; when I asked for news of Him, this reply was given to me:

"Thou askest a question. He will give the answer, though far distant."

At this I knew that I would set forth at once.

I gave it out that I was going on a pilgrimage to M'asúmih, a holy place between Káshán and Tihrán.

On foot I left the city, walking day and night. I slept, with a stone for my pillow, full of happiness, because of the purpose of my journey. When I needed money, I worked at my trade of coppersmith in the towns through which I passed. Thus Baghdád was reached, where I rested with my brother, he having already safely arrived.

For the first time, I saw with my outer, waking eyes, Jamál-i-Mubárak, as in my dream I had seen Him.

I was quite ill for a time, about a month, because of the hardships of the journey. Mírzá Músá (called Áqáyi Kalím, i.e., "Moses who talked with God" by the friends) cared for me until I recovered. My food was sent to me by the holy household.

Five or six friends used to take it in turns to prepare food; after a time we all joined in this plan; it saved trouble, and, moreover, economized the scanty provender we were able to obtain.

Morning and evening we came into the Blessed Presence.

Some mornings He would come to this house of the friends.

In the evenings we used to gather round Him on the river bank, where there was a small garden (Bahá'u'lláh had bought the land, and Áqáyi Kalím employed workers to cultivate and plant it). A sort of shed was made here, covered with branches of flowering trees; when sprinkled with water, it was cool and fragrant.

Bahá'u'lláh was very, very fond of this little garden, which was about half an hour's walk from the city of Baghdád. He often went to this garden, where He would be joined by the friends, one by one, very carefully, because of the unscrupulous and bitter enemies, who were always ready to seize pretexts for fresh persecutions.

In this garden we had many blessed meetings in the presence of Him we revered.

At this time He had two houses, one for the holy household, His own family, the other where the pilgrims and friends stayed.

One never-to-be-forgotten day Bahá'u'lláh came to the pilgrim house, and said to us "Áftábam! Áftábam! Dar Ámadam—I am the Sun! I am the Sun! I have arisen!"

As we heard these blessed words, it seemed as though all the happiness of the whole world had come to live in our hearts. As we looked upon His shining face, we were in an ecstasy—beside ourselves with joy. Our hearts were flaming within us!*

So enraptured were we, so high our hearts were beating that we could hardly sleep for thinking "In the morning! In the morning we are coming again into His Presence!"

We seemed to be living in an air of spiritual enchantment, of soul-stirring joy.

I can find no words to tell you of what our delight was.

Nothing on earth was of any importance, of any meaning, but that His Holy Presence was here with us.

A friend, being given a piece of bread by Bahá'u'lláh, asked "Give me spiritual food I implore." Some words were spoken to him, we knew not what. The friend became so excited and unbalanced that he committed suicide.

Bahá'u'lláh then said:

"How much better had he made other use of his enthusiasm; if he had gone to Persia to teach the Cause, rather than to uselessly take his own life!"

One day, when He was walking in the garden, we heard Him say: "No leaf, no flower, no fruit, no bark.

"All wonder why the gardener cultivates me, this tree."

This, I heard, was a quotation from His poems.

There was in the neighbourhood of Baghdád the holy shrine of an Imám; at Kázimayn. The friends used to follow Bahá'u'lláh at a distance, as he rode on a donkey to visit this shrine.

We were alert and ready to protect our Beloved should an enemy attack Him.

---

* This incident did not, apparently, convey to Mírzá Asadu'lláh that Bahá'u'lláh was "He Whom God shall make Manifest."—ED.

On some occasions the Persian Consul, and others of the Shi'ah sect, were at the shrine when Bahá'u'lláh arrived; they agitated themselves vastly, and were much perplexed, not comprehending the majesty in the personality of the wonderful visitor.

* * *

I was told that this Mírzá Asadu'lláh Káshání was a self-constituted guard, and hid a formidable weapon under his 'abá, as he followed the Beloved Master about in those days of danger, although Bahá'u'lláh had made a law that nobody was to carry arms!

* * *

Whilst Bahá'u'lláh was encamped in the Riḍván, there was much wind for some days.

His tent swayed; we thought it might be blown down, therefore we took it in turns to sit and hold the tent ropes so that it might be steady; night and day we held the ropes, so glad, in this way, to be near our Glorious Lord.

All the city came, friends and others, to see Him leave for the Riḍván. There was a great crowd. Weeping women pressed forward and laid their babes and young children at His feet. He tenderly raised those infants, one by one, blessing them, gently and lovingly replacing them in their sorrowing mothers' arms, and charging them to bring up those dear flowers of humanity to serve God in steadfast faith and truth.

What a soul-stirring day!

Men threw themselves in His path; if only His blessed feet might touch them as He passed.

Our Beloved One got into a boat to cross the river, the people pressing round Him waiting, not to lose one of the remaining chances of being in His Presence.

At length the boat put off, and we watched it with sorrowing hearts.

Then we were aware of an extraordinary exhilaration, some marvellous exaltation in the atmosphere of that day.

The reason for this phenomenon we were in due time to learn.

When we had seen that the boat was on the other side of the river, we started off to walk to the Riḍván, where we set up His tent, and five or six others for the friends. I helped Mírzá Muḥammad Báqir to cook, and to make tea for the friends.

The family of Bahá'u'lláh joined Him in the Riḍván on the ninth day; and on the twelfth day, in the afternoon, they went from us, under the escort of Turkish soldiers to an unknown destination.

Although Bahá'u'lláh had commanded the friends not to follow them, I was so loath to let Him go out of my sight, that I ran after them for three hours.

He saw me, and getting down from His horse, waited for me, telling me with His beautiful voice, full of love and kindness, to go back to Baghdád, and, with the friends, to set about our work, not slothfully, but with energy:

"Be not overcome with sorrow—I am leaving friends I love in Baghdád. I will surely send to them tidings of our welfare. Be steadfast in your service to God, who doeth whatsoever He willeth. Live in such peace as will be permitted to you."

We watched them disappear into the darkness with sinking hearts, for their enemies were powerful and cruel! And we knew not where they were being taken.

An unknown destination!

Weeping bitterly, we turned our faces towards Baghdád, determining to live according to His command.

We had not been, at that time, informed of the great event of the "Declaration," that our revered and beloved Bahá'u'lláh was He Who should come—"He Whom God shall make Manifest"—but we again felt that unspeakable joy, which surged within us, overcoming our bitter sorrow, with a great and mysterious radiancy.

Before the departure, the Governor of Baghdád had come to offer his services. "Is there not anything I can do?"

Bahá'u'lláh replied:

"One thing I ask of thee—protect the friends after I am gone. This only I wish from thee."

The Governor respected the wish of Bahá'u'lláh, and protected the friends at Baghdád, particularly on one occasion which led to our migrating to Mosul:

It happened in this way:

A year after the departure of the Holy One, the days of the "Feast of the Riḍván," which we were keeping with all the joy of our souls, coincided with the Muḥarram, the days of mourning for the martyrdom of Ḥusayn and his friends.

The Shi'ites, being angry that we were not joining the mourning, attacked us. One Bahá'í friend was killed, and several wounded, amongst whom was Badí', whose marvellous martyrdom was to take place later on.

The Válí (Governor of Baghdád), hearing of the tumult, gathered us into the Governorate for protection from the fury of the mob. He said to us:

"There are many places in the Turkish Empire; if you would be in safety, it is well to choose where to go."

So we knew that we must leave Baghdád.

"Go in two groups—one the week after the starting of the other—I will send a soldier to protect each of you whilst you sell some of your goods; pack up others and make preparations for the journey."

Some of the friends, and I with them, chose to go to Mosul, situated between Baghdád and Aleppo.

A number of soldiers were sent with us for our protection, and indeed they were needed, for, in all the towns and villages through which we went, the people stoned us, spat upon us, yelling execrations, crying "Accursed Bábís! Accursed Bábís!"

At length our journey ending, we were promptly locked into an inn—none allowed to go out, none to enter. This was for our protection, so furious were the people!

Thus we remained until the second party arrived.

Remembering the request of Bahá'u'lláh, the Governor of Baghdád had sent word to the Válí of Mosul, requesting him to protect and provide shelter for the Bábís. He accordingly had several houses placed at our service, which, though not comfortable, still gave us shelter.

There were about an hundred of us in all, men, women, and children.

As soon as possible we set about our various trades; I to that of coppersmith, and, on the whole, the people were not very unfriendly.

Before we left Baghdád a Tablet arrived, brought by one of the friends, from Adrianople, telling us of the welfare of Bahá'u'lláh, of the declaration in the Riḍván, and of the more public proclamation at Adrianople; so that we started on our toilsome journey with our hearts lightened of the terrible anxiety in which we lived, not knowing the fate of the Holy Family.

Now we were upheld by a preoccupation of the spirit, so that outside privations, stonings, cursings, scorn, and all other illusages, seemed to us of small importance as we remembered the joy of that day at the Riḍván, and now knew the sublime reason of that sacred atmosphere.

As we chanted our prayers of praise unto God that the Holy One was safe, that the Great Light which should come into the world had not been "blown out by contrary winds," we were full of happiness, for ourselves and for all humanity.

Time went on at Mosul; we were always hoping for further news.

One day a Tablet arrived by post, which, under the prevailing conditions, seemed marvellous, indeed miraculous.

This Tablet brought the tidings that our revered Beloved One, with His Family, were at 'Akká.

* * *

As soon as we knew that the Beloved Ones were at 'Akká, I started off with a Persian Bahá'í, who, having escaped from Dahají, had joined the band of exiles at Mosul. We determined to make our way to 'Akká. We walked six or seven hours a day, and coming to Aleppo we rested; thence we walked to Damascus.

Oh, how happy we were as we walked, each step bringing us

nearer to the presence of Jamál-i-Mubárak and Sarkár-i-Áqá.

Sometimes we sheltered for a night in the tent of a Bedouin, who welcomed us with unfailing kind hospitality; again we slept under the stars, with stones for our pillows, always with songs of joy in our hearts, because of our destination.

That preoccupation of the Spirit, as in our journey from Baghdád to Mosul, upheld us, and made all hardships so unimportant that we forgot them.

At length we came to Damascus, where, finding a friend from my native village, also a coppersmith, I tarried with him for ten days.

Then we started off again over the beautiful snowy Lebanon mountains, where the hospitable Bedouins were as ever our friends, and so we came to Beirut, where we rested for a week.

And now the last part of our pilgrimage from Beirut to 'Akká. I disguised myself as a dervish. Very seldom did I think it wise to ask to be directed, therefore we often wandered out of our way.

Our exaltation grew. Oh, the loveliness of the land through which we walked, the fragrance of the orange groves, the beauty of the many coloured flowers which carpeted the plains!

We stayed one night in the town of Sidon, surrounded with its luxuriant fruit trees, the scent of which is so delicious; then a night at Tyre. As we walked the "Ladder of Tyre" we saw 'Akká in the distance, shining in the sun, and there, in that place, were our Beloved Ones.

Great was the caution needed. We arrived separately.

My disguise allowed me to enter the city unquestioned. I wandered about in perplexity, for I did not dare to ask for information as to the abode of the Holy Ones. Fatigue was beginning to overwhelm me.

At length I went to the mosque, where I found a Shaykh who lived near by. I discovered that he was a Bahá'í; "Alláh'u'-Abhá." When he knew of my journey and of my aim, he said:

"Stay here with me, the Master will come when it is evening time."

I waited, breathless with anticipation.

Then from the mosque came our beloved Master!

He was young then and very beautiful.

"Aḥvál-i-Shumá? Marḥabá! Marḥabá! Khaylí Khush ámadíd." ("How are you? Welcome! Welcome! Your coming gives me most great pleasure and delight.")

His loving-kindness restored my soul. I was ready to sacrifice my life to *once* hear His "Marḥabá!"

"How tired you must be after that long, long, toilsome journey. I will send one of the friends to you in the morning."

So I rested in ecstatic peace, having achieved the desire of my heart.

In the morning Áqá Faraj came and took me to the Khán (inn) where four or five friends were staying. This was, of course, very secretly and cautiously arranged because of the threatened grave danger, at this time never absent from any suspected of being Bahá'ís. I rested quietly at the Khán, recovering from the physical fatigues of the journey.

After fifteen days, I was commanded to fetch my mother and my younger brother from Aleppo, where they were awaiting directions, having journeyed from Mosul, sometimes by steamer, and sometimes riding on mules.

How glad I was that my dear ones were to come into the presence of Jamál-i-Mubárak and the Master, Sarkár-i-Áqá! I joyfully departed on my errand, walking to Haifa, thence by boat to Alexandretta, thence to Aleppo. Returning with my family the same way, we arrived at Haifa. There we heard that my mother would be received into the holy household, to her extreme delight. My brother and I, however, were to remain at Haifa, not being suffered to go inside the town of 'Akká.

We therefore remained at Haifa, working at our trade of coppersmith. We opened a little shop. I went round to the houses, selling things that we had made.

My brother and I prospered at our work.

We used frequently to walk over by way of the sea, wading through the brook Kishon to 'Akká.

We would stand in a certain place, without the wall of the prison, and watch a particular window; sometimes we had the joy of seeing the hand of Bahá'u'lláh waving a greeting to us. We would then walk back to Haifa, delighted to have had our reward.

How we prayed that the Blessed One might have His freedom. It was heartbreaking to think of Him being imprisoned in the pestilential atmosphere of that most unhealthy town.

After some time, when rules were less strict, the Master asked me to come and live in 'Akká.

In these days Jamál-i-Mubárak was at liberty to walk freely about the town, and to live in His own hired house.

Our happiness was great when He would come to the Khán to speak to the friends, or when we were invited to the house of His Holiness, where He would receive us with such divine loving-kindness, and wonderful words of gladness and joy, that our hearts and souls were wrapt in an indescribable atmosphere of purity and peace.

No words could possibly convey to you the majesty and glory of His Presence. It is needless to attempt to do so; if only my spirit could speak. But you have known Sarkár-i-Áqá, you can understand something of what those days were to us.

* * *

The sincerity and simplicity of this dear old man seemed to make themselves felt in other ways than by the mere words. It might well be that his spirit was speaking; but it was a never-to-be-forgotten experience—one saw the scenes and breathed the atmosphere of the spirit which he described.

SAKÍNIH-SULTÁN KHÁNUM
told me other details of this time:

My husband, Jinábi-Zayn, was exiled from Tihrán for being a Bábí. We came to join these, whose happiness it was to live near Bahá'u'lláh at Baghdád. When He was taken away for "an unknown destination," we were of those who were bidden to remain.

At length, the time arrived when we were all to be driven forth. Jinábi-Zayn, who was a very learned man, incurred the especially malicious fury of the mob, which, in spite of the protection of the Governor, and incited by the fanatics, took every opportunity of injuring us.

They seized him, and scourged him severely. He, however, in company with a friend, escaped from Baghdád.

The infuriated mob seized all our belongings, so that we were able to save very few necessaries for the journey.

As we left the city, the people, filled with the hatred of bigotry, danced before us beating drums, and with other clashing noises the din was terrible. Those that went before, and those who followed after, shouted, yelled curses, and stoned us.

Thus we were driven forth in a headlong flight, the stones wounding many of us; the soldiers, who were supposed to protect us, being powerless to do so in the face of such unbridled fury.

As we fled, we lost many of our belongings, which we had with difficulty saved out of our looted and wrecked homes.

Many fell and were kicked and otherwise hurt; my poor sister had a knife stuck through her arm; a lady, riding on a mule, with her baby in the *takht-i-raván* (similar to a howdah) found that, in the confusion of the flight, the dear infant had gone!

At her entreaty, friends went back and found the sweet, wee girl, lying unhurt on the road; she was smiling, having been protected by her voluminous swaddling clothes.

We suffered much on this journey, both from hunger and thirst, having succeeded in bringing very little food with us in the turmoil of our departure.

The villages through which we passed were filled with bitter enemies, who reviled us, spat upon us, stoned us, rushed at us with sticks, yelling "Let the infidels die of hunger and thirst, let them die."

When we arrived at Mosul, the people of the town behaved in the same unfriendly manner, so that our condition was deplorable.

However, being locked into the Khán (the inn) to save us from injury from the people, the Válí, at the request of the Governor of Baghdád, had some food and water taken to us.

Eventually my husband and his friend arrived in so terrible a plight that we were aghast, and despaired for their lives.

Having escaped from Baghdád, they lost their way in the wilderness. So filled with malignity were the people they encountered, that they dared not ask their way, nor for food nor for water. Their sufferings were beyond description; driven by hunger and appalling thirst to venture near a village, the people rushed out to kill them, and they had to turn and flee for their lives.

Then, with strength almost gone, they reached Mosul.

They were brought to the Khán.

Five days they had struggled on without a drop of water; their tongues were badly swollen; they seemed about to die! We gave them what care we could, and they recovered.

The exiles at Mosul began to call my husband the "Father of the Exiles."

He was not able to do much to mitigate their misery, for all our belongings had been taken from us.

News had been taken to the "King of the Martyred" at Isfahán, explaining the plight of the Bábís at Mosul. He, with his usual kindness and generosity, promptly sent corn and other help to them, conditions thereby being vastly improved.

Stray fugitives, escaping from threatened death in Persia, joined us from time to time, until we were about one hundred and eighty persons.

These exiles gradually made their way to 'Akká and to Haifa.

Told by Siyyid 'Alí Yazdí

When I was a boy of fourteen (A.D. 1858) I remember a Bábí, a doctor named Radíu'r-Rúh; he had been in the presence of Jamál-i-Mubárak during each of the sojourns in Baghdád.

Radíu'r-Rúh created a profound sensation by going into a mosque on the day of mourning, the day of the commemoration of the martyrdom of Husayn.

He cried aloud:

"Oh, people! Ye are waiting for the Imám. But He has come! He is here! He is here!"

He then chanted "God is greatest. Muhammad is His Prophet."

The people said, "Why that chant on our day of mourning, O Radíu'r-Rúh?"

"Because the Promised One is here! You wait and wait, and know it not."

I remember seeing him as he rode off, carrying a flag over his shoulder; Bahá'u'lláh had sent him to teach in Persia.

He came to the village of Manshád, where he held meetings, with great caution, because of danger to everybody who was present, as well as to himself. I found out that there were meetings, that my father went in with others. I heard chanting when I listened; sometimes, when I watched them coming out, I saw that they had been weeping.

I ardently desired to know what it all meant.

One day I knocked at the door of Radíu'r-Rúh; he looked with surprise when I said: "What is happening? I want to know the meaning of all this; what are you doing—what?"

"My child, it cannot be told to you."

"But I want to know, I must know."

"If you know, and tell what you know, you will cause my death, that of your father, and of many, many others."

"I will tell nothing; only let me know, I promise to tell nothing."

"Very good," said Radíu'r-Rúh. "You shall know."

He taught me, and, my eyes being opened, I saw what he said was the truth, and I believed.

Ten days before his death, Raḍíu'r-Rúḥ came again to our village. He read a Tablet from Bahá'u'lláh.

"Human life without the spirit is absolutely of no importance—the spiritual life is the only real life."

The doctor Raḍíu'r-Rúḥ kissed this Tablet; to him it was a missive of command from on High.

"My stay in this world is now very short; it behoves me to make ready." He sent last messages to his family with various directions and requests.

When he was therefore prepared for his end, he was summoned to a village near by, where he was received by a fellow-doctor; this man offered him tea into which he had put strychnine.

In a few hours this fearless "Waiting Servant," this faithful disciple, rendered up that human life, which was to him of no importance, to attain, by being steadfast unto death, "the spiritual life, the only real life."

With his latest breath, in agony, he sang praises to God the Beloved, in that He had accepted the sacrifice of his life.

PART III

'ABDU'L-BAHÁ

"My father was much with Bahá'u'lláh.

"One night Bahá'u'lláh, as He walked back and forth in His room, said to my father:

" 'At stated periods souls are sent to earth by the Mighty God with what we call "the Power of the Great Ether." And they who possess this power can do anything; they have *all* Power. . . . '

"Jesus Christ had this Power.

"The people thought of Him as a poor young man, Whom they had crucified; but He possessed the Power of the Great Ether, therefore He could not remain underground. This ethereal Power arose and quickened the world. And now look to the Master, for this Power is His."

Recorded by Mírzá Valíyyu'lláh Khán Varqá, son of the martyred poet, Varqá.

CHAPTER I

1892 to 1908

After the passing, from this visible, mortal world, of Bahá'u'lláh, His devoted disciples turned their faces to the beloved Master, 'Abbás Effendi.

" 'Abbás Effendi" was the name by which He was known by all who came into His presence in those days, the dwellers in 'Akká and the country round about, and also by the many who came to ask His help and counsel in problems great and small.

To all comers He was the "Father of Compassion" and helpfulness; in His presence was rest; in His words peace and joy, love, and a wonderful wisdom.

Beyond the comprehension of the people, in whose midst He walked, to the pilgrims, who journeyed from Persia, Arabia, and gradually from America and Europe, the Master was also their adored Lord, Who had been appointed to establish the teaching of His Father.

The personality of Bahá'u'lláh, the pilgrims understood to have dwelt in a human temple, where the clouds of humanity veiled the mystery and the majesty of Divinity. They thought of Him as the Mouthpiece, the Manifestation of the Spirit of the Divine Father, Who had arisen to re-educate the world, which had forsaken the Law of Love, given to them nigh two thousand years ago by the Holy One, Christ Jesus, a humanity which had transferred their worship from the Lord of Compassion to that of the Golden Calf.

The pilgrims recognized that Bahá'u'lláh was "He whom God shall make Manifest."

He had fulfilled the prophecies, relative to this Day of God, the prophecies which were contained in the Holy books of the great religions of the world.

A mighty part of the Mission of Bahá'u'lláh was to bring about the cessation of "the fruitless strifes and the ruinous wars" and to usher in "the Most Great Peace."

He, "Whom God had made Manifest," had suffered persecutions, manifold tortures, imprisonment, and exile for forty years!

From behind the prison door His Voice had proclaimed His Sacred Mission. The Supreme Pen had written Laws for the guidance of the world of the future. The earthly, mortal work was finished. Bahá'u'lláh had returned to the Shelter of Heaven.

Before His Ascension, He had laid the charge upon 'Abbás Effendi, His eldest son, to go forth into all the world, to "Sound the solemn call to Regeneration, to carry the glad tidings of the renewal of the Gospel of Peace into every land of earth."

'Abbás Effendi henceforth took the title of 'Abdu'l-Bahá, literally "Servant of Glory."

Now the pilgrims who came from afar understood the glorious Mission which had been entrusted to Him, but the people of the land of Palestine knew not the Station of Bahá'u'lláh and of 'Abbás Effendi.

They saw only the Christ-like life; very few of them comprehended anything of the significance of the Great Ones Who walked in their midst.

The reason was this:

The Turkish Government, entirely misunderstanding the matter, gave ear to the false statements of prejudiced and bigoted religionists, and fearing any innovation, exacted a promise from Bahá'u'lláh that *no teaching should be given to the dwellers in that country*, where the Holy Ones were held as prisoners and exiles.

'Abdu'l-Bahá also continued to respect this promise, so that for the people of that country the Life of the Holy Ones, as lived amongst them, was the Teaching for them. Some souls, by intuition, divined the secret of the stupendous event which was taking place, but for the most part they did not become aware.

At this time many and great difficulties beset 'Abdu'l-Bahá, mainly through those enemies who were of His own kindred and "of His own Father's house." The enemies would approach the various Governors of the Prison City with differing results.

1892 TO 1908

Some of these Governors, being intelligent, and having, moreover, a great admiration for the Master, would reply to the calumnies of these persons:

"I advise you not to make these accusations against your brother; He is a great and wonderful person, of Whom you should be very proud; I do not wish to listen to these obviously untrue tales; do not trouble me again with such things."

Another Governor, not so intelligent, would give ear to the insidious suggestions made by this enemy. For instance:

" 'Abbás Effendi has gone to Haifa.

"He has many English and American friends.

"He is building a strong fortification on Mount Carmel. Very soon the whole of Palestine and Syria will be in his hands, and the Turkish Government will be driven out."

Such insinuations seem too absurd to consider, but they constituted ground for fresh persecutions.

Thus 'Abdu'l-Bahá and His family were recalled from Haifa, where they were enjoying the freshness of the air, and, with their dear little children, were again immured in the pestilential atmosphere of the prison city of 'Akká.

The Turkish officials at one time tried persistently to entrap the Master into saying something which they would be able to misrepresent as incriminating, but the wisdom of His replies never failed.

On one occasion an unfriendly Governor, hating these peaceful, honest Bahá'ís, thought of a plan for destroying their means of livelihood. He gave orders to the police: "There are fifteen shops owned by Bahá'ís; go to-morrow morning early, lock them up and bring the keys to me."

The Master called the Bahá'ís to Him that same evening and said:

"Do not open your shops to-morrow, but wait and see what God will send to us."

The next morning the Governor waited for the keys. Again he sent them. "Go," he said to the police, "and see if the shops are open." The police announced that the shops were closed.

He waited and waited; at ten o'clock all the shops were still unopened, those shops which were always accustomed to open and be ready for trade at seven o'clock. The Governor was greatly perplexed. His plan did not seem to be working as he had schemed.

The Muftí (the chief mullá) came to the Governor whilst he waited.

"How are you?" said the Governor.

"Quite well," was the reply, "but very sad; because of a telegram from Damascus, I am full of sorrow."

"Show it to me," said the Governor.

To his consternation he saw that the telegram was from the Válí of Damascus, deposing him from his place as governor, and directing that he be conducted by the police to Damascus.

In fear, sorrow, and amazement he went to his own house to make such preparation as was possible for the hurried and unlooked for journey.

The shops of the friends were saved.

'Abdu'l-Bahá, hearing of the misfortune which had befallen the Governor, went to visit him.

"You must not be sad because of this; everything in this world changes. Can I do anything for you?" He asked of the erstwhile Governor.

"Now that I am being taken away from them, there will be none to care for those I love. My dear family will be sad, lonely, and helpless, with nobody to counsel and aid them in their sore need."

"Do not be filled with grief, but tell me where you wish your family to go."

"If only they could go to Damascus?"

"Now, trust in me, and let your heart be lightened of its distress; I will gladly send an honourable escort with your wife and children to Damascus; you will find that they will be there soon after your own arrival."

The Master sent the family with a trustworthy escort, providing mules and everything needed for the comfort of the journey—quite a formidable undertaking in those days. The command was worded: "Take these persons safely and with great respect to join the Governor at Damascus." A telegram was despatched after they had set out: "I have sent your family to Damascus. They will very soon arrive in safety."

When they arrived in Damascus the Governor, being greatly

rejoiced, enquired of the escort as to the cost of the journey.
"It is nothing; I am but obeying the command of the Master."
The Governor then wished to give the escort a present for himself.
"I desire no recompense; I am but obeying the Master's command, I can accept nothing."
When invited to stay the night for rest and refreshment, the reply was:
"I obey the Master's command to return without delay."
"Then I pray you take a letter, which I will write at once to the Master."
"O 'Abdu'l-Bahá," the letter read, "I pray you pardon me. I did not understand. I did not know you. I have wrought you great evil. You have rewarded me with great good."
Thus was this enemy, who had indeed wrought great evil to the prisoners, repaid by being loaded with benefits.
Always did 'Abdu'l-Bahá obey this Tablet of Bahá'u'lláh:
"Be generous in prosperity, and thankful in adversity. Be worthy of the trust of thy neighbour, and look upon him with a bright and friendly face. Be a treasure to the poor, an admonisher to the rich, an answerer of the cry of the needy, a preserver of the sanctity of thy pledge. Be fair in thy judgment, and guarded in thy speech. Be unjust to no man, and show all meekness to all men. Be as a lamp unto them that walk in darkness, a joy to the sorrowful, a sea for the thirsty, a haven for the distressed, an upholder and defender of the victim of oppression. Let integrity and uprightness distinguish all thine acts. Be a home for the stranger, a balm to the suffering, a tower of strength for the fugitive. Be eyes to the blind, and a guiding light unto the feet of the erring. Be an ornament to the countenance of truth, a crown to the brow of fidelity, a pillar of the temple of righteousness, a breath of life to the body of mankind, an ensign of the hosts of justice, a luminary above the horizon of virtue, a dew to the soil of the human heart, an ark on the ocean of knowledge, a sun in the heaven of bounty, a gem on the diadem of wisdom, a shining light in the firmament of thy generation, a fruit upon the tree of humility."

'Abdu'l-Bahá lived forty years of His sanctified life in the prison fortress town, obeying this holy Tablet, not only in the letter but in the spirit.

* * *

When the dreaded Committee of Investigation arrived from Constantinople, they abode in a large garden, near the tomb shrine of Bahá'u'lláh.

Enemies of the Master at once busied themselves in sending documents full of false accusations. The people of 'Akká, being panic-stricken and full of fear, were careful to avoid any communication with the Master and His family; nobody dared to pay visits to them.

'Abdu'l-Bahá wrote to the Committee, informing them that there were many enemies, who were capable of forging and posting a letter in His name, full of untrue statements. The Committee assured Him that they would beware of and suppress any such document.

After the investigations in 'Akká were completed, the Committee proceeded to Haifa, where they examined the building on Mount Carmel.

In the meantime they were awaiting the official *farmán*, confirming the sentence of banishment of the Master to the far-off island of Fízán. But, instead of that *farmán*, the Committee received the command to return at once to Constantinople, in consequence of an attempt to assassinate the Sultán, 'Abdu'l-Ḥamíd, by placing a bomb in his path!

In consequence of this recall, it came to pass that the very boat which had been prepared to take 'Abdu'l-Bahá into perpetual banishment took the investigators hurriedly away to Beirut, thence to Constantinople.

Arrived there, they presented their report to the Sultán.

The main points were three:

1. 'Abbás has made 'Akká a Mecca, and Haifa a Medina unto himself.

2. He has made a banner with "Yá Bahá'u'l-Abhá" emblazoned upon it; with this he is endeavouring to foment a rebellion among the Arabs.
3. He, 'Abbás, is establishing his government in that neighbourhood.

Such was the report presented to His Majesty the Sultán, at Constantinople.

But his government, being too much occupied with the investigation of the conspiracy against the life of the Sultán, did not take up the matter of the "'Akká and Haifa Accusations," as they were legally called.

Meanwhile the persecution of the Master continued unabated. No one dared to go near Him, but a few of the Bahá'í friends.

His days were spent in chanting prayers and in planting trees in the garden.

One day the Governor of 'Akká sent for the Master, Whom he questioned about some political documents which He was supposed to have received. To which the reply was:

"Assuredly, and I speak naught but the truth, no such papers have ever been received by me. If, however, you wish to bring a false accusation against me, you have only to write it down and I will sign it. For I have no fear of death, it is, indeed, my life's greatest desire, for it would be following the example of the most dearly beloved Báb to be martyred for my love of God."

This answer was communicated to the Válí of Beirut.

At this time the Master wrote to the Sublime Porte at Constantinople, replying to the three accusations, contained in the report of the Committee of Investigation.

I

"To make a 'Mecca' of one town, and a 'Medina' of another town is not in the power of my hands to accomplish, therefore it is an absurd accusation.

II

"The statement that I have established a government in this place, with myself as king, is quite the greatest honour you could possibly confer upon me, and the highest praise.

"For a prisoner, so carefully watched and guarded, day and

night, to be able to institute a government would be absolutely miraculous, therefore the accusation is truly a tribute to my ability.

III

"Concerning the banner which I am supposed to have had made, with that special emblem upon it—it is very strange that neither the Válí, nor any other Government official has ever seen it.

"Moreover, for me to possess such a flag, and to carry it far and wide among the Arabs to raise a revolt, would need the help of the Angels of God to render it invisible to the sight of all others."

When the Sultán eventually received the report of that Committee of Investigation, he sentenced the Master to banishment, but before the decree was carried out the "Young Turk" revolution took place, the Sultán was deposed, and the religious, with the political prisoners, were set at liberty.

This release took place in August 1908.

Those fateful days in the autumn of 1908 were passed by the Master's family and friends in constant anxiety and fear of danger to His very life; whilst the people of 'Akká were panic-stricken and full of fear.

At this time there was much activity going forward: the Governor of the town was dismissed, and replaced by a new Governor of 'Akká, who was appointed in Beirut.

This man was very unfriendly to the Master, and did not permit any of His friends to approach Him.

In a short time this antagonistic official was recalled to Beirut, and another new Governor had arrived in 'Akká; whilst in Beirut the unfriendly person's conduct as an official gave great offence, and he was dismissed from his post. On hearing of his downfall, the Master straightway sent a special messenger to enquire as to his health and to assure him of His good wishes; He also sent a very precious ring as a present. This envoy was charged to tell the unfortunate man that, although in captivity, 'Abdu'l-Bahá was ready to do everything in His power for him.

Such was the Master's kindness, disregarding always the bitter persecution directed against Himself.

The man was much ashamed of his behaviour, and begged the Master to forgive him all the harmful deeds he had wrought against Him.

The Master forgave all the evil done to Himself, but the people of Beirut were not ready to overlook his behaviour, and rejoiced in his downfall.

It was during these dark days that one of the government officials asked the Master to give an 'abá (cloak) to him.

"I have only this 'abá, which I am wearing, I will gladly give it to you."

The man replied that he did not like that 'abá, but wanted a better one.

"I do not possess a better one, but if you wish," said the Master, "I will give you money to buy a good 'abá for yourself."

This offer did not content the man, so 'Abdu'l-Bahá promised to send and buy a new 'abá for him, meanwhile letting him keep His only one!

In spite of all this kindness, the man continued to speak evil concerning the Master, to bring false accusations against Him, to make more rigorous the prison rules, and in many ways to harass and annoy the noble prisoner. He set soldiers to watch all those who tried to approach the Master, and to prevent their meeting Him.

Whilst this official busied himself in working evil against 'Abdu'l-Bahá he offended a brother official, who accused him to the Válí of Beirut, of certain treacheries; for instance, of possessing a book by which he could foretell future events. By this book he prophesied "that the Sultánate would not last more than two years."

This aroused the suspicions of the Válí, who sent an escort of soldiers to arrest that faithless public servant, also to seize all his possessions and papers, and to bring him and his belongings, including the prophetic book, to Beirut.

* * *

During the latter part of this time when all the people of the place had grown to look upon Him with a great reverence, witnessing His perfect Christ-like life, He had much additional suffering heaped upon Him through the bitter hatred of His half-brothers.

The Master one day being asked a question concerning these enemies, replied:

"I do not wish to mention them, much less to speak against them; only do I wish to say unto you that calumny and persecution are of no importance. As nothing can prevent the fall of rain from heaven to give life to the gardens of earth, so no human power is able to prevent the fulfilment of the Word of God."

And so we leave them, for as these are some memories of the Divine Cause, not of its traitors, its betrayers, its opposers, or its enemies, it is not the place to discuss the abundant evidence of increased severity, of imprisonment, of even death sentences passed upon 'Abdu'l-Bahá through the intrigues of these enemies, the subtle poison of whose malign and cunningly-devised misrepresentations were persistently poured into the ears of officials. These persons, however inclined to be in themselves friendly, were not proof against what was described to them as the dangerous influence of the new reforming teaching.

The day came when the Master was forbidden to visit even the tomb-shrine of Bahá'u'lláh, where He had been wont to spend in prayer such time as He spared from the daily and nightly ministering service to the poor, the grief-stricken, and the sick in body, soul, and spirit.

One of His daughters related that being deprived of these visits, which were the most prized intervals in His arduous days, gave Him more pain than the imprisonment itself:—

One day, a party of nine (we, my mother, Khánum, my three sisters, two Persian, and one English, friends) were passing the Master's door. He came out and said:

"Where are you going?"

"To the shrine; to Bahjí—it is the day of the ascension of Bahá'u'lláh."

"Yes. Yes. Pray for me."

None could describe how touched we were that our Beloved One should turn back into His little room, whilst we went on to celebrate the day in prayer and chanting. Oh, the pity of it, that the Master was not permitted to visit the tomb-shrine of His Father, even on the Day of His ascension.

The party of nine determined to pray a prayer of power at the shrine for the whole of the night, with the special intention —the release of 'Abdu'l-Bahá.

Very soon, suddenly, the release came.

The day before 'Abdu'l-Ḥamíd was dethroned, we were seated at lunch; always in a state of terrible anxiety, the atmosphere seemed charged with dread and danger.

A soldier passed the window; he was bringing a letter. It was for the Master calling Him to the house of the Governor. The much-feared Committee of Investigation had returned, unrelenting and cruel, and began to terrorize the people in advance.

'Abdu'l-Bahá arose to obey the call, to be arraigned before such a tribunal.

"Do not be unhappy, my dear ones," and He smiled that calm, loving smile, which filled our hearts with peace, even in that dire hour.

"Do not be unhappy; I shall come back to you."

Those waiting hours were spent in an extraordinary state of mind. Outwardly all was hopeless. We were tortured by the spectre of the possible, nay most probable fate of the Master. We waited—waited. Mírzá Muḥsin (a son-in-law of 'Abdu'l-Bahá) went to the Court House to obtain news. Still we waited, upheld by the words, spoken as He left us:

"Do not be unhappy; I shall come back to you."

At length He came. But He told us nothing.

All through the hours of that night we could hear the Beloved chanting and praying. The night seemed endless. At dawn He called us: "Make some tea and then go to Haifa. Carry the news that everything is changed, that all is well."

Thus the burden was lifted from our hearts.

On that day the Sultán, 'Abdu'l-Ḥamíd, was dethroned. In two days the news reached 'Akká. "The Young Turk Party are in power."

The great gun was fired from the fortress of 'Akká.

"That was God's gun," said 'Abdu'l-Bahá.

All prisoners, religious and political, were released. The Master was free!

* * *

Forty years in captivity!
Entering the prison city of 'Akká a young man of twenty-four years. Released at sixty-four!
Was ever so great a victory over material conditions? The opposing forces utterly routed!
The radiant spirit of 'Abdu'l-Bahá, undaunted and eager!
He began to make plans for journeying to the western world in accordance with His Father's sacred charge to bring to mankind the knowledge of the Divine Plan for establishing the "Kingdom of God, where His Will shall be done on earth as it is in Heaven." He was ready to go forth with that vital transforming spirit which would change a World, now wet with tears, into the delectable Paradise of Love and Justice.
Oh, the marvel of such a preparation for such a Mission! Was ever such unfaltering, unswerving determination?

CHAPTER II

'Abdu'l-Bahá in London

To the Bahá'ís of Britain:

TABLET FROM 'ABDU'L-BAHÁ

O ye Sons and Daughters of the Kingdom! Your letter, which was written by heavenly inspiration, has arrived. Its contents are full of interest, and its message expresses the feelings of radiant hearts. Verily, the Bahá'ís of London are steadfast believers and faithful in service.

They shall not slacken with years, nor shall their light grow dim.

For they are Bahá'ís. They are children of Heaven. They are of God. Surely they will be the means of uplifting God's word and of fostering the oneness of the world of humanity.

They will proclaim the equality of man and spread the Divine Teachings.

It is easy to accept the Kingdom of God; to endure therein with steadfastness is difficult, for temptations are great and strong.

The English have always been resolute, not swerving in the face of difficulties. Having taken up a cause, they are not ready, for trivial reasons, either to leave it or to lose heart and enthusiasm.

Verily, in all their undertakings they show firmness.

O my friends, though you dwell in the West, praise be to God, you have heard the Divine Call from the East, and like unto Moses and the burning bush, you have become aglow with the fire, lighted in the "Tree of Asia."*

You have found the Right Path. You have become as shining lamps, and have entered into the Kingdom of God.

Now in thanksgiving for this bounty, you have arisen to offer prayers for blessings to fall upon all mankind: that, by the light

---
* Rev. 22: 2.

of the Star of the Kingdom of Abhá, the eyes of all may be opened and their hearts, like unto mirrors, reflect the splendour of the Sun of Truth.

This is my hope—that the breath of the Holy Spirit may so inspire your hearts, that your tongues may begin to reveal the mysteries and to expound the truth and the meaning of the Holy Books.

May the Bahá'ís, by the Divine Teachings, become physicians to heal the long-standing infirmities of the world, to restore sight to the blind, hearing to the deaf, and life to the dead, and to awaken those that sleep.

Be assured that the blessings of the Holy Spirit will descend upon you, and that the hosts of the Kingdom of Abhá will come to your succour.

Upon you be the glory of the Most Glorious!

Signed: 'ABDU'L-BAHÁ 'ABBÁS.

Written by 'Abdu'l-Bahá at Ramleh, Egypt,
on the 9th May, 1911.
Translated into English by Y. Dáwúd.

The beloved Prisoner was free! Free to obey the charge laid upon Him by Bahá'u'lláh to go forth into all the world to carry the message of the Renewal of Peace and Unity, of Joy and Service, and to call mankind to immediate action for averting the "Great Woe."

Would His strength be sufficient for these journeys? Our hearts sank as we thought of His captivity in the pestilential air of 'Akká. Entering it as a young man of twenty-four; leaving that death-dealing atmosphere at the age of sixty-four (August 1908).

News came of His sojourn in Alexandria from one who said of Him: "Seeing 'Abdu'l-Bahá and His most holy life has made me believe in Christ. Never before did I think His existence possible. Now I can understand."

As we thought upon all these marvels, we waited and wondered whether it was to be our privilege to see Him. Would it be given to us to hear the teaching of Bahá'u'lláh from 'Abdu'l-Bahá Himself?

Should we travel to Egypt, or would He come to Europe? If He were to come to London, where would be the roof to shelter Him? We who had quietly prepared our home in the hope that He might deign to sojourn there awhile, sent the invitation. Soon a telegram came:

" 'Abdu'l-Bahá arriving in London 8th September.* Can Lady Blomfield receive Him?"

And now at last 'Abdu'l-Bahá was coming into the western world, even to us in London!

He arrived, and who shall picture Him?

A silence as of love and awe overcame us, as we looked at Him; the gracious figure, clothed in a simple white garment, over which was a light-coloured Persian *'abá*; on His head He wore a low-crowned *táj*, round which was folded a small, fine-linen turban of purest white; His hair and short beard were of that snowy whiteness which had once been black; His eyes were large, blue-grey with long, black lashes and well-marked

---
* 8th September, 1911.

eyebrows; His face was a beautiful oval with warm, ivory-coloured skin, a straight, finely-modelled nose, and firm, kind mouth. These are merely outside details by which an attempt is made to convey an idea of His arresting personality.

His figure was of such perfect symmetry, and so full of dignity and grace, that the first impression was that of considerable height. He seemed an incarnation of loving understanding, of compassion and power, of wisdom and authority, of strength, and of a buoyant youthfulness, which somehow defied the burden of His years; and such years!

One saw, as in a clear vision, that He had so wrought all good and mercy that the inner grace of Him had grown greater than all outer sign, and the radiance of this inner glory shone in every glance, and word, and movement as He came with hands outstretched.

"I am very much pleased with you all. Your love has drawn me to London. I waited forty years in prison to bring the Message to you. Are you pleased to receive such a guest?"

I think our souls must have answered, for I am not conscious that anyone uttered an audible word.

The history of 'Abdu'l-Bahá's stay in our house lies in the relating of various incidents, connected with individuals, who stand out from amongst the crowd of those persons who eagerly sought His Presence.

Oh, these pilgrims, these guests, these visitors! Remembering those days, our ears are filled with the sound of their footsteps—as they came from every country in the world! Every day, all day long, a constant stream. An interminable procession!

Ministers and missionaries, Oriental scholars and occult students, practical men of affairs and mystics, Anglican-Catholics and Nonconformists, Theosophists and Hindus, Christian Scientists and doctors of medicine, Muslims, Buddhists, and Zoroastrians. There also called: politicians, Salvation Army soldiers, and other workers for human good, women suffragists, journalists, writers, poets, and healers, dressmakers and great ladies, artists and artisans, poor workless people and prosperous merchants, members of the dramatic and musical world, these all came; and none were too lowly,

nor too great, to receive the sympathetic consideration of this holy Messenger, who was ever giving His life for others' good.
In this short chronicle I must be content to omit many details and only touch lightly on such personalities as pass before my eyes in the memories of those unforgettable days.

First of all there were the Bahá'í friends, who assembled to greet the Master. These arrived eager and elated nearly every day during His sojourn, often bringing a friend or relation; Mrs. Thornburgh-Cropper, Miss Ethel Rosenberg, Miss Gamble, Miss Herrick, Mrs. Scaramucci, Miss Elsie Lee, Mr. Catanach, Mr. Cuthbert, Miss Juliet Thompson, Mr. Mountfort Mills, Mr. Mason Remey, Mrs. Claudia Coles, Miss Yandell, Miss Julia Culver, Mrs. Louise Waite, the Reverend Cooper Hunt, Miss Drake Wright, Mrs. Movius, and many others.
Foremost amongst our visitors were Monsieur and Madame Dreyfus-Barney, the brilliant French scholar and his no less brilliant American wife, who spoke Persian with 'Abdu'l-Bahá, translated for Him, and were altogether helpful, courteous, and charming.
Very important arrivals were the pilgrims from Persia, who had journeyed far to attain the Presence of the Master. Now at last this was possible, after long years of confinement, of danger, and of persecution. Several were sons of those who "steadfast unto death had been martyred for the Cause of God."
These survivors of the Martyrs were accorded a very special and loving welcome by 'Abdu'l-Bahá, Who was deeply affected as they entered His Presence. We were all overcome by the poignant emotions of such meetings.
As a contrast to these faithful souls, came a man of imposing appearance, also a Persian, Jalálu'd-Dawlih, who had caused two young brothers to be cruelly tortured and killed for refusing to deny their faith in what they held to be the Truth of God. This man entreated to be received by 'Abdu'l-Bahá, at Whose feet he fell prostrate, imploring pardon for his inhuman crimes.
When all was understood, this was a heart-rending episode.

Another day came a deputation from the Bramo-Somaj

Society, inviting the Master to address them. 'Abdu'l-Bahá was much pleased with the enlightened spirit of their movement.

Members of the Muslim Community of Great Britain came to pay their respects, and at their request 'Abdu'l-Bahá visited the mosque at Woking, where an important gathering of their friends gave an enthusiastic welcome to Him Who, albeit the bearer of the new Message to all the religions of the world was descended from the ancient line of nobles in Islám.

Members of the Persian Legation came to see Him from time to time, entertained Him, and were also entertained by Him.

Another Persian nobleman, Dúst Muḥammad Khán (Mu'ayyiru'l-Mamálik) was a constant visitor, and sometimes accompanied the Master to His country meetings.

A workman who had left his bag of tools in the hall was welcomed with smiling kindness by 'Abdu'l-Bahá. With a look of sadness the man said: "I don't know much about religious things, as I have no time for anything but my work."

"That is well. Very well. A day's work done in the spirit of service is in itself an act of worship. Such work is a prayer unto God."

The man's face cleared from its shadow of doubt and hesitation, and he went out from the Master's presence happy and strengthened, as though a weighty burden had been taken away.

The late Maharajah of Jalawar, an enlightened and cultured prince, paid many visits to 'Abdu'l-Bahá. He gave an elaborate dinner and reception in His honour, to which we also were invited. The Maharajah and members of his suite sometimes dined at our house with the Master, who delighted all the guests with His beautiful courtesy, recounting interesting stories, often full of humour; He always loved to see happy, laughing faces. And what grace He possessed—as of a king—this serene and dignified Personage Who had spent a lifetime in prison!

'Abdu'l-Bahá was always very glad to welcome visitors from India.

He would speak to them of the "Spiritual Sun of Truth, which has always shone from the eastern horizon, and again of

the great Spiritual Teachers, who have all arisen in the East."
The Message of Krishna was a Message of Love; every true
Prophet of God has given the same message, that of Love. We
must all strive to spread this Love among the sons of mankind.

"It would be well for the Western peoples to turn to the East
for illumination," He would say again and again.

"The East and the West should unite to give to each other
what is lacking in each. This exchange of gifts would form a
true civilization, where spiritual ideals would be translated
into action in the material world."

Professor Edward Granville Browne, who had written much
concerning the Bábís and the Bahá'ís, came from time to time,
speaking in Persian with the Master, Who was delighted to see
him, and talked over many things, especially the momentous
occasion when that intrepid Cambridge Orientalist succeeded
in obtaining permission to enter the presence of Bahá'u'lláh.*

Mr. Wellesley Tudor-Pole, who had visited the Master in
Alexandria, with the clear insight of a student of things sacred
and mystic, had recognized the inspiring influence which
emanated from 'Abdu'l-Bahá. Mr. Tudor-Pole had helped us
to understand something of the power of Bahá'u'lláh, working
in the realm of thought, to awaken the hearts and minds of
those who, through inner training, had attained capacity.
These explanations were very illuminating to us, who were
waiting and hoping for the coming of 'Abdu'l-Bahá.

Soon after His arrival in London, 'Abdu'l-Bahá received
Archdeacon Wilberforce in audience. This was a remarkable
interview. Our dear friend, the Archdeacon, sat on a low chair
by the Master. 'Abdu'l-Bahá spoke to him in His beautiful
Persian. He placed His hand on the head of the Archdeacon,
talked long to him, and answered many questions. Evidently
His words penetrated further than the outer ears, for both
were deeply moved. On this occasion the invitation was given
for 'Abdu'l-Bahá to speak to the congregation of St. John the
Divine, at Westminster, on the following Sunday.

The beloved Messenger from the East passed through the

---

* This occasion is described in the Introduction to *The Traveller's Narrative*, by Professor E. G. Browne, who translated that interesting book from the Persian.

midst of the crowded church, hand in hand with Archdeacon Wilberforce, up to the chancel, where they stood together, two men of God, one from the East and one from the West, united in their loving service to the "Ruler of the throne and of the dust." 'Abdu'l-Bahá's beautiful voice filled the church with its powerful vibrations. The translation was read by the Archdeacon in his own impressive way. This was indeed a soul-stirring event, far-reaching in its influence!

Dr. Platon Drakoules, who had invited the first Bahá'í gathering in England to meet at his chambers in Oxford, paid several visits to the Master.

Among other guests were Mr. Albert Dawson, editor of an interesting paper, *The Christian Commonwealth*, dealing with religious and ethical matters. The Rev. R. J. Campbell was one of the earliest to arrive. At his invitation 'Abdu'l-Bahá, for the first time in His life, addressed a Western audience. This took place at the City Temple. On this occasion Mr. Wellesley Tudor-Pole read the translation.

Mrs. Annie Besant visited the Master one day, also Mr. A. P. Sinnett, who came several times, and they each invited 'Abdu'l-Bahá to address the Theosophical Society.

Sir Richard and Lady Stapley were frequent visitors. Mr. Eric Hammond came several times. He was the author of that interesting book *The Splendour of God*, dealing with the Bahá'í Message, published in *The Wisdom of the East* series.

Miss Alice Buckton was an earnest visitor. She had written *Eager Heart*, a very interesting Christmas mystery play. The performance of this mystery play at the Church House, Westminster, was honoured by the presence of 'Abdu'l-Bahá. This was a memorable occasion, as it was the first time He had ever witnessed a dramatic performance.

The Master wept during the scene in which the Holy Child and His parents, overcome with fatigue, and suffering from hunger, were met by the hesitation of Eager Heart to admit them to the haven of rest which she had prepared, she, of course, failing to recognize the sacred visitors.

The Master afterwards joined the group of players.

It was an arresting scene. In the Eastern setting the Messenger, in His Eastern robes, speaking to them in the beautiful Eastern words of the Divine significance of the events which had been portrayed.

Another interesting visitor was Mrs. Pankhurst, who was much cheered by her interview, for the Master told her to continue her work steadfastly, for women would very shortly take their rightful place in the world.

Mr. Stead had a long and earnest conversation with 'Abdu'l-Bahá. I see also passing before me Mr. Francis Skrine, author of a book on the Bahá'í Message, Lady Wemyss and her sister, Lady Glenconner, Princess Karadja, Mrs. Douglas Hamilton, Mrs. Forbes, Baroness Barnekow, Mr. David Graham Pole, Miss Constance Maud, Miss Mary Maud, Mrs. Charles Blomfield and her tiny girl. From time to time children were brought, who received an especially loving welcome from the Master.

Other guests were the Rev. Roland Corbet, the Rev. Rhonddha Williams, Mr. Claude Montefiore, Dr. Hector Munro, Miss Felicia Scatchard, Miss Louise Heron, Miss Eve Faulkener, Mrs. Cecil Headlam, Mrs. Alexander Whyte, Miss Leggatt and her sister, Miss MacLeod, Madame Bricka, Lady Evelyn Moreton, and Miss Katie Wingfield.

Mr. and Mrs. Felix Moscheles, who were very eager to hear the Master's teaching on the imperative need for a universal language, arranged a meeting at their studio, at which many Esperantists were present:

The Ranee of Sarawak, Colonel and Mrs. Seymour, Mr. Keightley, Lady Agnew, Sir Michael Sadler, Mírzá Nayyir Afnán, and many, many others who came were privileged to share in the joyous atmosphere created by the presence of the Master.

One evening in the drawing-room of Mrs. Gabrielle Enthoven, the Master asked her whom he called "Hamsayih" (neighbour): "What is your great interest in life?"

She replied: "The Drama."

'Abdu'l-Bahá said: "I will give you a play. It shall be called the *Drama of the Kingdom*."

The Master then gave a plan, from which a play has been written by my daughter, Mary. This has been approved by the Reviewing Committees of the National Spiritual Assemblies of the Bahá'ís of the British Isles, and of the United States and Canada.

Day by day friends brought offerings of flowers and fruit, so that the dinner table was laden with these beautiful tokens of love for 'Abdu'l-Bahá. Whilst cutting off bunches of grapes and giving them to various guests, He talked to us of the joy of freedom, of how grateful we should be for the privilege of dwelling in safety, under just laws, in a healthy city, with a temperate climate, and brilliant light—"there was much darkness in the prison fortress of 'Akká!"

After His first dinner with us He said: "The food was delicious and the fruit and flowers were lovely, but would that we could share some of the courses with those poor and hungry people who have not even one."

What a lesson to the guests present!

We at once agreed that one substantial, plentiful dish, with salad, cheese, biscuits, sweetmeats, fruits, and flowers on the table, preceded by soup and followed by coffee or tea, should be quite sufficient for any dinner. This arrangement would greatly simplify life, both as to cookery and service, and would undeniably be more in accordance with the ideals of Christianity than numerous dishes unnecessary and costly.

'Abdu'l-Bahá was accompanied by a secretary, Mírzá Maḥmúd, and Khusraw, His faithful servant.

He rose very early, chanted prayers, took tea, wrote Tablets, and dictated others. He then received those who flocked to see Him, some arriving soon after dawn, patiently waiting on the door-steps until the door would be opened for their entrance.

On an early day of His visit a telegram came from the Tihrán Bahá'í Assembly:

"That the holy feet of 'Abdu'l-Bahá have crossed your threshold receive our felicitations. Blessed are ye."

* * *

A book entitled *Abdu'l-Bahá in London* was compiled soon after His visit, and contains many of His addresses. I will therefore describe some episodes and incidents which came under my own observation, and which, as I believe, are not elsewhere recorded.

One striking fact was that 'Abdu'l-Bahá never asked for donations, and even refused to accept money or any costly gifts that were offered to Him.

One day in my presence a lady said to Him: "I have here a cheque from a friend, who begs its acceptance to buy a good motor-car for your work in England and Europe."

The Master replied: "I accept with grateful thanks the gift of your friend." He took the cheque into both His hands, as though blessing it, and said "I return it to be used for gifts to the poor."

"We have never seen the like before. Surely such deeds are very rare," it was whispered amongst the friends.

In all the arrangements for the comfort of the numerous guests, Miss Beatrice Platt, Dr. Lutfulláh Ḥakím, and my daughters, Mary and Ellinor, were occupied from morning till night. They also took notes of the addresses of 'Abdu'l-Bahá, and made appointments for interviews with Him.

We very swiftly grew into the habit of calling Him "the Master," a name used by Bahá'u'lláh when speaking of Him, and afterwards by His family and His intimate friends, though He Himself preferred to be called " 'Abdu'l-Bahá" ("Servant of the Glory").

"Come ye people into the Kingdom of God, for this day the doors are open, and the station of Servitude is the highway thereto."

This station of Servitude—how great! How marvellous! We very gradually began to have a tiny glimmer of comprehension of what Service could mean, as the life of this Servant unfolded itself daily before our eyes.

The Master's custom was to receive the visitors by twos or by threes, or individually, during the early hours of the morning. Then, about nine o'clock, He would come into the dining-room whilst we were at breakfast to greet us. "Are you well? Did you sleep well?"

We tried to prevail upon Him to take some breakfast with us

(we were always concerned that He ate so very little). At last one day He said He would like a little soup—then we had it brought in every morning. He smiled and said: "To please you I will take it. Thank you, you are very kind." Then to the servitor who offered it to Him: "I give too great trouble," He said.

In a few minutes He would go to His room, where He would resume the chanting of prayers and dictating of Tablets in reply to the vast number of letters which incessantly arrived.

Visitors having gradually gathered in the drawing-room (about ten o'clock), 'Abdu'l-Bahá would come to us, pausing just inside the door, smiling round at the guests with a look of joyous sympathy which seemed to enfold each and all who were present; they rose simultaneously, as though the kingship of this Messenger were recognized by an inner perception.

"How are you? My hope is that you are well. Are you happy?"

Speaking so to us, He would pass through our midst to His usual chair. Then He would talk rather *with* us than *to* us; so did He reply to unspoken questions, causing wonderment in those who were waiting to ask them—weaving the whole into a beautiful address, in the atmosphere of which all problems and pain and care and doubt and sorrow would melt away, leaving only happiness and peace.

The power of Divine Love we felt to be incarnated in Him, Whom we called "the Master."

Now came the hour when He would receive those who had asked for appointments for private audiences. Careful time-tables were made and strictly adhered to, for very numerous were these applicants for so unique an experience, how unique, only those knew when in the presence of the Master, and we could partly divine, as we saw the look on their faces as they emerged—a look as though blended of awe, of marvelling, and of a certain calm joy. Sometimes we were conscious of reluctance in them to come forth into the outer world, as though they would hold fast to their beatitude, lest the return to things of earth should wrest it from them.

"My sorrow is still with me," said one woman clad in deepest mourning, "but He has taken away the sting, and turned it into joy."

One day a woman asked to be permitted to see the Master. "Have you an appointment?"

"Alas! No."

"I am sorry," answered the over-zealous friend who met her in the hall, "but He is occupied now with most important people, and cannot be disturbed."

The woman turned away, feeling too humble to persist in her appeal, but, oh! so bitterly disappointed. Before she had reached the foot of the stairway, she was overtaken by a breathless messenger from 'Abdu'l-Bahá.

"He wishes to see you, come back! He has told me to bring you to Him."

We had heard His voice from the door of His audience room speaking with authority:

"A heart has been hurt. Hasten, hasten, bring her to me!"

Another day, whilst several personages were talking with 'Abdu'l-Bahá, a man's voice was heard at the hall door.

"Is the lady of this house within?" The servitor answered "Yes, but——" "Oh please, I must see her!" he interrupted with despairing insistence. I, overhearing, had gone into the hall.

"Are you the hostess of 'Abdu'l-Bahá?" he asked.

"Yes. Do you wish to see me?"

"I have walked thirty miles for that purpose."

"Come in and rest. After some refreshment you will tell me?"

He came in and sat down in the dining-room. In appearance he might have been an ordinary tramp, but as he spoke, from out the core of squalor and suffering, something else seemed faintly to breathe.

After a while the poor fellow began his pitiful story:

"I was not always as you see me now, a disreputable, hopeless object. My father is a country rector, and I had the advantage of being at a public school. Of the various causes which led to my arrival at the Thames embankment as my only home, I need not speak to you."

"Last evening I had decided to put an end to my futile, hateful life, useless to God and man!"

"Whilst taking what I had intended should be my last walk, I saw 'a Face' in the window of a newspaper shop. I stood looking at the face as if rooted to the spot. He seemed to speak to me, and call me to him!"

"Let me see that paper, please," I asked. It was the face of 'Abdu'l-Bahá.

"I read that he is here, in this house. I said to myself, 'If there is in existence on earth that personage, I shall take up again the burden of my life.' "

"I set off on my quest. I have come here to find him. Tell me, is he here? Will he see me? Even me?"

"Of course he will see you. Come to Him."

In answer to the knock, 'Abdu'l-Bahá Himself opened the door, extending His hands, as though to a dear friend, *whom He was expecting.*

"Welcome! Most welcome! I am very much pleased that thou hast come. Be seated."

The pathetic man trembled and sank on to a low chair by the Master's feet, as though unable to utter a word.

The other guests, meanwhile, looked on wonderingly to see the attention transferred to the strange-looking new arrival, who seemed to be so overburdened with hopeless misery.

"Be happy! Be happy!" said 'Abdu'l-Bahá, holding one of the poor hands, stroking tenderly the dishevelled, bowed head.

Smiling that wonderful smile of loving compassion, the Master continued:

"Do not be filled with grief when humiliation overtaketh thee.

"The bounty and power of God is without limit for each and every soul in the world.

"Seek for spiritual joy and knowledge, then, though thou walk upon this earth, thou wilt be dwelling within the divine realm.

"Though thou be poor, thou mayest be rich in the Kingdom of God."

These and other words of comfort, of strength, and of healing were spoken to the man, whose cloud of misery seemed to melt away in the warmth of the Master's loving presence.

As the strange visitor rose to leave Him Whom he had sought and found, a new look was upon his face, a new erectness in his carriage, a firm purpose in his steps.

"Please write down for me His words. I have attained all I expected, and even more."

"And now what are you going to do?" I asked.
"I'm going to work in the fields. I can earn what I need for my simple wants. When I have saved enough I shall take a little bit of land, build a tiny hut upon it in which to live, then I shall grow violets for the market. As He says 'Poverty is unimportant, *work is worship*.' I need not say 'thank you,' need I? Farewell." The man had gone.

* * *

Certain of those who thronged to see the Master, having travelled from far countries, were naturally anxious to spend every possible moment with Him, Whose deeds and words appealed to them as ever-filled with grace and love. Therefore it came about that day after day, whilst the Master was teaching, the luncheon gong would sound, and those who remained would be invited to sit at food with Him. We grew to expect that there would be nineteen guests at table, so often did this number recur.

These were much-prized times; 'Abdu'l-Bahá would continue the interrupted discourse, or tell some anecdote, often humorous, meanwhile frequently serving the guests with His own hands, offering sweets, or choosing various fruits to distribute to the friends.

The following touching incident took place one day when we were seated at table with the Master.

A Persian friend arrived who had passed through 'Ishqábád. He presented a cotton handkerchief to 'Abdu'l-Bahá, Who untied it, and saw therein a piece of dry black bread, and a shrivelled apple.

The friend exclaimed: "A poor Bahá'í workman came to me: 'I hear thou goest into the presence of our Beloved. Nothing have I to send, but this my dinner. I pray thee offer it to Him with my loving devotion.' "

'Abdu'l-Bahá spread the poor handkerchief before Him, leaving His own luncheon untasted. He ate of the workman's dinner, broke pieces off the bread, and handed them to the assembled guests, saying: "Eat with me of this gift of humble love."

Of the guests who remained to lunch or dinner, the Master would often hold out His hand to the humblest or most diffident, lead them into the dining-room, seat him or her at His right hand, smile and talk until all embarrassment had passed away, and the guest felt as though all uneasiness had changed into the atmosphere of a calm and happy home.

Every detail of one evening remains in the memory of those who were present.

Two ladies had written from Scotland asking if it were possible that 'Abdu'l-Bahá would spare them one evening.

They accepted my invitation to dinner. Having come straight from the train, and being about to return the same night, every moment was precious.

The Master received them with His warm, simple welcome, and they spontaneously, rather than consciously, made more reverent curtsies than if in the presence of the ordinary great personages of the earth.

Everybody was feeling elated at the prospect of a wonderful evening, unmarred by the presence of any but the most intimate and the most comprehending of the friends.

Not more than half an hour had passed, when, to our consternation, a persistent person pushed past the servitors, and strode into our midst. Seating himself, and lighting a cigarette without invitation, he proceeded to say that he intended writing an article for some paper about 'Abdu'l-Bahá, superciliously asking for "Some telling points, don't you know." He talked without a pause in a far from polite manner.

We were speechless and aghast at the intrusion of this insufferable and altogether unpleasant bore, spoiling our golden hour!

Presently 'Abdu'l-Bahá rose and, making a sign to the man to follow Him, went to His own private room.

We looked at one another. The bore had gone, yes, but alas! so also had the Master!

"Can nothing be done?" Being the hostess, I was perturbed and perplexed. Then I went to the door of the audience room, and said to the secretary: "Will you kindly say to 'Abdu'l-Bahá that the ladies with whom the appointment has been made are awaiting His pleasure."

I returned to the guests and we awaited the result.

Almost immediately we heard steps approaching along the corridor. They came across the hall to the door. The sound of kind farewell words reached us. Then the closing of the door, and the Beloved came back.

"Oh, Master!" we said.

Pausing near the door, He looked at us each in turn, with a look of deep, grave meaning.

"You were making that poor man uncomfortable, so strongly desiring his absence; I took him away to make him feel happy."

Truly 'Abdu'l-Bahá's thoughts and ways were far removed from ours!

His desire that everyone should be happy showed itself in many ways. "Are you well? Are you happy?" he always asked.

One day the sound of peals of laughter came from the direction of the kitchen. The Master went quickly to the cheery party.

"I am very much pleased that you are so happy. Tell me, why are you laughing?"

It appeared that the Persian servant had remarked "In the East women wear veils and do all the work," to which our English housekeeper had replied: "In the West women don't wear veils, and take good care that the men do at least some of the work. You had better get on with cleaning that silver."

The Master was delighted, laughed heartily, and gave each of them a small gold coin, *"for being happy."*

At the invitation of the Lord Mayor of London, 'Abdu'l-Bahá paid him a visit at the Mansion House, and was greatly pleased with the interview, in the course of which many subjects were discussed; the freedom and happiness of the people; the efforts made to improve social conditions; prisons and prisoners. When the Lord Mayor told Him how people were working to improve the treatment of these poor creatures in prison, and to secure help for them when they were released, the Master said:

"It is well with a country when the magistrates are as fathers to the people.

"There is a great spiritual light in London, and the ideal of justice is strong in the hearts of the people.

"I am always pleased to remember an instance of this sense of justice, which so amazed the Eastern people of the place.

"A certain Páshá, having most unjustly and cruelly beaten one of his servants, was arrested and brought before that just man who represented Britain. To the intense surprise of the Páshá, he himself was sentenced to a term of imprisonment, and told that he richly deserved the punishment. He could not think it possible that so great a person as himself could be sent to prison, and offered a large bribe for his release. This was sternly refused. A much larger sum was offered with the same result, and the unjust lord was compelled to accept the punishment awarded him for his cruelty to his servant.

"The news of this incident, being noised abroad, did much to show the Eastern people that British justice is in reality the same for the rich and for the poor, and therefore worthy of all respect."

The Lord Mayor remarked that he was delighted to hear so pleasing a story of British administration in the East. "Sometimes, alas! there are adverse criticisms," he added.

* * *

During the early days of 'Abdu'l-Bahá's visit to London, many were the attempts to photograph Him. Men with cameras waited round the door, watching for an opportunity. On one occasion I expostulated with them: "Do you think it very courteous to insist on photographing a guest from a distant country against His will?"

"No, Madam," was the reply, "but if others succeed and I fail, my chief will think me a fool."

When I told this to 'Abdu'l-Bahá, He laughed heartily and said: "If the photographs must be, it would be better to have good ones. Those in that paper are very bad indeed."

Thereupon he consented with His unfailing, smiling grace, to be photographed. "To please the friends," he said. "But to have a picture of oneself is to emphasize the personality, which is merely the lamp, and is quite unimportant. The light burning within the lamp has the only real significance."

He signed a photograph, writing His name on the white part of his turban. "My name is my crown," said 'Abdu'l-Bahá— "Servant of God, the Most Glorious."

* * *

'Abdu'l-Bahá often went to the houses of the friends, where again others were invited to meet Him, so that many were the meetings other than at His "English home" which took place.

Mrs. Thornburgh Cropper placed her charming motor-car at His service. It was always ready, in the early morning, at any hour of the day, or late hour of the evening.

It was especially touching to see Mrs. Thornburgh Cropper and Miss Ethel Rosenberg, who had visited Him in the prison fortress of 'Akká, and who had been the first to bring the Message to London, coming day after day, as though transported with gratitude that He was now free to give His Message to those who were hungering and thirsting after righteousness, who were not content that the grand Christian ideals should continue to be "words only," but that they should be translated into action, to the healing of the woes of the world.

For us, every day was filled with joyous interest and marvelling, where simple happenings became spiritual events. One day we were invited to accompany the Master to East Sheen, where a number of friends were gathered, invited by Mr. and Mrs. Jenner. Their three small children clambered on to His knee, clung round His neck, and remained as quiet as wee mice whilst the Master spoke, He meanwhile stroking the hair of the tiny ones and saying:

"Blessed are the children, of whom His Holiness Christ said: 'Of such are the Kingdom of Heaven.' Children have no worldly ambitions. Their hearts are pure. We must become like children, crowning our heads with the crown of severance (from all material things of the earth); purifying our hearts, that we may see God in His Great Manifestations, and obey the laws brought to us by those, His Messengers."

After we had enjoyed the hospitality of the parents of those sweet children, the Master, always loving trees and pastures, went into Richmond Park, where He watched a race on ponies between some boys and a girl. When the latter won, He clapped His hands, crying out "Bravo! Bravo!"

On the way back the evening light was waning as we crossed the Serpentine bridge. Rows of shining lamps beneath the trees, stretching as far as our eyes could see into the distance, made that part of London into a glowing fairyland.

"I am very much pleased with this scene. Light is good, most good. There was much darkness in the prison at 'Akká," said the Master.

Our hearts were sad as we thought on those sombre years within that dismal fortress, where the only light was in the indomitable spirit of the Master Himself! When we said "We are glad, oh! so full of gladness that you are free," He said: "Freedom is not a matter of place, but of condition. I was happy in that prison, for those days were passed in the path of service.

"To me prison was freedom.

"Troubles are a rest to me.

"Death is life.

"To be despised is honour.

"Therefore was I full of happiness all through that prison time.

"When one is released from the prison of self, that is indeed freedom! For self is the greatest prison.

"When this release takes place, one can never be imprisoned. Unless one accepts dire vicissitudes, not with dull resignation, but with radiant acquiescence, one cannot attain this freedom."

* * *

Those of us who were included in the kind invitation of Mr. and Mrs. Tudor-Pole to accompany 'Abdu'l-Bahá on His visit to the Clifton Guest House, Clifton, will forever remember the wonderful three days under that hospitable roof. Many of their friends and neighbours were invited to meet the Eastern guest Who had suffered long years of persecution "in the path of God."

This visit has already been described in our host's own words in *'Abdu'l-Bahá in London*, and we shall always be grateful that we were privileged to share in the sunshine of those days.

One refreshing evening was spent at the house of a friend in Chelsea, who had steadfastly refused to invite anybody to meet 'Abdu'l-Bahá. "He shall have *one* quiet, restful evening without being surrounded by people. Besides, we really want to have Him to ourselves," she said.

So our hostess, her sister, and little niece made the Master very happy. He was delighted to watch the lighted boats passing up and down the river Thames. Our hostess was a real musician, and an authoress. 'Abdu'l-Bahá said to her:

"All Art is a gift of the Holy Spirit. When this light shines through the mind of a musician, it manifests itself in beautiful harmonies. Again, shining through the mind of a poet, it is seen in fine poetry and poetic prose. When the Light of the Sun of Truth inspires the mind of a painter, he produces marvellous pictures. These gifts are fulfilling their highest purpose, when showing forth the praise of God."

A reception was given by Sir Richard and Lady Stapley in honour of 'Abdu'l-Bahá. A picturesque and symbolic decoration was that of a large iced cake with flights of snow-white doves radiating from it. One of these doves was given by the Master to each guest as a souvenir of the Eastern Harbinger of Peace, Who spoke earnestly to us of the duty of each one of those assembled to work, body and soul and spirit, for the Most Great Peace.

"When a thought of war enters your mind, suppress it, and plant in its stead a positive thought of peace. These thoughts, vital and dynamic, will affect the minds of all with whom you come into contact, and like doves of peace, will grow and increase till they spread over all the land."

The devotion of the Master's followers was wonderful, and sometimes took embarrassing ways of showing itself.

As we were starting to the entertainment, one of those who dearly loved 'Abdu'l-Bahá, Siyyid Asadu'lláh, followed Him. Finding the car full of invited guests, he sprang on to the roof, and arrived with us! When we were announced, the host and hostess hid their surprise, and welcomed the faithful friend.

At a sign, an extra seat was placed at the table for him, who refused to be separated from his Master.

Knowing nothing, and caring less, for conventionalities, he spent a happy evening in the presence of the Beloved One.

* * *

'Abdu'l-Bahá did not accept gifts of money, but a handkerchief, a box of bon-bons, baskets of fruit, and lovely flowers gave Him great pleasure. These were constantly brought to His "English home." These offerings of love gained His smiling thanks, and were quickly distributed among the friends.

One day a pair of soft, red-leather slippers, folded into a little case, were offered to Him by the daughters of the hostess. These were soon given to a Persian prince, who, no doubt, treasured them always as the gift of the Master.

The pastor of a Congregational church in the east end of London invited the Master to give an address one Sunday evening. The congregation seemed spell-bound by the power which spread like an atmosphere from another, higher world.

* * *

The visit to Oxford was one of notable interest. The meeting between 'Abdu'l-Bahá and the dear, revered higher critic, Dr. T. K. Cheyne, was fraught with pathos. It seemed almost too intimate to describe, and our very hearts were touched, as we looked on, and realized something of the sacred emotions of that day.

'Abdu'l-Bahá embraced the Doctor with loving grace, and praised his courageous steadfastness in his life's work, always striving against increasing weakness, and lessening bodily health. Through those veiling clouds the light of the mind and spirit shone with a radiant persistence. The beautiful loving care of the devoted wife for her gifted, invalid husband touched the heart of 'Abdu'l-Bahá. With tears in His kind eyes He spoke of them to Mrs. Thornburgh-Cropper and myself on our way back to London:

"She is an angelic woman, an example to all in her unselfish love. Yes, she is a perfect woman. An angel."

This lady was Elizabeth Gibson Cheyne, the very specially gifted poetess.

* * *

One day after a meeting when, as usual, many people had crowded round Him, 'Abdu'l-Bahá arrived home very tired. We were sad at heart that He should be so fatigued, and bewailed the many steps to be ascended to the flat. Suddenly, to our amazement, the Master ran up the stairs to the top very quickly without stopping.

He looked down at us as we walked up after Him, saying with a bright smile, from which all traces of fatigue had vanished:

"You are all very old! I am very young!"

Seeing me full of wonder, 'Abdu'l-Bahá said:

"Through the power of Bahá'u'lláh all things can be done. I have just used that power."

That was the only time we had ever seen Him use that power *for Himself*, and I feel that He did so then to cheer and comfort us, as we were really sad concerning His fatigue.

Might it not also have been to show us an example of the great Reserve of Divine Force always available for those of us who are working in various ways in the "Path of the Love of God and of Mankind." A celestial strength which reinforces us when our human strength fails.

Many were the "Signs" spoken of by those friends gifted with the clairvoyant sense.

"I have just seen a great light, as a halo shining round the Master's head! Wonderful! Wonderful!"

"Have you not seen it yourself?" said one of these friends.

I replied, "In the sense you mean, no. I am not gifted with a constant clairvoyance, but to me He is always clothed in a sacred light."

"But," she persisted, "there must be miracles. Many miracles, are there not?"

"Yes, of course. But 'Abdu'l-Bahá says:

" 'Miracles have frequently obscured the Teaching which the Divine Messenger has brought. The Message is the real miracle. The phenomenal miracles are unimportant, and prove nothing to anybody but the witnesses thereof, and even they will very often explain them away! Therefore miracles have no value in the teaching of religion.' "

"Yes, I understand," she answered, "but when a dear friend was being carried to the operating room to undergo a serious operation, 'Abdu'l-Bahá seemed to walk before her, smiling encouragement, and stayed whilst the doctors did their work. The dreaded ordeal was overpast, and she who had been despaired of, even by the doctors, recovered most unexpectedly. Are you not surprised?"

"No, for this reason; on the day she left London, to join her mother, that lady's daughter came to implore 'Abdu'l-Bahá to 'bear in mind the critical hour of the operation, and to come to her mother's help.' I am of course not surprised that He granted her request."

Another friend said: "At that gathering which I attended, the radiant light emanating from 'Abdu'l-Bahá spread over the whole hall. It looked like showers of golden drops, which fell upon every person in the assemblage."

We who observed and pondered these things grew to take the unprecedented happenings as a part of the whole, not with surprise, but rather with thankfulness that such things could be.

* * *

A woman had grown to love 'Abdu'l-Bahá. She had, however, not yet seen Him. She wrote imploring Him to help her, and, if possible, to send her a sign for her comfort, as she was in very great distress of mind. One day shortly afterwards she went to the Bahá'í friend who had told her of the great Educator: "You have a message for me?" she said.

"Yes, I have; it is this: I seemed to hear 'Abdu'l-Bahá's voice at the early hour of dawn this morning. This is what I heard:

" 'Tell her that walking from henceforth in the Celestial Garden she will evermore be bathed in the sunlight of God. No future occurrences will have power to really hurt, for the Protection surrounding her will so shield her that no evil will have any possibility of penetrating through her armour. In this armour there will be no flaw.' "

This message she wrote down at the time on the fly-leaf of her Bible (in April 1912, at Bex in the Valley of the Rhône).

The following December, during the second visit of 'Abdu'l-Bahá to London, this lady came to see Him. He talked to her of happy, pleasant things, smiling His welcome. When she rose to leave, I said: "Master! She is so very unhappy!"

The Master then put His hand on her shoulder and spoke to her the very words of the Message, which had been written down in her Bible many months before. "It is my message," she said, trembling.

'Abdu'l-Bahá looked at us with a smile, full of loving pity, as though at children, who were surprised at some unusual token of their father's power and love.

* * *

One day, whilst I was driving with Mrs. Cropper and the Master, she said: "Master, are you not longing to be back at Haifa with your beloved family?" He smiled and said:

"I wish you to understand that you are both as truly my dear daughters, as beloved by me, as are those of whom you speak."

Our hearts thrilled with joy and awe as He spoke. "How can we serve to be even a little worthy of so high an honour?"

* * *

"Will this misery-laden world ever attain happiness?" a visitor asked one day. The Master replied:

"It is nearly two thousand years since His Holiness the Lord Christ taught this prayer to His people: 'Thy Kingdom come, Thy will be done *on earth*, as it is in Heaven.' Thinkest thou that He would have commanded thee to pray for that which would never come? That prayer is also a prophecy."

" 'Abdu'l-Bahá, *when* will the Kingdom come? How soon will His Will be done on earth as it is in Heaven?"

"It depends on how intensely you, each and every one of you, serve day and night. Ye are all torches that I have lighted with mine own hands. Go forth, light others till all the separate waiting servants are linked together in a great Unity.

"Those who are working alone are like ants, but when they are united they will become as eagles.

"Those who work singly are as drops, but, when united, they will become a vast river carrying the cleansing water of life into the barren desert places of the world. Before the power of its rushing flood, neither misery, nor sorrow, nor any grief will be able to stand. Be united! Be united! It is rather dangerous to be an isolated drop. It might be spilled or blown away."

* * *

In Scotland 'Abdu'l-Bahá gave several public talks, emphasizing different aspects of the Bahá'í Teaching. One very definite impression received from that visit was of His power to refresh Himself from some spiritual source when His strength had been overtaxed.

'Abdu'l-Bahá had spoken to a large group in the afternoon, and when He mounted the platform in the evening, before a packed hall, He looked very tired. He remained seated in silence for a few moments, after Mr. Graham Pole had reverently introduced Him. Then, seeming to gather strength, He arose, and with voice and manner of joyous animation, and eyes aglow, He paced the platform with a vigorous tread, and spoke with words of great power.

The following is a message to the Theosophists, who received Him with so much enthusiasm during His stay in Scotland:

"Give my most friendly greetings to all the Theosophists. You have risen to help humanity because you are freeing yourselves from superstition and you are casting ignorance far from your minds. You wish the welfare of mankind, and this object is a mighty one. Every man that in this day rises to save his brothers is nearing the threshold of God, for all the Manifestations and Prophets of God have striven to bring about unity among men, and they have worked for harmony.

"The foundation of the Divine teaching is this unity and harmony. Moses strove for unity among men; the Christ did all to promote this understanding, and Muḥammad proclaimed the necessity of this union. The Buddha also worked for the same great goal. The Gospel, the Qur'án, and all Holy Writings are the basis for this unity. The foundation of the religions of God is one; the faith of God is one: to bring between men love and understanding. Bahá'u'lláh has renewed the teachings of the Prophets and of the Manifestations, and has again proclaimed the Oneness of the foundation upon which the religion of God is established.

"He is bringing together different nations, and He has been able to unite antagonistic sects. The spirit of Bahá'u'lláh is bringing all the members, and all the organs of the body of humanity, to a complete understanding. As you are members of this body of humanity striving to bring about the accomplishment of this great aim, I pray God to assist you."

* * *

The last morning came. The secretaries and several friends were ready to start for the train.

'Abdu'l-Bahá sat calmly writing. We reminded Him that the hour to leave for the train was at hand. He looked up, saying:

"There are things of more importance than trains," and He continued to write.

Suddenly in breathless haste a man came in, carrying in his hand a beautiful garland of fragrant white flowers. Bowing low before the Master, he said:

"In the name of the disciples of Zoroaster, The Pure One, I hail Thee as the 'Promised Sháh Bahrám'!"

Then the man, for a sign, garlanded 'Abdu'l-Bahá, and proceeded to anoint each and all of the amazed friends who were present with precious oil, which had the odour of fresh roses.

This brief but impressive ceremony concluded, 'Abdu'l-Bahá, having carefully divested Himself of the garland, departed for the train.

We had witnessed a solemn act in the Mysterious Sacred Drama of the World.

'Abdu'l-Bahá's sojourn in London was ended.

We stood bereft of His presence.

Of the friends who gathered round Him at the train, one had been a constant visitor, a charming Eastern potentate,* dignified and picturesque in his jewelled turban. He was an example of earthly kingship, one of the many other great personages of the world, all of whom, absent and present, were so small, so insignificant, when compared with the Ambassador of the Most High, as He stood, clad in a simple garment, speaking courteous words of farewell, smiling that love-laden smile which comforted all hearts.

Discarding preconceived ideas, a new consciousness seemed to awaken when in His presence.

Some of the minds, though as yet so finite, reached out to a recognition of the Light of the great Manifestation, now being diffused by 'Abdu'l-Bahá on all Humanity. To us He was impregnated with that Light, "as a vesture wrapped about him, like a garment round him thrown."

Small wonder that we mortals were overwhelmed with awe, as we drew near to the heavenly Messenger of that Immortal Spirit of Truth and Light, which had come to save the children of men from chaotic destruction.

Would Humanity awaken? Or would they continue to sleep "unaware"?

* * *

A question, natural, and often asked, is this:
"Where are those people who crowded to 97 Cadogan

---
* The Maharajah of Jalawar.—ED.

Gardens, during the two visits of 'Abdu'l-Bahá, and how have they answered His call?"

"I have come with a torch in my hand, seeking out those who will arise and help me to bring about the Most Great Peace."

Who shall say how much or how little of the Message given by the Servant of God was understood by those persons, well-known and unknown, gentle and simple, who sought His presence in those days?

States of consciousness and powers of vision being so varied, one visitor would come to hear and to see "some new thing" out of curiosity, hoping to witness a magic happening, an astounding phenomenon.

Of another kind was a man who, being on his way to Japan, heard that 'Abdu'l-Bahá was in England. He broke his journey at Constantinople, and hastened to London for the joy of spending one evening in His presence.

Still another type of mentality was that of a popular preacher. Often voicing his hope and desire that a Great Messenger would again come to the world, he answered an invitation to visit the Master by sending regrets as he was "engaged to attend a garden party."

It is not ours to know how many were conscious of the vital breath of that atmosphere of "Love and Wisdom and Power," which was always around the Master, more penetrating and significant than even His words, although they were spoken with authority.

Of those who came into touch with that pervading influence, some were awed and transformed. Their very souls seemed wrapt by an unforgettable experience. The power of this atmosphere was overwhelming, but could neither be described nor defined.

Some of the Western visitors felt this hitherto unknown or unaccustomed atmosphere of the Spirit with moving gratitude and awe. To the Eastern guests this wonder was as the air they breathed. They accepted the Power with the reverence of the Oriental soul, trained to recognize the influence of holiness manifest in Him, Who had suffered long years in the Path of God, and Who had at length succeeded in bringing the Message into the open air of the world.

Minds and motives must needs be varied because their quality depends upon the stage of advancement of each in spiritual evolution. Such an awakened consciousness alone determines the capacity to recognize Spiritual Truth.

The appeal of the Word of God to the spirit of man being so intimately sacred, it is not our province to judge any other human being in this matter.

"The earth is full of the signs of God; may your eyes be illumined by perceiving them," said 'Abdu'l-Bahá.

For our comfort and encouragement we are able to perceive these signs as stars of hope and fulfilment on every hand, whilst they are developing on the crowded stage of the world since 'Abdu'l-Bahá's coming to the West with His warnings and His injunctions.

"The Great Woe" (the World War) proves the truth that when spiritual civilization is neglected and material civilization alone is cultivated, the whole edifice collapses into ruin, there being no firm foundation.

"And great is the fall thereof."

That terrific catastrophe shows that too few were the helpers who arose in answer to the Master's Call.

* * *

Talk Given at 97 Cadogan Gardens, London, England
16th January, 1913

"The Cause has become very great. Many souls are entering it—souls with different mentalities and range of understanding. Complex difficulties constantly rise before us. The administration of the Cause has become most difficult. Conflicting thoughts and theories attack the Cause from every side. Now consider to what extent the believers of God must become firm and soul-sacrificing. Every one of the friends must become the essence of essences; each one must become a brilliant lamp. People all around the world are entering the Cause, people of various tribes and nations and religions and sects. It is most difficult to administer to such heterogeneous elements. Wisdom and Divine insight are necessary. Firmness and steadfastness are needed at such a crucial period of the Cause.

"All the meetings must be for teaching the Cause and spreading the Message, and suffering the souls to enter into the Kingdom of Bahá'u'lláh. Look at me. All my thoughts are centred around the proclamation of the Kingdom. I have a lamp in my hand searching throughout the lands and seas to find souls who can become heralds of the Cause. Day and night I am engaged in this work. Any other deliberations in the meetings are futile and fruitless. Convey the Message! Attract the hearts! Sow the seeds! Teach the Cause to those who do not know. It is now six months that Siyyid Asadu'lláh implored that I write a few lines to my sister, my daughters. I have not done this because I find I must teach. I enter all meetings, all churches, so that the Cause may be spread. When the 'Most Important' work is before our sight, we must let go the 'Important' one. If the meeting or spiritual assembly has any other occupations the time is spent in futility. All the deliberations, all consultations, all the talks and addresses must revolve around one focal centre, and that is: Teach the Cause. Teach. Teach. Convey the Message. Awaken the souls. Now is the time of laying the foundation. Now must we gather brick, stone, wood, iron, and other building materials. Now is not the time of decoration. We must strive day and night and think and work; what can I say that may become effective? What can I do that may bring results? What can I write that may bring forth fruits? Nothing else will be useful to-day. The interests of such a Glorious Cause will not advance without such undivided attention. While we are carrying this load we cannot carry any other load!"

* * *

TABLET FROM 'ABDU'L-BAHÁ TO THE FRIENDS SENT TO US BY "LUTFULLÁH"* IN MARCH 1912

Cry aloud and say:
O friends, a hundred times Glad Tidings that the Light of Reality has shone and enlightened the world.

* Dr. Lutfulláh Hakím.

The Proclamation of the Kingdom has reached you.
The ears heard and shook with this great sound!
The Doors of the Kingdom were opened.
The Heavenly Troops have arrived Army by Army, and they help the Bahá'ís (friends of God).
Anyone who is free from ambition and (earthly) desire will be victorious on this plane, and anyone who is pure and holy from the suggestions of evil, and is a refined (purified) soul, he will shine in reality like the Star of the Most High!
Then, O friends, strive with all your might to make yourselves free from ambitions until you become brimful of joyfulness like a cup of wine from the bounties of Bahá'u'lláh—the Blessed Beauty—that you may be the cause of the illumination of the world!

'Abdu'l-Bahá 'Abbás.

CHAPTER III

'Abdu'l-Bahá in Paris

Much has been written of the journeys of 'Abdu'l-Bahá, 'Abbás Effendi. Having been released from the prison fortress of 'Akká, after forty years of captivity, He set Himself to obey the sacred charge laid upon Him by His Father, Bahá'u'lláh. Accordingly, He undertook a three years' mission into the Western world. He left the Holy Land and came to Europe in 1911. During that and the two following years He visited Switzerland, England, Scotland, France, America, Germany and Hungary.

When the days of 'Abdu'l-Bahá's first visit to London (in the autumn of 1911) were drawing to a close, his friends, Monsieur and Madame Dreyfus-Barney, found an apartment for His residence whilst in the French capital. It was charmingly furnished, sunny, spacious, situated in the Avenue de Camœns (No. 4), whence a flight of steps led into the Trocadero Gardens; here the Master often took solitary, restful walks. Sheltered in this modern, comfortable, Paris flat, He Whom we revered, with a secretary, servitors, and a few close friends, sojourned for an unforgettable nine weeks.

Who is this, with a branch of roses in His hand, coming down the steps? A picturesque group of friends (some Persians, wearing the *kuláh*, and a few Europeans), who are following Him, see little children coming up to Him. They hold on to His *'abá* (cloak), confiding and fearless. He gives the roses to them, caressingly lifting one after another in His arms, smiling the while that glorious smile which wins all hearts.

Again, we saw a cabman stop his fiacre, take off his cap and hold it in his hand, gazing amazed, with an air of reverence, whilst the majestic figure, courteously acknowledging his salutation, passed by with that walk which a friend had described as "that of a king or of a shepherd."

Another scene. A very poor quarter in Paris—Sunday morning—groups of men and women inclined to be rowdy. Foremost amongst them a big man brandishing a long loaf of bread in his hand, shouting, gesticulating, dancing.

Into this throng walked 'Abdu'l-Bahá, on His way from a mission hall, where He had been addressing a very poor congregation at the invitation of their pastor. The boisterous man with the loaf, suddenly seeing Him, stood still. He then proceeded to lay about him lustily with his staff of life, crying "Make way, make way! He is my Father, make way!" The Master passed through the midst of the crowd, now become silent and respectfully saluting Him. "Thank you, my dear friends, thank you," He said, smiling round upon them. The poor were always His especially beloved friends. He was never happier than when surrounded by them, the lowly of heart.

Who is He?

Why do the people gather round Him?

Why is He here in Paris?

I hope to indicate, albeit inadequately, something of that Messenger, the "Trusted One" Who came out of an Eastern prison to bring His Father's message to the bewildered nations of earth. During the Paris visit, as it had been in London, daily happenings took on the atmosphere of spiritual events. Some of these episodes I will endeavour to describe as well as I can remember them.

Every morning, according to His custom, the Master expounded the principles of the Teaching of Bahá'u'lláh to those who gathered round Him, the learned and the unlearned, eager and respectful. They were of all nationalities and creeds, from the East and from the West, including Theosophists, agnostics, materialists, spiritualists, Christian Scientists, social reformers, Hindus, Súfís, Muslims, Buddhists, Zoroastrians, and many others. Often came workers in various humanitarian societies, who were striving to reduce the miseries of the poor. These received special sympathy and blessing.

'Abdu'l-Bahá spoke in Persian, which was translated into French by Monsieur and Madame Dreyfus-Barney. My two daughters, Mary and Ellinor, our friend Miss Beatrice Platt, and I, took notes of these "Talks" from day to day. At the request of the Master, these notes were arranged and published in English.* It will be seen that in these pages are gathered together the precepts of those Holy Souls Who, being Individual Rays of the One, were, in divers times and countries, manifested here on earth to lead the spiritual evolution of human kind.

The words of 'Abdu'l-Bahá can be put on to paper, but how describe the smile, the earnest pleading, the loving-kindness, the radiant vitality, and at times the awe-inspiring authority of His spoken words? The vibrations of His voice seemed to enfold the listeners in an atmosphere of the Spirit, and to penetrate to the very core of being. We were experiencing the transforming radiance of the Sun of Truth; henceforth, material aims and unworthy ambitions shrank away into their trivial, obscure retreats.

'Abdu'l-Bahá would often answer our questions before we asked them. Sometimes He would encourage us to put them into words.

"And now your question?" he said.

I answered: "I am wondering about the next world, whether I shall ask to be permitted to come back here to earth to help?"

"Why should you wish to return here? In My Father's House are many mansions—many, many worlds! Why should you desire to come back to this particular planet?"

The visit of one man made a profound impression upon us: "O 'Abdu'l-Bahá, I have come from the French Congo, where I have been engaged in mitigating the hardships of some of the natives. For sixteen years I have worked in that country."

"*It was a great comfort to me in the darkness of my prison to know the work which you were doing.*"

Explanations were not necessary when coming to 'Abdu'l-Bahá! One day a widow in deepest mourning came. Weeping bitterly, she was unable to utter a word.

---

* When the "'Talks'" were ready, the book was sent to 'Abdu'l-Bahá for His comments. He read them through and was well pleased with the English translation. He wished them to be published without delay. Accordingly, the book came out in May 1912 and is now obtainable from Bahá'í Publishing Trust, London. In 1939 *Talks of 'Abdu'l-Bahá in Paris* was translated into French by Madame Hesse. With the assistance of Mrs. Lynch and of Madame Dreyfus-Barney the book was published in Geneva. It is found to be of great use in teaching the various seekers in Paris and other towns in France.

Knowing her heart's grief, "Do not weep," said 'Abdu'l-Bahá, wiping away the tears from the poor face. "Do not weep. Be happy! It will be well with the boy. Bring him to see me in a few days."

On her way out, this mother said: "Oh, my child! He is to go through a dangerous operation to-day. What can I do?"

"The Master has told you what to do. Remember His words: 'Do not weep, it will be well with the boy. Be happy, and in a few days bring him to see me.'"

In a few days the mother brought her boy to the Master, perfectly well!

One evening at the home of Monsieur and Madame Dreyfus-Barney, an artist was presented to 'Abdu'l-Bahá.

"Thou art very welcome. I am happy to see thee. All true art is a gift of the Holy Spirit."

"What is the Holy Spirit?"

"It is the Sun of Truth, O Artist."

"Where, where, is the Sun of Truth?"

"The Sun of Truth is everywhere. It is shining on the whole world."

"What of the dark night, when the Sun is not shining?"

"The darkness of night is past, the Sun has risen."

"But, Master, how shall it be with the blinded eyes that cannot see the Sun's splendour? And what of the deaf ears that cannot hear those who praise its beauty?"

"I will pray that the blind eyes may be opened, that the deaf ears may be unstopped, and that the hearts may have grace to understand."

As 'Abdu'l-Bahá spoke, the troubled mien of the artist gave place to a look of relief, satisfied understanding, joyous emotion.

Thus interview followed interview. Church dignitaries of various branches of the Christian Tree came, some earnestly desirous of finding new aspects of the Truth—"the wisdom that buildeth up, rather than the knowledge that puffeth up." Others there were who stopped their ears, lest they should hear and understand.

One afternoon, a party of the latter type arrived. They spoke words of bigotry, of intolerance, of sheer cruelty in their bitter condemnation of all who did not accept their own particular dogma, showing themselves obsessed by "the hate of man, disguised as love of God," a thin disguise to the penetrating eyes of the Master. Perhaps they were dreading the revealing light of Truth which He sought to shed upon the darkness of their outworn ecclesiasticism. The new revelation was too great for their narrowed souls and fettered minds.

The heart of 'Abdu'l-Bahá was saddened by this interview, which had tired Him exceedingly. When He referred to this visit there was a look in His eyes as if loving pity were blended with profound disapproval, as though He would cleanse the defiled temple of Humanity from the suffocating diseases of the soul. Then He uttered these words in a voice of awe-inspiring authority:

"Jesus Christ is the Lord of Compassion, and these men call themselves by His Name! *Jesus is ashamed of them!*"

He shivered as with cold, drawing His '*abá* closely about Him, with a gesture as if sternly repudiating their misguided outlook.

The Japanese Ambassador to a European capital (Viscount Arawaka—Madrid) was staying at the Hotel d'Jéna. This gentleman and his wife had been told of 'Abdu'l-Bahá's presence in Paris, and the latter was anxious to have the privilege of meeting Him.

"I am very sad," said Her Excellency. "I must not go out this evening as my cold is severe, and I leave early in the morning for Spain. If only there were a possibility of seeing Him."

This was told to the Master, Who had just returned after a long, tiring day.

"Tell the lady and her husband that, as she is unable to come to me, I will call upon her."

Accordingly, though the hour was late, through the cold and the rain He came, with His smiling courtesy, bringing joy to us all, as we awaited Him in the Tapestry Room of the Hotel d'Jéna.

'Abdu'l-Bahá talked with the Ambassador and his wife of conditions in Japan, of the great international importance of that country, of the vast service to mankind, of the work for the abolition of war, of the need for improving conditions of life for the worker, of the necessity of educating girls and boys equally.

"The religious ideal is the soul of all plans for the good of mankind. Religion must never be used as a tool by party politicians. God's politics are mighty, man's politics are feeble."

Speaking of religion and science, the two great wings with which the bird of human kind is able to soar, He said: "Scientific discoveries have increased material civilization. There is in existence a stupendous force, as yet, happily, undiscovered by man. Let us supplicate God, the Beloved, that this force be not discovered by science until spiritual civilization shall dominate the human mind. In the hands of men of lower material nature, this power would be able to destroy the whole earth."

'Abdu'l-Bahá talked of these and of many other supremely important matters for more than an hour. The friends, wondering, said: "How is it possible that, having spent all His life imprisoned in an Eastern fortress, He should so well understand world problems and possess the wisdom to solve them so simply?"

Truly we were beginning to understand that the majesty of greatness, whether mental, or spiritual, is always simple.

One day, I received a disquieting letter: "It would be well to warn 'Abdu'l-Bahá that it might be dangerous for Him to visit a certain country, for which I understand He proposes to set forth in the near future."

Having regard to the sincere friendship of the writer, and knowing that sources of reliable information were available to him, this warning obviously could not be ignored. Therefore, as requested, I laid the matter before the Master.

To my amazement, He smiled and said impressively: "My daughter, have you not yet realized that never, in my life, have I been for one day out of danger, and that I should rejoice to leave this world and go to my Father?"

"Oh, Master! We do not wish that you should go from us in that manner." I was overcome with sorrow and terror.

"Be not troubled," said 'Abdu'l-Bahá. "These enemies have no power over my life, but that which is given them from on High. If my Beloved God so willed that my life-blood should be sacrificed in His path, it would be a glorious day, devoutly wished for by me."

Therefore the friends surrounding the much-loved Master were comforted, and their faith so strengthened, that when a sinister-looking man came up to a group who were walking in the gardens and threateningly said: "Are you not yet sufficiently warned? Not only is there danger for 'Abdu'l-Bahá, but also for you who are with Him," the friends were unperturbed, one of them replying calmly: "The Power that protects the Master protects also His other servants. Therefore we have no fear."

The man departed, abashed, saying nothing more.

Two days before the close of 'Abdu'l-Bahá's visit, a woman came hurriedly into the gathering at the Avenue de Camoens: "Oh, how glad I am to be in time! I must tell you the amazing reason of my hurried journey from America. One day, my little girl astonished me by saying: 'Mummy, if dear Lord Jesus was in the world now, what would you do?' 'Darling baby, I would feel like getting on to the first train and going to Him as fast as I could.' 'Well, Mummy, He *is* in the world.' I felt a sudden great awe come over me as my tiny one spoke. 'What do you mean, my precious? How do you know?' I said. 'He told me Himself, so in course He *is* in the world.' Full of wonder, I thought: Is this a sacred message which is being given to me out of the mouth of my babe? And I prayed that it might be made clear to me.

"The next day she said, insistently and as though she could not understand: 'Mummy, darlin', why isn't you gone to see Lord Jesus? He's told me two times that He is really here, in the world.' 'Tiny love, Mummy doesn't know where He is, how could she find Him?' 'We see, Mummy, we see.'

"I was naturally perturbed. The same afternoon, being out for a walk with my child, she suddenly stood still and cried out, 'There He is! There He is!' She was trembling with excitement and pointing at the windows of a magazine store where there was a picture of 'Abdu'l-Bahá. I bought the paper, found this address, caught a boat that same night, and here I am."

The above was written down as it was related to me. This is the second instance which came to my knowledge of the pictured face of 'Abdu'l-Bahá arresting the beholder with a compelling force. The first incident was that of a man in deadly despair, about to take his own life; and now this innocent child.

It was of great interest to notice the effect the presence of 'Abdu'l-Bahá had upon some children. One little girl whispered, "Look, that is Jesus when He was old." Perhaps their unstained nature sensed the breath of holiness which was always with Him, and caused these little ones to liken Him to the most Holy One of Whom they were conscious.

One day, a certain man, a Persian of high degree, came to 'Abdu'l-Bahá: "I have been exiled from my country. I pray you intercede for me that I may be permitted to return."

"You will be allowed to return."

"Some of my land has been bought by one of the Bahá'í friends. I desire to possess that property once more."

"It shall be given back to you and without payment."

"Who is the young man standing behind you? May he be presented to me?"

"He is Mírzá Jalál, son of one of the martyred brothers of Isfahán."

"I had no part in that crime."

"The part you took in that event, I know. Moreover, your motive I know."

This man, with his fellow-conspirator, the "Wolf" (so named because of his ruthless cruelty and greed), had borrowed large sums of money from the two noble and generous brothers of Isfahán. To accuse them of being followers of Bahá'u'lláh, to bring them before a tribunal which condemned them to be executed, and to have the brothers put to death, was their plot *to avoid being required to repay the loans.*

After the death of the "Wolf" some documents were discovered, relating to the borrowed money. This, with the addition of the interest which had accumulated, now amounted to a considerable sum. The lawyer who was in charge of the affair wrote to the son of the martyr, asking into what bank the moneys should be paid. The reply sent, with the approval of 'Abdu'l-Bahá, was that he declined to accept repayment of money which had been one reason for the shedding of his father's blood.

Mírzá Jalál was now married to a daughter of 'Abdu'l-Bahá.

Whilst these episodes were taking place, we who witnessed them seemed to be in a higher dimension, where they were natural indications of the presence of the Light which in all men is latent and in 'Abdu'l-Bahá transcendent.

The constant awareness of an exhilaration, which carried us out of our everyday selves, and gave us the sense of being "one with the Life Pulse, which beats through the Universe" is an experience to be treasured rather than an emotion to be described.

The reader will understand that it is impossible to find fitting words for the thoughts and feelings which were with us in those Paris days.

CHAPTER IV

'Abdu'l-Bahá in War-time
Abú-Sinán
The Story of Mírzá Jalál
Hájí Ramaḍán
Bahá'í Villages
The Master

PRAYER OF 'ABDU'L-BAHÁ

"Oh Lord, this is a mountain to which Thou hast given the name Carmel in the Torah, and Thou hast attributed it to Thyself in the Tablets and the Scriptures.

"O Lord, verily I invoke Thee, in this supreme threshold, under the wing of the gloomy nights; pray to Thee with throbbing heart and flowing tears, imploring, supplicating Thee, and cry: 'O my Lord, verily the fire of battle is raging in the valleys, hills, and streams, and the conflagration of war is burning even under the seas and high in the air, destroying and devastating.'

"We hear only the sighs of the maidens and the cry of the orphans, the moaning of the mothers, and the tears of the fathers . . . and this is only because of our heedlessness of Thy commemoration, and our neglect of Thy Love. Verily we have been occupied with ourselves. The intoxication of passion seized us. We have taken the road of neglect and blindness; have abandoned the path of guidance, and have chosen the path of obstinacy. . . .

"Oh my Lord, do not deal with us according to our offences—remove the veil, scatter this dense cloud on the horizon; extinguish these fires; subdue this flood, staunch the bloodshed, that these hurricanes may cease, the thunderbolts be extinguished, the torrents quelled, the land become visible, so may the souls find composure, and we will thank Thee for Thy abundant favour, O thou dear Lord, O Thou Forgiver."

ABÚ-SINÁN

The joy when 'Abdu'l-Bahá arrived safely back in Haifa (in December 1913) cannot be described. How the friends flocked about Him! He had now greater work than ever; letters to be answered increased and multiplied. From all those places which He had visited, letters came asking for explanation and begging for advice. From many other parts of the earth came appeals imploring Him to visit them also.

To these correspondents the Master replied with His unfailing patience. So it came about that His family saw little of Him in those months after His return from the world Mission.

Eight months after this came the war.

Soon after its outbreak, Haifa, which was still under Turkish rule, was panic-stricken. Most of the inhabitants fled inland, fearing bombardment by the Allies.

Those Bahá'í friends who were merchants suffered great losses, for all their stores of tea, sugar, etc., were commandeered by the Government, without payment.

The friends, in spite of the reassurances of the Master that no guns would be turned on Haifa, were living in constant fear, and the children, having heard terrible stories which were being told everywhere, grew quite ill, always looking round and about with frightened eyes.

At this time, the Master decided that it would be well to accept an invitation of the Shaykh of Abú-Sinán to remove the Bahá'ís and their children to that peaceful, healthy village, out of reach of the dreaded bombarding. In this village also, the very limited resources of the friends would, with strictest economy, be sufficient for their daily needs, with the help of the corn from 'Abdu'l-Bahá's storing.

Shaykh Sálih placed his house at the disposal of 'Abdu'l-Bahá and His family, Who received the most cordial welcome from this gracious and courteous chief of the Druze village of Abú-Sinán.

The other Persian friends were gladly taken into various houses of the village, where they found themselves in most happy surroundings.

Their food was of the simplest: lentils, dried beans, delicious olives and their oil, and sometimes milk, eggs, and even some goat's meat. The fresh pure air was, of course, wonderfully good for their health, and they quickly recovered calm nerves and strength of body.

The strictest economy was the rule, from necessity, there being so many mouths to feed, some of whom, being in terrible distress, had to be cared for and saved from sheer starvation.

'Abdu'l-Bahá had taught the friends to grow nourishing vegetables, which, with the corn from His village of 'Adasíyyih— where there were marvellous crops—kept many from perishing of hunger.

The Master's life was very full at this time. Not only did He care for the friends of Abú-Sinán, but in 'Akká and Haifa all the poor looked to Him for their daily bread. Even before the war the spectre of starvation had not been very far from many of these pitiful people, but now when all the breadwinners (Germans and Turks) had been taken for the army, the plight of the women and children was desperate, for alas! there were no government "separation allowances."

Nothing and no one but the Master stood between them and certain death from hunger.

He also instituted a dispensary at Abú-Sinán, and engaged a doctor, Ḥabíb'u'lláh Khudábakhsh. This doctor was qualified to perform operations and to give instruction in hygiene.

'Abdu'l-Bahá did not neglect the education of the children. He arranged schools where they were taught by some of the most gifted of the Bahá'í friends.

These were truly unquiet days. From time to time the Bahá'ís were in danger of being compelled to join the army. Even the young boys of the Master's family, who were at school in Beirut, had their names taken down. Many were the telegrams sent to Constantinople, claiming exemption for the Persians as being of a neutral nation.

In spite of all the difficulties which surrounded them, the sojourn at Abú-Sinán village was a time of great happiness. Was not the Beloved One more with them than ever before? It was many years since His family had seen so much of their Father.

From the balcony of the house in Abú-Sinán the Master's family watched for His return on the days when He went to Haifa and 'Akká. The Shaykh and his handsome sons would walk down the steep, rocky road to welcome 'Abdu'l-Bahá as soon as His carriage came into sight, and they led their finest horse for their guest to ride, when the carriage could climb no further.

He was always a fearless horseman, and to ride was a joy for Him. Riding swiftly on a beautiful Arab horse must have given Him a sense of restoration of vigour, after the fatigue of these strenuous days.

All the friends would run out to the steep, hilly road to greet Him, clustering round Him, the children dancing with gladness that He was come, vieing with each other to get nearest to Him. These were the first days of real freedom many of them had really ever known.

The Master would bring any news from the outside world that was available, and would first visit the ladies' wing of the house, asking about the health of each one separately. There were some American guests in those early days, but 'Abdu'l-Bahá thought it unwise for them to remain. They left by the last boat which went from Haifa to Alexandria in January 1915. All were much relieved when these dear American friends had succeeded in reaching safety.

The Shaykh and his sons would gather in the *díván*. This was the reception room, vast and comfortable, of the masculine portion of the family. Here, with their friends and guests, they waited to hear any news the Master might bring.

They loved Him, trusted Him, and honoured Him, with all their hearts, feeling and believing that His wisdom grasped the future as well as the present.

Prayers were chanted at these gatherings, the Druze friends joining with the Bahá'ís.

For five months there was no word from any part of the outside world.

Sometimes the Governor of 'Akká, or the Commandant, the Chief Magistrate, the Mufti, or the Páshá, would come to visit 'Abdu'l-Bahá, staying one or two nights, as guests at the village. All consulted Him on many questions regarding the feeding or otherwise caring for the people during this time of difficulty, and many other problems were discussed. Great was His wisdom. Here, too, He answered many questions and explained many incidents which had not hitherto been made clear. Questioned by one of the visiting officers from 'Akká, 'Abdu'l-Bahá told the following:

"Sultán 'Abdu'l-Ḥamíd wished to strike terror into my heart; he sent to tell me that I should be imprisoned for ever, or executed, or sent to a far-off penal colony. I answered his threats by a message which read: 'Please assure 'Abdu'l-Ḥamíd that he cannot imprison me whilst my spirit is unfettered. Even in the grave I should not be imprisoned, for my spirit, free from the limitation of the material body, would be still more free. The threat to send me to the island of Fízán, far from family and friends, where my only companions would be murderers and other malefactors, also has no terror for me; from amongst those poor, ignorant children of God the Pardoner, I should lead many back to my Father's House to receive forgiveness and Peace.' "

The narrative here is continued by Túbá Khánum:

On the 19th of January, 1915, Faḍlu'lláh Khán, a friend of Báqir Khán of Shíráz, Persia, came with great difficulty to obtain some news of the Master and the Bahá'í friends. This was the last neutral friend we saw for a long time.

Faḍlu'lláh took the last Tablet from the Master to Cairo and to all the friends—then no more communications.

At the dinner hour we often listened to words of wisdom from the lips of 'Abdu'l-Bahá that were like sacred gems being slowly strung on the consciousness of the Druze villagers and of the guests in their care.

One day He spoke of healing:

"There is spiritual healing and there is also material healing. Unless these two work together a cure is impossible. The material element is medicine; spiritual healing is of God.

Man must work in unison with the laws ordained by Providence. All good things that take place are based on Divine Wisdom."

'ABDU'L-BAHÁ IN WAR-TIME

The Naw-Rúz* is a sacred day, and 'Abdu'l-Bahá prepared the feast at Bahjí, the shrine of Bahá'u'lláh. He Himself cooked it. All the friends were bidden. They walked those few miles from Abú-Sinán in two parties, the women in one party, the men in the other.

'Abdu'l-Bahá explained the day to His guests:

"There are two equinoxes, the vernal (Aries) and the autumnal (Libra). Before this vernal season, the earth, mountains, and gardens are as dead; this season brings life.

"In Persia the great vernal feast has been respected from far-off ages. King Jamshíd first built a gigantic fire-place and instituted a banquet on this day, and from this time the day of Naw-Rúz gradually came to be kept as a national feast. All victories were celebrated on this anniversary, and foundation stones of important buildings were laid on this day of the Naw-Rúz."

At the end of the feast the Master chanted prayers at the shrine of Bahá'u'lláh, and at sunset we dispersed and walked back to Abú-Sinán.

A few days later on the Mutișarrif (Governor) of 'Akká and a group of friends came to visit the Master. They talked of the war. As they all sat at dinner that evening, 'Abdu'l-Bahá spoke as follows:

"All this trouble is because humanity has wandered far from the true teaching of God.

"Nations are divided through superstition and tradition. Religions are divided through tradition and superstition. All superstition is the result of people's imagination. For instance, the Shí'ites await a promised one who is invisible; they believe that he is the Imám Mihdí, who with servants and soldiers are abiding in Jábulqá and Jábulsá, two imaginary cities of the East and the West. Each of these cities has twelve gates. The Imám Mihdí spends six months of the year in either city. When he appears he will fill the earth with justice and mercy, destroying enmity and oppression.

---
* Bahá'í New Year—21st March.

"The Sunnís believe that the Mihdí will come from an unknown place and suddenly appear at Mecca with a sword in his right hand; he will disperse the people (infidels) into different parts of the earth.

"Parsees believe that Kay-Khusraw will appear from a mountain.

"Christians believe that the Promised One will descend from the sky.

"The Jews say that the Messiah must be a descendant of David. They speak of a city named Sabbath, round which flows a river of sand; this sand stops flowing on Saturdays. The gates of this city are all closed. Moses said: 'After me, a man like unto me will appear.' He came. But the Jews are still waiting. They have waited three thousand years.

"Materialists maintain that a Superman will arise, who must be perfect in wisdom, and in all respects above and beyond the best of men. All peoples are awaiting a Promised One.

"When the wise man regards this world, he realizes that this earth has not existed for only six thousand years. Science has proved that stars have a fixed orbit, therefore there are many 'heavens,' in which are 'many mansions.'

"The Truth of Divinity is everlasting. God's bountiful qualities and names are eternal in the Divine Sovereignty.

"Would it be possible for a king to exist without subjects? Or creatures without a Creator? If the Divine Creator be eternal, then His creatures, made after His own image, into whom He breathed the breath of Life, are likewise eternal.

"Change and transformation are qualities essential to material things. As physical man comes under the category of material things, these qualities affect him. Therefore it follows that change and transformation must take place in the administration of laws which affect mankind. Whenever there is a change there must be a rebirth into new conditions.

"The physical sun sets, and the earth is in darkness. Should the sun not arise again, death would overtake all things in the world. Heat and light are the essential qualities of the sun; without heat and light the sun would be a vast colossal orb of darkness.

"Man should weigh all questions with the power of the intellect.

"History, which is a great science, should be written by academies, not by individuals, liable to be influenced by emotions."

Speaking of the name "Druzes," the hospitable dwellers in Abú-Sinán, the Master said: "A few hundred years ago, Darzí, a tailor, came from Persia to Syria, where he established the Druze cult. 'Druze' is a corruption of the word 'Darzí.' "

One of the stories that 'Abdu'l-Bahá told us at that time was the following:

"There was a woman who was one of the disciples of His Holiness the Báb; she had seven sons; six of them had been martyred. She dreamed a dream, and behold, she saw her seventh son, the only one left. He was being brought to her with a dagger in his heart.

"When she awoke from her dream she prayed: 'O God, the Compassionate! I gave six sons unto Thee. I cannot lose my only son, the last one left to me. Oh spare him! Do not take him also!'

"As she prayed, a young woman, who was a friend, came to her: 'Why lamentest thou?' she asked.

" 'I have lost six sons, who were martyred for their Faith. I am begging God not to take my last one,' she answered.

" 'If I were worthy, and had beautiful sons, I would give them all to my God,' the young friend said.

"In course of time a boy, Ashraf, was born to her also. He grew up to be a joy and comfort to his mother. He was loved and admired by all for his beauty, both of body and of soul.

"When he was about twenty-two years old, he was arrested, having become a disciple of the Báb.

"He was condemned to be crucified.

"As he, Ashraf, was being nailed to the cross the people begged him to deny his Master. He steadfastly refused, saying: 'Nay, rather do I wish to be sacrificed for my God.'

"Then his mother was brought to him.

"She had been told that he had denied his faith—this was to her an unspeakable tragedy. But when she saw her beautiful, beloved only child being nailed to the cross, she cried:

" 'My Ashraf! I owe thee to our God. I promised you to Him before you were born. I brought you up and educated you and taught you [holy things] for this day. If you had consented to deny your God, my very motherhood would have cursed you. But now my mother-blessing will follow you into the Presence of our God.'

"So spake Umm-Ashraf.

"The people cried 'Crucify him.' Then turning towards her the mob cried 'And now let us kill this foolish mother.'

"They fell upon her. Still she cried aloud, rejoicing that she had given her dearest treasure for the Cause of God—and they beat her till she, too, died.

" 'There are many mirrors reflecting the Light, but though all the mirrors should be shattered, the Light would remain.' "

* * *

This seems the place to relate the story of 'Abdu'l-Vahháb, as told at Abú-Sinán, by 'Abdu'l-Bahá.

One day, whilst at Káẓimayn, through which He passed on his first journey to Karbila and Baghdád, Jamál-i-Mubárak was appealed to by a young man, 'Abdu'l-Vahháb, who was much attracted to Him, saying:

"One request, my Lord. My father and my mother have come to spend their latter days, and to die, in this holy place. They are very fanatical! I pray that they may be given grace to drink of the Chalice of Life."

Bahá'u'lláh answered: "Persuade your father to come to me."

To his father the youth went, saying:

"O my father, there is here an honourable person from Tihrán, who, although wearing a *kuláh*, not a turban, is a surging sea of divine knowledge; he has a shining countenance, and a radiance of joy and happiness is with him, surely we should go to see him."

His father, as soon as he came into the presence of Jamál-i-Mubárak, exclaimed:

"Oh! Lord, we have heard One calling us to faith, therefore we believe. Forgive us our sins." (From the Qur'án.)

Immediately he, having understood and believed, began to teach publicly, and became a famous Bábí.

'Abdu'l-Vahháb (the son) implored to be allowed to accompany Bahá'u'lláh; he was, however, directed to remain with his parents, whose love for him was very great. 'Abdu'l-Vahháb continued to ask his father's permission to join Bahá'u'lláh. To this at length the father agreed, and the young man made his way to Tihrán, where he was unable to find his beloved Lord.

He, meanwhile, proceeded to teach the people openly in the street, ignoring all personal risk.

Now took place the deplorable incident of the insane youth shooting at the Sháh.

Mírzá 'Abdu'l-Vahháb was instantly seized and thrown into the horrible prison, where very soon Bahá'u'lláh Himself arrived, having been arrested at His village, Níyávarán, whence He had been made to walk barefoot, with heavy chains on His neck, and fetters on His limbs; in this condition, without His *kuláh*, did the friends see their Beloved.

Mírzá 'Abdu'l-Vahháb spent a few days in that dungeon in great joy and happiness, for was he not in the presence of Him, Whom he recognized as his Lord?

Each day would the executioner come and call out certain names.

'Abdu'l-Vahháb's turn came. He arose and danced in the prison, knowing that his hour of martyrdom had come. He kissed the beloved hand, and gave himself over into the hands of the executioner and his assistant torturers.

When the news reached his father, he bowed his head and thanked God that his sacrifice had been accepted at the Divine Threshold.

He is amongst those martyrs who were so great an amazement to the people of Tihrán.

It is related that the torturers said "Let us nail red horseshoes on to his feet, we then shall see where his joyful dance will be."

This was done! But never did he flinch, and passed to his Crown of Martyrdom, praising God with his last breath.

Little wonder that the people of Tihrán were filled with astonishment and awe.

FIRST VISIT OF RÚHÁ KHÁNUM TO ABÚ-SINÁN, AFTER THE
PASSING OF 'ABDU'L-BAHÁ. EARLY SPRING OF 1922.

Abú-Sinán is about an hour's drive from Haifa over fields,
with rough tracks—that is after we passed by 'Akká. Our car
seemed to be taking flying leaps over rocks, then we climbed
winding, almost perpendicular roads. Nothing but a Ford car,
with a perfect driver, knowing every inch of the way, which
was our Khusraw, could safely have accomplished the tests of
that motor drive.

The Shaykh of the place, with some of his sons and nephews,
came out to welcome us.

We were conducted to the Shaykh's house, which, with its
adjoining guest house, is a veritable palace. In the court-yard
we were received with great cordiality by the ladies of the
families—the wife of the Shaykh, her daughters, daughter-in-
law, and their children.

We mounted many, many steps on the outside of the house,
and arrived at a very large, beautifully-proportioned room.
Under the large windows, round two sides of this reception
chamber, were fixed divans.

As we arrived, the younger ladies brought soft, square cushions
covered in wonderful brocade of apple-green and gold; these
they placed on the divans for the comfort of their honoured guests.

They were full of joy to see Rúhá Khánum, who had not
paid them a visit since the passing of her adored Father. Her
sorrow overflowed her heart afresh, as these dear Druze ladies
wept with her, and she looked round the room, where the
Master had so often taught and comforted His people during
the dread and fear-laden days of the war.

This was their refuge till some of that ghastly time was overpast, and the Master knew that it would be safe to return to their
homes at Haifa, bringing their children, now restored to health.

The view from these windows is glorious, and the whole
atmosphere of the place full of calm and rest. No marvel that

the dear ones were happy in that haven, in the presence of their Beloved One, and cared for by these devoted, lovely creatures.

Across one end of this room were book-cases filled with beautifully bound books.

How I longed to know what they contained! Sacred writings naturally; but their religion is secret, none but the initiated are ever permitted to either enter their houses of worship, or to read their holy books. They are not Christians, although they reverence the Lord Christ; they are not Jews, but they reverence Moses and some of the other Israelitish prophets: Nabí-Shu'ayb, the father-in-law of Moses, is one of the Saints whom they esteem.

But Khiḍr, a prophet of pre-Mosaic times, is greatly honoured by the Druzes. He, according to their sacred legend, having drunk of the Water of Immortality, is now alive, and will live for evermore. He dwells in the Invisible Kingdom, but assumes bodily form and appears to those who love him in their dreams.

The places where Khiḍr is seen in dreamland are held sacred. These holy places are numerous. Muslims also hold these shrines in veneration, make pilgrimages to them, praying for such benefits as healing, and vowing to return and give thanks, when their prayers are granted.

The Cave of Elijah on Mount Carmel is one of the shrines, where Khiḍr is also honoured both by Druzes and Muslims. Important pilgrimages are made to this cave at certain seasons of the year, where a lamb is sacrificed in memory of Abraham and of Isaac, whom they look upon as friends of Khiḍr, also associated with Moses and Elijah.

What their beliefs are, and their mode of worship, no outside person is ever permitted to know.

But their religion is deep and real, as shown in their lives.

The Druzes are kind, courteous, and nobly hospitable. Strict, very strict, in their morality—the husband of one wife; no lapse from virtue is permitted—the penalty would be terrible, even death.

No Druze family would suffer dishonour. They never marry outside their own religion; the penalty for this (which, however, very rarely occurs) would be fearful.

There is a tragic story told of a Druze maiden who fell in love with a Muslim and secretly married him. Her brothers inflicted the punishment on their sister—poor, beautiful 'Afífih—they killed her!

No Druze, either man or woman, can with impunity break any of their religious laws.

They may neither smoke nor drink alcohol. Shaykh Yúsif, the eldest son of Shaykh Sálih, is now the chief Druze. Shaykh Sálih was deposed from that position because on a visit to some town he had learned to smoke cigarettes! He even dresses differently, wearing a red fez and a brown, fur-lined coat.

The Druzes wear a white amice, under the zombaz, a long, black coat, which, with a large, snow-white turban, has a pleasing and dignified effect. Both men and women are extraordinarily fine, noble-looking, strong, and healthy people.

Their fine physique is due in great measure to the pure, clean lives they lead. They keep to a vegetarian diet, very seldom eating meat; they observe the strictest morality, take no wine, spirits, nor tobacco. Tilling the ground, growing corn, olive oil, and fruit for their simple needs, spending most of their days in the fresh, pure, bracing air, they certainly do nothing to induce weakness or ill-health.

The ladies are amazingly lovely, with slight, graceful figures, regular features, wonderful eyes with long lashes, deep ivory-coloured skins. I have never seen so many beautiful women together without one plain face among them. For even the grandmother and great-grandmother were beautiful! The dress is certainly most becoming; there is the white amice, very soft muslin-embroidered, and edged with fine lace. Then an ivory-coloured, fine, supple silk, embroidered with coloured flowers, only showing in front, where the zombaz, a long coat, floated back as they walked with their free, graceful step; this zombaz is sometimes black or dark blue velvet; the head is covered with a large, flowing, white, soft veil; this is bound firmly round the head with a band, it might be dark blue, embroidered with gold, forming a sort of coronet; it is tied at the back of the head, the ends falling below the knees, over the snowy veil, nearly reaching the ground. They never show their hair, and it is a mark of great respect to draw their veil over the mouth.

An enchanting baby, one year old, was brought in; even her hair was not to be seen. She wore a quaint little silk bonnet with white frills round the lovely baby face, and a curtain covered the neck. I wanted to see Baddúrah's head, but the beautiful grandmother, Sit 'Afífih, only pushed the bonnet a wee bit back, and I did not like to insist by asking again.

As soon as we arrived, sweet iced water was offered to us in pretty glasses. After a while tea came, with delicious Arabian pastry, cakes, sweets, and nuts, followed by very sweet coffee.

They pressed Rúḥá Khánum and the other visitors, of whom there were three, to stay for at least a few days. Their hospitality is spontaneous kindness itself.

When they found we were really unable to accept their invitation, we were taken to the *díván*, another comfortable and large reception room. Here we were presented by Rúḥá Khánum to Shaykh Sáliḥ, a courtly, charming, and fascinating man, ninety years old, who wept bitterly as he welcomed us, for he had a great reverence and love for 'Abdu'l-Bahá.

Then came the Shaykh of the Khalwa—the sacred House of Prayer—which is entered by none but the Druzes who are initiated.

This is Yúsif, the eldest son of Shaykh Sáliḥ, who had taken the place of his father, when he was deposed for smoking! He also was deeply moved as he spoke of the Master with loving devotion. Three younger brothers were then introduced to us and numbers of their sons, quite a large party of as splendid-looking men as I have ever seen.

They had come to Haifa to the funeral of 'Abdu'l-Bahá, also to the forty days memorial feast, and were now overcome with emotion as they spoke of Him, and the never-to-be-forgotten days, when He had hallowed their roof by sheltering under it. When at last we rose to depart, they all came out into the court-yard, the ladies were standing apart, and an enchanting group they made.

Our two friends were anxious to be allowed to take a photograph, but when asked, the Shaykh consented *for themselves*, but *not* for the ladies, which was disappointing.

I shall always remember that visit to Abú-Sinán—the refuge of the Haifa friends and their children, during the terror-days of the war.

The Story of Mírzá Jalál Isfahání, Son-in-Law of
'Abdu'l-Bahá, Son of the "King of the Martyrs"

At the beginning of the year 1916, at about seven o'clock one morning, 'Abdu'l-Bahá sent me for His faithful coachman. "Tell Isfandíyár to have my carriage brought, and you and Khusraw be ready to accompany me to Nazareth in half an hour." We did as He commanded, and at the appointed time 'Abdu'l-Bahá left His home in Haifa, accompanied by Khusraw and me. That day the health of 'Abdu'l-Bahá was not very satisfactory, as one could see by the signs of weariness on His blessed face. However, the Commander-in-chief of the Syrian and Palestine fronts was in Nazareth. He was Jamál Páshá, and 'Abdu'l-Bahá was determined to meet him there, so in spite of His great fatigue and physical weakness, the Beloved started on His journey.

At one in the afternoon we arrived at a small village, called Majdal.

"Have you any acquaintance in this village?" the Master asked.

"Yes, Master, the headman of the village is a good Christian and an acquaintance of mine."

The Master then told me to inform him of His arrival, and ask shelter and time to rest in his house. I went at once to the home of the headman of the village, who was called Khúrí, and told him of the arrival of 'Abdu'l-Bahá. The headman, and many of the notables of the village ran towards the Master's carriage, and with great respect helped Him to alight. 'Abdu'l-Bahá, His attendants, the host, and some of the notables entered the house and sat in the guest room. The Master told Khusraw to make tea and prepare a repast. The food had been brought from Haifa, and the host produced some honey, yoghourt, olives, and eggs. 'Abdu'l-Bahá tasted only a few spoonfuls of honey, a little broth, and some olives, and after the meal He slept about an hour. Arising, He washed His hands and bathed His face with cool water, and came again to sit in the guest room. He spoke words of wisdom to the host, and to the notables, and advised them on many of their problems and difficulties caused by the war.

The host thanked 'Abdu'l-Bahá for His advice, and for the great honour bestowed upon his humble dwelling and upon himself by this visit.

"Your visit at such a time of distress, and particularly to this house, will bring heavenly bounties and support and confirmation to all the dwellers in this village. Now I have one more request to make of you."

"What is your request?" said 'Abdu'l-Bahá. "It will be a happiness to grant it if I have the power."

The Master was always courteous to every creature. He was the symbol of what Bahá'u'lláh had said long ago. "Courtesy is my garment with which we have adorned the temples of our favourite servants."

"The headman continued: "I have only one child, a girl of fourteen, who has been consumptive for two years. All the physicians have pronounced her a hopeless case. Days and nights her mother and I and our relatives can do nothing but weep, wail, and moan. God has not given us another offspring. If your Holiness would pray for the restoration of my only child to health, I feel that a new life would be bestowed upon her, as has been bestowed upon us all by your sympathy and wise advice. We feel sure that the prayers of your Holiness are acceptable to God, and we know that 'Abdu'l-Bahá's bounties shower on all men, regardless of their deserving." At this point the headman burst into tears.

'Abdu'l-Bahá immediately arose from His seat.

"Where is your little girl?"

"In the other room," the headman answered.

'Abdu'l-Bahá went into the other room and saw the young girl lying on a bed on the floor, in the middle of the room. The members of her family were seated about her. Some were acting as nurses, and some only wept. 'Abdu'l-Bahá approached the head of the bed, and sat down beside her. He took the little hand and felt the pulse. The temperature was very high. The child coughed incessantly, and spat blood. She was like a creature of skin and bones. She was in a condition of utter weakness. 'Abdu'l-Bahá laid His blessed hand upon the child's forehead and caressed her. Turning to Jalál, He said, "Bring a cup of tea." This was done at once. 'Abdu'l-Bahá drank some of the tea, and prayed for about five minutes. He Himself gradually poured the rest of the tea with a spoon into the maiden's mouth, and twice placed His hands on her forehead. Once more He prayed, this time for about ten minutes.

Then with a movement of great authority He arose, and turned to the parents, saying in a loud voice of command: "Be assured God will grant a complete cure to your daughter. Do not be perturbed, and neither weep nor moan. With utmost assurance nurse her. Before long she will be in perfect health."

He then returned to the guest room, and comforted the people present with words of great wisdom for half an hour. Then bidding them farewell, He walked out of the house, and stepped into the carriage. Khusraw and I also took our seats.

'Abdu'l-Bahá told Isfandíyár to drive on to Nazareth. All the people of the village, men, women, and children were crowding about the carriage, and until the last second of His remaining there were begging and pleading with the Master for His prayers and blessings.

On the night of that day the maiden perspired a great deal, and gradually the fever abated. According to the word of her father, within two months his daughter was restored to complete health, and in the year 1922 she was married to a Christian man of 'Akká, who is a government official. She is now the mother of three healthy children. Since then, at 'Akká, Haifa, and at Nazareth, the father of the girl has recounted this story many times, and always ends his tale with:

"My daughter was given back to me by His Holiness 'Abbás Effendi."

'Abdu'l-Bahá continued on His way, arrived at Nazareth in the evening at seven o'clock, and took up His residence at the German Hotel.

The next day the Master was invited to lunch at the home of one of the notables of the town of Nazareth. He was one of the Fahúm family. On that day Jamál Páshá, and nearly two hundred of the war leaders, were present at the lunch where the

'ABDU'L-BAHÁ IN WAR-TIME

Master sat down at one o'clock and arose from the table at four. During all those hours 'Abdu'l-Bahá was speaking in Turkish on philosophical and scientific subjects, and on heavenly teachings. So intense was His utterance that all stopped eating while they listened to His blessed words.

"Who is this great and learned Shaykh who is so well-informed in science?" they asked. So moved and attracted were they by His blessed utterance that all endeavoured to draw near to Him, the better to hear every word. Jamál Páshá, who had been His great enemy because of false accusations, had not paid the proper respect to 'Abdu'l-Bahá when He had first arrived. Now, however, having heard the Master speak so learnedly and wisely, he was most deferential and full of all kinds of politeness. When the time came for the Master to rise, Jamál Páshá most courteously held the Beloved's arm to assist Him to leave the table, and himself led the way to the reception room, and seated the Master comfortably.

Finally, after answering more questions, and giving wondrous light on many subjects, the Master arose to bid farewell to His host. Jamál Páshá accompanied Him out of the house, and to the bottom of the steps, and would have gone further with the Master, but was thanked with great kindness and urged by 'Abdu'l-Bahá to return. This was that Jamál Páshá who was not accustomed to rise from his seat to pay respect to any one. His Holiness 'Abdu'l-Bahá was excessively fatigued, and remained that night at the German Hotel at Nazareth. The next day, His work of making a friend of an old enemy having been accomplished, He returned to Haifa.*

---

* This episode is translated from the Persian of Mírzá Jalál Isfahání.—ED.

Ḥájí Ramaḍán

Early in 1917 rumours, vague though most alarming, reached us in London regarding Palestine conditions. Great was our anxiety for our beloved 'Abdu'l-Bahá. Often to comfort myself I repeated His words: "Have you not realized that never in my life have I been for one day out of danger? . . . Be not troubled, these enemies have no power over my life, but that which is given to them from on high." Often I found myself saying these words as though for some inner comfort.

During these very difficult and dangerous days of the war 'Abdu'l-Bahá was desirous of sending a Tablet to the friends in Tihrán, there to be copied and despatched to the Bahá'ís in different parts of the world. Everywhere the friends were anxious to hear of the Master, of Whose fate terrible rumours were whispered.

Who would be chosen for this mission?

None of the friends available could have any probable chance of succeeding in so arduous an enterprise. Carrying a letter in war-time from one, whose watchful enemies were always on the alert for opportunities of mischief, seemed an impossible task. Loss of liberty, and even of life itself, would inevitably be the penalty of such an attempt on behalf of 'Abdu'l-Bahá.

Now there stepped forth an Arabian Bahá'í, named Ḥájí Ramaḍán:

"I implore Thee, O my Master, to accept this service from me. Insignificant am I, and nearly blind, who would suspect me? A humble old man, seventy-five years old. No family have I, my wife is dead, my boys are dead; my property and my shop I have given to my sons-in-law. What money I have left I wish to be used for the poor. Nothing have I to bind me to this world, so in perfect freedom I offer this my service. I only, it seemeth to me, have any chance of succeeding as Thy messenger. I pray Thee, accept me!"

"Thou only art at this time available, and I entrust thee with this Tablet," said the Master.

Ḥájí Ramaḍán began his journey with the precious treasure hidden most carefully, and his heart filled with joy. For forty-five days he walked. Finally, he reached Tihrán with the glorious news of the safety of the Beloved One and His family.

After resting awhile, he set off on the return journey, which was even more difficult. He wended his way through Kirmánsháh and Baghdád disguised as a pedlar. There was gold in the bottom of the bags! Letters were sewn inside the lining of his *abá*!

At one stage of his journey he was an eye-doctor, working wonders, according to the child-like belief of the wild Arabs amongst whom he passed, with his simple remedies (boracic acid lotion).

Very little rest did he dare to take, because of the risk of discovery, so he persisted, defying fatigue, danger, and the burden of his seventy-five years. At the end of his intrepid, daring return journey he arrived and laid the gold and the letters with which he had been entrusted, intact, at the feet of the Master!

"Behold by what poor and humble children of God are great events served," said 'Abdu'l-Bahá, embracing him.

After some rest this gallant friend again started on a mission, but alas! he never arrived. And no tidings of the fate of brave and loving Ḥájí Ramaḍán ever reached the friends. From time to time others were sent to seek him, but all in vain.

The valiant Arab, old and nearly blind, with the soul of a shining and chivalrous knight, will never be forgotten by the friends, and his name will live in song and story as the centuries unroll their days and nights.

* * *

Tablet of 'Abdu'l-Bahá, sent through Tihrán, by the heroic bearer, Ḥájí Ramaḍán, to assure the friends of uninterrupted Communion of the Spirit:

November 1917.

"What though the doors be closed, the roads and the ways

barred, and the usual means of communication be no longer existing, yet the streams of union and nearness of heart flow on without ceasing in the ecstasy of spiritual communion.

"Even though the rays of Light and the reflecting Mirrors be far apart, yet there is no severance, for the union, by the rays and bounties of the reflection, remains firm and unfailing.

"The Bahá'ís ought to show forth in their works such determination and steadfastness that the world of humanity may greatly marvel, saying: 'Behold what firmness and uprightness, what strength and vigour are theirs.'

"By night and by day the thoughts of this servant are ever filled with fragrant spiritual memories of the friends, and his constant and fervent prayers to His Holiness the Merciful are that He will so greatly bless them with the infinite confirmations of the Holy Spirit, that every drop may surge like the sea, and every atom be made to shine, visible in the light of the Sun.

"This can only come to pass through the grace of God the Beloved.

"Convey to the friends each and all from me the utmost longing to see them.

"Praise be to God that, with the aid and favour of His Holiness the Almighty, our days are passed in the best of health on Mount Carmel at the house of His Honour Áqá 'Abbás-Qulí.

"Because of the many inquiries (by the friends) as to the health and safety of the Bahá'ís of this place, and because of the usual means of communication being severed, His Honour Ḥájí Ramaḍán, has been sent with this Tablet, since he only is, at this time, able to undertake the journeyings."

(Signed) *'Abdu'l-Bahá 'Abbas.*

'ABDU'L-BAHÁ IN WAR-TIME

BAHÁ'Í VILLAGES

The Master bought from time to time some land in various villages. Aṣfíyá and Dáliyá, near Haifa—these two properties He bestowed upon Ḍíyá'u'lláh and Badí'u'lláh, the two younger half-brothers, at the request of Bahá'u'lláh.

Land was also acquired in the villages of Samrih, Nughayb, and 'Adasíyyih, situated near the Jordan.

A comparatively small sum, a few hundred pounds only, was required for the purchase of these properties. Groups of Bahá'ís live on this land, where they grow corn. Zoroastrian Bahá'ís are established in 'Adasíyyih; they occupy themselves in cultivating the land. A tenth part of the corn they produce is sent to the Master's household, so that bread is always assured.

These people are industrious and prosperous, growing a sufficiency of the fruits of the earth for their own use, and selling that which remains.

The peace of these tillers of the ground is not always unbroken. A raid of wild Arabs used not to be infrequent.

They would descend upon the village, steal everything they could find, carrying off, not only the corn and oil, but furniture, clothes, even the doors, and the simple agricultural tools, as well as driving off all the cattle and horses. At these times the women and children would be packed into wagons, and conveyed with all possible haste out of the very real danger of capture.

These fugitives would arrive at Haifa, claiming protection from the Master; it was a difficult task to find food and shelter for these suddenly arrived guests. On at least one occasion he caused the chief Shaykhs of the tribes guilty of these depredations to be arrested, much to their amazement, and to be compelled to restore to the poor villagers at least some part of the stolen property.

In the village of Nughayb some of the kinsfolk of the Holy Family live; they cultivate the land, the produce of which gives them the wherewithal to live.

The dwellers in these villages looked always to the Master for protection, guidance, and direction in every detail of their simple lives.

During the war the Arabs were less frequent in their raids. They were afraid, if they ventured too near, that they might be seized and carried off into an unknown life—that of the soldier, the idea of which was a terror to themselves, and indirectly a cause of tranquillity to the villagers.

Preparation for war conditions had been made by 'Abdu'l-Bahá even before His return to Palestine, after His world tour. The people of the villages Nughayb, Samrih, and 'Adasíyyih were instructed by the Master how to grow corn, so as to produce prolific harvests, in the period before and during the lean years of the war.

A vast quantity of this corn was stored in pits, some of which had been made by the Romans, and were now utilized for this purpose. So it came about that 'Abdu'l-Bahá was able to feed numberless poor of the people of Haifa, 'Akká, and the neighbourhood, in the famine years of 1914–1918.

We learned that when the British marched into Haifa there was some difficulty about the commissariat. The officer in command went to consult the Master.

"I have corn," was the reply.

"But for the army?" said the astonished soldier.

"I have corn for the British Army," said 'Abdu'l-Bahá.

He truly walked the Mystic way with practical feet.*

---

* Lady Blomfield often recounted how the corn pits proved a safe hiding-place for the corn, during the occupation of the Turkish army.—ED.

'ABDU'L-BAHÁ IN WAR-TIME

THE MASTER

I, Mrs. Florian King, said to the Master:
"O Beloved, Paradise would be black for me without Thee or Thy Presence. To me Thou art Bahá'u'lláh, Thou art Muḥammad, Thou art Jesus, Thou art Moses, Thou art Buddha."
He held out His hand, saying:
"Come take my hand."
His face was shining, shining. Verily transfigured!
I asked if I might kiss His hand.
"No, my daughter, it is not permitted; the personality is not to be worshipped; the Light it is which is of importance, not the lamp through which it shines."
This he said with a smile of most holy radiance.

* * *

One day 'Abdu'l-Bahá said to the friends: "Your names are better known in the Heavenly Realm than they are in this world." Again He said: "I know the station, the needs, and the condition, of every soul in the world, therefore I know how hard *your* life has been."

* * *

"WE WANT TO SEE OUR FATHER"
THE STORY OF THE SAD TURKISH OFFICIAL AND HIS FAMILY

A Turkish official living in Haifa lost his position when the British occupation took place. He became very poor; he, with his wife and children, were in great want.

They came to ask the help of 'Abbás Effendi, Who did much to soften their hardship.

At length the poor man became ill; the Master sent a doctor to him, medicine, and many comforts.

When about to die he asked for 'Abbás Effendi, and called his children. "Here," he said, "is your father, who will take care of you when I am gone."

One morning four little children came to the house of 'Abbás Effendi; they said:

"We want our father." The Master heard their voices and recognized them.

"Oh! we have come to you, our other father is dead, and now you will take care of us, and be our father."

The Master brought them in and gave them tea and cakes and sweets. He then went with the little ones to their home. The father was not really dead, but had merely fainted; the children thought that he had passed away. However, the next day he died.

The Master charged Himself with the whole responsibility of the doctor, nurse, and funeral.

Then He provided the sad family with food, clothing, their travelling tickets, and other expenses, to Turkey.

This is one instance of the Master's care for all who came to Him, sorrowing and in misery.

On all sides we heard stories of the Master's care for the people.

Christians said "He lived the life of Christ amongst us for forty years."

Muslims cried "He was our Comforter, our Father, Brother, Friend. We shall never cease from mourning Him."

Jewish friends tell how they found themselves, when in His presence, wrapped round in such an atmosphere of love that they felt they had found the true home of the heart and soul.

And how shall *we* speak of Him?

* * *

Jú'án (literally "I am hungry" in Arabic) was the constant moan of a woman who sat in a Haifa street.

A broken leg! The people called her "Jú'ání." None to care for her, starving she lay, full of pain, pleading for help.

Two weeks later, Jú'ání having ceased her pitiful moaning, a woman had this tale to tell:

"The Master called me to take care of poor Jú'ání—to find a room for her. To wash and comfort her with good food, clean clothes, and a doctor. Now she has died, and the Master arranged for her funeral."

* * *

The Master was told:
"There is a poor young Arab man sick of consumption. The Master went to see him; every comfort was taken to him, good food was prepared for him every day; Dr. Nicola was directed by the Master to give all needful attention and medicine. When he died, 'Abbás Effendi arranged that the coffin from the mosque (usually borrowed) should be retained for the young man himself.
"The mother and the sister, overcome with gratitude, cried: 'O Master, Thou art like as God unto us.'"

* * *

The Master was averse to divorce.
In reply to a question, He said "It is not that divorce should be more easy, but that marriages should be more difficult." In all the years that Bahá'u'lláh and 'Abdu'l-Bahá were dwelling in Syria there was not one case of divorce among the Bahá'ís.
The wife of an Armenian Bahá'í implored the Master to allow her husband to divorce her; many were her accusations against her husband.
The Master said to her:
"You are a Christian, how can you ask to be separated? Christ Jesus, Whom I reverence, came not to part but to unite."
At length, seeing that the woman loved another man, the Master said:
"You may divorce her, she is no longer your wife."
When the woman fled with the man, taking much of her husband's money with her:
"You now see the reason for my consent," said the Master.

Another instance:
'Abdu'l-Qásim, the gardener of the Riḍván, wished to marry an Arab peasant woman; he was advised by Bahá'u'lláh not to do so. But as he was very much in love with her, consent was at length given.

In a few years he came saying:
"I want to divorce Jamílih, and marry a younger woman."
"It is absolutely forbidden, you have married her; you must take care of her to the last moment of your life."

When the British arrived in Haifa, where the blockade had caused a perilous condition for the inhabitants, it was discovered that 'Abdu'l-Bahá had saved the civilian population from starvation. Provisions which He had grown, buried in under-ground pits, and otherwise stored, had been given out to the civilians of every nation living in Haifa. 'Abdu'l-Bahá did this in a military way as an army would give rations, and deep was the gratitude of those women and children who had been saved by His power to see into the future of tragedy and woe as early as 1912, when He began the preparations for the catastrophe which was to overtake that land in 1917 and 1918. When Haifa was finally occupied by the British, reserve provisions had not yet come for the army, and someone in authority approached the Master, as already mentioned.

The British Government, with its usual gesture of appreciating a heroic act, conferred a knighthood upon 'Abdu'l-Bahá 'Abbás, Who accepted this honour as a courteous gift "from a just king."

The dignitaries of the British crown from Jerusalem were gathered in Haifa, eager to do honour to the Master, Whom every one had come to love and reverence for His life of unselfish service. An imposing motor-car had been sent to bring 'Abdu'l-Bahá to the ceremony. The Master, however, could not be found. People were sent in every direction to look for Him, when suddenly from an unexpected side He appeared, alone, walking His kingly walk, with that simplicity of greatness which always enfolded Him.

The faithful servant, Isfandíyár, whose joy it had been for many years to drive the Master on errands of mercy, stood sadly looking on at the elegant motor-car which awaited the honoured guest.

"No longer am I needed."

At a sign from Him, Who knew the sorrow, old Isfandíyár rushed off to harness the horse, and brought the carriage out at the lower gate, whence 'Abdu'l-Bahá was driven to a side entrance of the garden of the Governorate of Phœnicia.

So Isfandíyár was needed and happy.

* * *

OF LIFE AFTER DEATH

"Know thou of a truth that the Soul, after its separation from the body, will continue to progress until it attaineth the presence of God, in a state and condition which neither the revolution of ages and centuries, nor the changes and chances of the world can alter. It will endure as long as the Kingdom of God, His Sovereignty, His Dominion and Power shall endure."

Bahá'u'lláh.

A woman, full of sorrow and despair, came to 'Abdu'l-Bahá:
"I pray you remove my doubt, and give me consolation, I have lost my beloved husband."

The Master answered her:

"If you have a bed of lilies-of-the-valley that you love and tenderly care for, they cannot see you, nor can they understand your care, nevertheless, because of that tender care, they flourish.

"So it is with your husband. You cannot see him, but his loving influence surrounds you, cares for you, watches over you. They, who have passed into the Divine Garden, pray for us there, as we pray for them here."

Another day a woman came to 'Abdu'l-Bahá and told Him of a dream.

"Last night, Master, I dreamed that I was in a garden of such beauty that it seemed beyond the power of the most perfect human gardener to have created it. In this garden I saw a beautiful girl, about nineteen, who was caressing the flowers. As I came into the garden she lifted her lovely head and came towards me with outstretched arms, as though in great love and joy at my visit. I look at her amazed, and then I saw a startling resemblance to the tiny daughter I lost many years before."

'Abdu'l-Bahá smiled His miraculous smile:

"My child, you have been permitted to see your daughter as she is now, walking in the sacred garden of one of the worlds of God. This is a bounty of God to you. Rejoice and be happy."

Riḍváníyyih Khánum related that when her child was ill, the Master came and gave two pink roses to the little one, then, turning to the mother, He said in His musical voice so full of love: "Be patient."

That evening the child passed away.

"Riḍváníyyih," said the Master, "there is a Garden of God. Human beings are trees growing therein. The Gardener is Our Father. When He sees a little tree in a place too small for her development, He prepares a suitable and more beautiful place, where she may grow and bear fruit. Then He transplants that little tree. The other trees marvel, saying: 'This is a lovely little tree. For what reason does the Gardener uproot it?'

"The Divine Gardener, alone, knows the reason.

"You are weeping, Riḍváníyyih, but if you could see the beauty of the place where she is, you would no longer be sad.

"Your child is now free, and, like a bird, is chanting divine joyous melodies.

"If you could see that sacred Garden, you would not be content to remain here on earth. Yet this is where your duty now lies."

When my own mother made the "great change" from one world of God to another, 'Abdu'l-Bahá wrote a very beautiful tablet to me, in which He spoke of my mother as being "in the garden of rejuvenation." One day a friend, who had not yet heard of the tablet of the Master, told me of a vivid dream she had of my mother, whom she had known and loved. "I seemed to be in a marvellous garden, where every type of rare and beautiful flower was in bloom. Moving about among the flowers was a young girl. She seemed to be in a state of inexpressible joy over the loveliness of her garden. Her voice, as she chanted, was full of the ecstasy of a complete happiness. She listened to the song of birds, and inhaled the odour of the flowers as though she were filling her soul with their fragrance. Suddenly she turned towards me, as though conscious that someone was there beside herself. The young girl facing me with an enchanting smile was your mother, in the full beauty of youth."

* * *

NEW YEAR TABLET FROM 'ABDU'L-BAHÁ

Nawrúz, 21st March, 1918.

O ye Children of the Kingdom! It is the New Year. A year is the expression of the cycle of the sun, but now is the beginning of a cycle of the Sun of Reality! A new cycle, a new age, a new time, and therefore it is very blessed.

I wish the Blessing to appear and become manifest in the faces and characters of all the believers in God, so that they may also become a new people, and having found new life, and been baptized with Fire and Spirit, may make the world a new world—so that the old earth may disappear and the new earth become manifest; the old ideas depart and new thoughts come; old garments be cast aside, and new garments be put on; former politics, whose foundation is war, be discarded; and new politics, founded upon peace, raise the standard of victory, the new star shine, and the new sun's gleam illumine and radiate; so that new flowers may bloom, the new spring become known, the new breeze blow, the new bounty descend, the new tree bring forth the new fruit, the new voice be raised, and its new sound reach all ears.

I desire for you all that you will receive this great assistance, and partake of this Bounty; that in Spirit and heart, you will strive and endeavour until the World of War become the World of Peace; the World of Darkness the World of Light; Satanic conduct be turned into Heavenly behaviour, the ruined places become builded up; the sword be turned into the olive branch; the flash of hatred be changed into the Flame of the Love of God, and the roar of the gun become the Voice of the Kingdom.

That the soldiers of death may become the soldiers of Life!

That all the nations of the world may be united in one nation; all races as one Race.

And all the National Anthems be harmonized into one melody.

Then this material realm will be Paradise, the earth will be Heaven, and the world of Satan will become the World of Angels.

Upon thee be greeting and praise.

* * *

One day, during the war, two men were passing along the way of the sea beyond Jordan which lies between Haifa and 'Akká. They were talking together, when their attention became attracted by the venerable figure of a man lying, as though overcome with weariness, on the sands, near the edge of the tideless sea.

They gazed silently; the body was completely relaxed, one arm supporting the beautiful head with its hair of spun silver. The face bore traces of great sorrow, but was softened by an ineffable tenderness. Great nobility of character lay upon the brow. There seemed a spiritual light of rare beauty about Him. He was resting in deep slumber.

The sleeper was 'Abdu'l-Bahá.

CHAPTER V

Danger to 'Abdu'l-Bahá, His Family and Friends, and How it was Averted

In the spring of 1918, I was much startled and deeply disturbed by a telephone message: "'Abdu'l-Bahá in serious danger. Take immediate action." It came from an authoritative source. There was not a moment to be lost. Every available power must be brought to bear to save the Master.

I went at once to Lord Lamington. His sympathetic regard for 'Abdu'l-Bahá, his understanding of the ramifications and "red tape" necessary for "immediate action" were of priceless value.

A letter was immediately written to the Foreign Office explaining the importance of 'Abdu'l-Bahá's position, His work for true peace, and for the spiritual welfare of many thousands of people. Through the influence of Lord Lamington, and his prompt help, the letter, with its alarming news, was at once put into the hands of Lord Balfour.

That very evening a cable was sent to General Allenby with these instructions, "Extend every protection and consideration to 'Abdu'l-Bahá, His family and His friends, when the British march on Haifa."

So a terrible tragedy was averted, by the promptness and understanding of Lord Lamington and the power of Lord Balfour, his colleagues in the Cabinet here in London, and by the devotion, efficiency, and promptitude of Major Tudor-Pole at the Turkish end, for Haifa was still in the hands of the Turks.

The Turks had been so aroused by the enemies of the Master that they had threatened to crucify Him, and all His family, on Mount Carmel.

When General Allenby took Haifa, several days before it was believed possible for him to do so, he sent a cablegram to London which caused everybody to wonder, and especially filled the hearts of the Bahá'ís in all the world with deep gratitude to the Almighty Protector.

The cable of General Allenby was as follows: "Have to-day taken Palestine. Notify the world that 'Abdu'l-Bahá is safe."

* * *

EXTRACT FROM A LETTER OF LADY BLOMFIELD TO LORD LAMINGTON

14th March, 1939.

Dear Lord Lamington,

It was a great pleasure to meet you at the Saudi Arabian reception.

I was reminded of that time in the spring of 1918, when having received the terrible message, " 'Abdu'l-Bahá in serious danger, take immediate action," I hurried to ask your advice and help.

How an urgent letter was at once written to Lord Balfour, how you had it delivered into his own hands, how instructions were cabled that same evening to Lord Allenby to "extend every consideration and protection to 'Abdu'l-Bahá, His family, and His friends when the British march on Haifa," all this is a matter of history. Also that Lord Allenby marched on Haifa two days before he had planned to do so, thereby preventing the dire tragedy which had been fixed for that date.

I afterwards heard that a British officer, Major Tudor-Pole, had sent that terrifying message. He had discovered that "the enemy High Command had sentenced 'Abdu'l-Bahá and His family to be crucified on Mount Carmel," and that the day appointed for the carrying-out of the decree was the second day after Allenby's entry into Haifa.

A guard was immediately placed round the home of the Master, and it was made known that "prompt retribution would follow any attempt to injure Him or any of His family." So that the London part and the Haifa part of this episode fitted into each other through this sequence:

DANGER TO 'ABDU'L-BAHÁ

1. Major Wellesley Tudor-Pole's discovery.
2. His message of urgency which came to me.
3. Your wonderful help in knowing what to do, and in *doing it*.
4. Lord Balfour's prompt instructions to Lord Allenby.
5. Lord Allenby's energy, foresight, and wisdom.

And the vile intent was frustrated. How grand a privilege for Britain, who was able to do this service to the "Servant of God" through the chosen instruments of "The Protector, The Supreme."

I have before me the letter of Major Tudor-Pole describing the Haifa end of this episode, also speaking of the profound impression created by the Master's calm, serene aloofness above all the turmoil and danger of the conditions of that time.

My account of these days needs your letter for its completion and intense interest. For the generations of the future I am anxious to have as detailed a story of those critical days as it is possible to obtain.

Lord Lamington to Lady Blomfield.
Dear Lady Blomfield,

I thank you for your letter of the 14th instant, and I am glad to hear that you are compiling a volume on Bahá'ísm.

I could not usefully add to your account and description of 'Abdu'l-Bahá.

There was never a more striking instance of one who desired that mankind should live in peace and goodwill and have love for others by the recognition of their inherent divine qualities.

At Haifa, in 1919, I well remember seeing a white figure seated by the roadside; when he arose and walked the vision of a truly and holy saintly man impressed itself on me. I think it was on this occasion that he took his signet ring from off his finger and gave it to me.

(Signed) *Lamington.*

* * *

The story from the side of Haifa is told by Major Tudor-Pole, V.C.

"It must have been in the early spring of 1918 that I began to feel acute anxiety for 'Abdu'l-Bahá's safety at Haifa, and that of His family and followers there. I came out of the line in December 1917 during the attack on Jerusalem, and being temporarily incapacitated for active service, was transferred to Intelligence, first at Cairo and later at Ludd, Jaffa, and Jerusalem.

Subject to verification of dates, it was during March 1918 that information reached me from our own espionage service that the Turkish Commander-in-Chief, whose H.Q.S. were then between Haifa and Beirut, had stated his definite intention to "Crucify 'Abdu'l-Bahá and His family on Mount Carmel" should the Turkish Army be compelled to evacuate Haifa and retreat northwards.

With an advance base at and around Jaffa, we were beginning to prepare for a move towards Haifa and the north at that time. For several reasons, including shortage of men and munitions, the British advance was delayed well into the summer of 1918.

Meanwhile, the news reaching me concerning 'Abdu'l-Bahá's imminent danger became more and more alarming. I tried to arouse interest in the matter among those who were responsible for Intelligence Service activities (including General Clayton, Sir Wyndham Deedes, and Sir Ronald Storrs—the latter having been made Governor of Jerusalem). I also brought the matter before my own chief, General Sir Arthur Money (Chief Administrator of Occupied Enemy Territory). None of these personages knew anything about 'Abdu'l-Bahá, nor could they be made to realize the urgent need to ensure His safety.

At this time chance brought me into touch with an officer whose social and political connexions in London were strong. Through his courtesy and interest I was enabled to get an urgent message through to the British Foreign Office.

Through friends associated with the Bahá'í Cause in England, an independent avenue of approach to the ruling powers in London was discovered.

By these means Lord Balfour, Lord Curzon, and others in the Cabinet were advised as to the critical situation at Haifa. Lord Lamington's influence proved of special help at this time.

DANGER TO 'ABDU'L-BAHÁ

The upshot of these various activities bore fruit, and the Foreign Office sent a despatch to General Allenby instructing him to ensure the safety of 'Abdu'l-Bahá and His family and entourage so soon as the British Army captured Haifa.

This despatch passed through my hands in Cairo *en route* for Army Headquarters at Ludd, and was duly passed on to be dealt with by the Headquarters Staff there. No one at Headquarters had heard of 'Abdu'l-Bahá or of the Bahá'í Movement, and Intelligence was requested to make urgent enquiry. In due course this demand for information reached the Headquarters of Intelligence at the Savoy Hotel, Cairo, and ultimately (when enquiries elsewhere had proved fruitless) was passed to me for action. As a result, General Allenby was provided with full particulars in regard to 'Abdu'l-Bahá's record and the history of the Movement of which He was the Master.

Allenby at once issued orders to the General Commanding Officer in command of the Haifa operations to the effect that immediately the town was entered, a British guard was to be posted at once around 'Abdu'l-Bahá's house, and a further guard was to be placed at the disposal of His family and followers. Means were found for making it known within the enemy lines that stern retribution would follow any attempt to cause death or injury to the great Persian Master or to any of His household.

I believe that this warning played its part in safeguarding 'Abdu'l-Bahá's welfare at that time.

When Haifa was ultimately taken, these instructions for posting a guard were duly carried out, and all dangers of death or accident were thereby averted.

It is not possible to say for certain whether disaster would have resulted otherwise, but as the town was full of Turkish spies for some time after its capture (many of whom knew of the Turkish Commander-in-Chief's firm intention to massacre 'Abdu'l-Bahá and His family at that period), action with this end in view might have been seriously and successfully attempted, were it not for the taking of the precautions referred to above.

The honour and protection shown to the Bahá'í leader at

that time were greatly appreciated by Him, and considerably helped British prestige in Persia and elsewhere in the Near and Middle East. He told me this Himself.

It was a wonderful experience in the midst of the chaos of war conditions to visit the Master at His Mount Carmel home, which even at that time was a haven of peace and refreshment. I can remember Him, majestic yet gentle, pacing up and down His garden whilst He spoke to me about eternal realities, at a time when the whole material world was rocking on its foundations. The divine power of the spirit shone through His presence, giving one the feeling that a great prophet from Old Testament days had risen up in a war-stricken world, as an inspirer and spiritual guide for the human race.

One or two incidents which happened shortly afterwards, connected with the capture of Haifa, are worthy of record.

During the British advance from the south, field batteries were placed in position on high ground immediately to the south-east of Mount Carmel, the intention being to shell Haifa at long range over Mount Carmel itself. Some of the Eastern Bahá'ís living on the northern slopes of Mount Carmel becoming agitated, went to 'Abdu'l-Bahá's residence and expressed fear as to the tragic course of possible events. According to an eye-witness of this scene (from whom I obtained the story when I reached Haifa), 'Abdu'l-Bahá calmed His excited followers and called them to prayer. Then He told them that all would be well, and that no British shells would cause death or damage to the population or to Haifa and its environs. As a matter of historical fact, the range of the field batteries in question was inaccurate, the shells passing harmlessly over the town and falling into the Bay of 'Akká beyond.

Another incident of those stirring times is worthy of record, although I am not able to vouch for its complete accuracy at first hand. Before the fall of Haifa, 'Abdu'l Bahá was discussing the British campaign with a few of His followers in His garden one day. He then predicted that, contrary to the general expectation, the taking of Haifa and the walled town of 'Akká would come about almost without bloodshed. This prediction was verified by the facts. He also stated that the Turks would surrender 'Akká (supposed to be impregnable) to two unarmed

British soldiers. The resultant facts so far as I was able to gather them were as follows:—

Subsequent to the entry of our troops into Haifa, the front line was pushed forward half-way across the Bay of 'Akká, and outposts were placed in position on the sands of the Bay some four miles from 'Akká itself. 'Akká, as a fortified and walled town, was believed to be filled with Turkish troops at this time. Very early one morning two British Army Service soldiers, who had lost their bearings in the night, found themselves at the gates of 'Akká, believing erroneously that the town was already in British hands. However, the Turkish rearguard troops had been secretly evacuated only eight hours earlier, and the Mayor of the town, seeing British soldiers outside the gates, came down and presented them with the keys of the town in token of surrender! It is credibly stated that the dismayed Tommies, being unarmed, dropped the keys and made post haste for the British lines!

It is interesting to remember that even during the darkest periods of the Great War 'Abdu'l-Bahá's faith in a British triumph never wavered. Indeed, there is no doubt that He possessed foreknowledge not only of the principal events connected with the war itself, but also predicted correctly happenings belonging to the war's aftermath in regard to Palestine in particular and the world in general. He was providentially spared for some years longer to continue sowing the seeds of a spiritual understanding of the significance of universal peace and brotherhood, which seeds will undoubtedly bear a rich harvest of fruit during years that still lie ahead of us.

(Signed) *W. Tudor-Pole.*

* * *

LETTER FROM SIR HERBERT SAMUEL, G.C.B., C.B.E.*

In 1920 I was appointed as the first High Commissioner for Palestine under the British Mandate, and took an early opportunity of paying a visit to 'Abdu'l-Bahá Effendi at his home in Haifa.

---
* Now Viscount Samuel of Carmel.

I had for some time been interested in the Bahá'í movement, and felt privileged by the opportunity of making the acquaintance of its Head. I had also an official reason as well as a personal one. 'Abdu'l-Bahá had been persecuted by the Turks. A British regime had now been substituted in Palestine for the Turkish. Toleration and respect for all religions had long been a principle of British rule wherever it extended, and the visit of the High Commissioner was intended to be a sign to the population that the adherents of every creed would be able to feel henceforth that they enjoyed the respect and could count upon the goodwill of the new Government of the land.

I was impressed, as was every visitor, by 'Abdu'l-Bahá's dignity, grace, and charm. Of moderate stature, his strong features and lofty expression lent to his personality an appearance of majesty. In our conversation he readily explained and discussed the principal tenets of Bahá'ísm, answered my inquiries and listened to my comments. I remember vividly that friendly interview of sixteen years ago, in the simple room of the villa, surrounded by gardens, on the sunny hillside of Mount Carmel.

I was glad I had paid my visit so soon, for in 1921 'Abdu'l-Bahá died. I was only able to express my respect for his creed, and my regard for his person, by coming from the capital to attend his funeral. A great throng had gathered together, sorrowing for his death, but rejoicing also for his life.

(Signed) *Herbert Samuel.*

* * *

LETTER FROM SIR RONALD STORRS, K.C.M.G., C.B.E., FIRST GOVERNOR OF JERUSALEM SINCE PONTIUS PILATE

I met 'Abdu'l-Bahá first in 1909, on my way out from England and Constantinople through Syria to succeed, in Cairo, Harry Boyle as Oriental Secretary to the British Agency. (The episode is fully treated in my *Orientations*, published by Ivor Nicholson & Watson.) I drove along the beach in a cab from Haifa to 'Akká and spent a very pleasant hour with the patient but unsubdued prisoner and exile. When, a few years later, he was released and visited Egypt, I had the honour of looking after him and of presenting him to Lord Kitchener, who was deeply impressed by his personality, as who could fail to be?

The war separated us again until Lord Allenby, after his triumphant drive through Syria, sent me to establish the Government at Haifa and throughout that district. I called upon 'Abbás Effendi on the day I arrived and was delighted to find him quite unchanged. When he came to Jerusalem he visited my house and I never failed to visit him whenever I went to Haifa. His conversation was indeed a remarkable planning, like that of an ancient prophet, far above the perplexities and pettinesses of Palestine politics, and elevating all problems into first principles.

He was kind enough to give me one or two beautiful specimens of his own handwriting, together with that of Mishkín Kalam, all of which, together with his large, signed photograph, were unfortunately burned in the Cyprus fire.

I rendered my last sad tribute of affectionate homage when, early in 1921,* I accompanied Sir Herbert Samuel to the funeral of 'Abbás Effendi. We walked at the head of a train of all the religions up the slope of Mount Carmel, and I have never known a more united expression of regret and respect than was called forth by the utter simplicity of the ceremony."

(Signed) *Ronald Storrs.*

P.S.—You may care to know that I employed several of 'Abbás Effendi's followers on the Military Governorate at Haifa, where I believe more than one of them still continues to render excellent service.

* * *

---

* This is evidently a slight lapse of memory by Sir Ronald Storrs, since the funeral of 'Abdu'l-Bahá took place in November, 1921.

A tale is told of British occupation in Palestine which may one day be related to the children of the future as legend, but is now believed as fact.

British guns were trained on Jerusalem. The Turks were in control of the sacred city.

The British command hesitated to fire on the "City of God." A message was sent to headquarters: "What shall we do?"

The answer came back, "Pray."

Not a gun was fired.

When the British arrived in Jerusalem at dawn, it had been evacuated by the Turks, and not a sacred place had been desecrated.

PART IV

VARIOUS DOCUMENTS

LETTER FROM SITÁRIH KHÁNUM TO HER DAUGHTER PARVÍN
(MRS. BASIL HALL). HOUSE OF BAHÁ'U'LLÁH, 'AKKÁ

2nd May, 1922.

I came here yesterday by train—Díyá Khánum, Ṭúbá Khánum, Rúḥá Khánum, with their three little boys (Ríyáḍ, Fu'ád, and Ḥasan), and a few servants made up our party.

It is impossible to convey in any words the interest of this visit.

Rúḥá Khánum and I went to the Barracks, and saw the very courteous Military Governor, a British officer in khaki, who himself arranged to conduct our party, when the rest should arrive, over all parts of the ancient fortress castle, the prison dwelling of Bahá'u'lláh, 'Abbás Effendi, Their families, and the seventy devoted disciples, who would not consent to be separated from Him, whom they hailed as their Lord, as "Him Whom God should make Manifest," but followed Him into exile, prison, or death.

In the afternoon Mihrangíz Khánum, Shoghi Effendi's younger sister, and I sallied forth, guided by the son of an old believer, Áqá Riḍá Qannád, who had been with his Master throughout the terrible early days; this Persian Bahá'í took us to see the Khán. This was an inn, where the pilgrims used to stay in that time, when, at length, rules being a little relaxed, and the believers having discovered where their Beloved One was imprisoned, made long, arduous journeys, hoping to see Him. Here we came to the long, stone-floored room, where the friends used to spread out their bedding and rest, also the rows of little rooms where families encamped. There was a room where a school for little children was afterwards arranged —poor little scholars—from early morning till sunset in an airless room, with dull studies, nothing interesting, nothing amusing; no breaks now and then for play! Such scanty, tasteless scraps called dinner!

After the Ascension of Bahá'u'lláh there was also a room set apart for the little girls, who were, if possible, in a worse case than even the boys.

The Khán is a wonderfully picturesque building, built round a large court-yard, with rows of rounded arches and columns on three sides.

Here the Master's custom was to assemble all the poor, especially the children, of 'Akká, on Feast Days, both Christian and Muslim, also on the anniversary of the Sultán's coronation. Here He regaled them with sweets, cakes, fruit, and tea. He had the middle fountain filled with *sharbat*, which was a great treat. After this, we went through the narrow, winding streets of this unique historic town to the great mosque. There we met a polite Shaykh, who had become a devoted friend of 'Abbás Effendi; he turned back with us, and showed us the little room where the Master used to retreat, when He wished to meditate in peace and quiet.

It was here that the Páshá of Yaman lived and died in exile. Of him more in another place.

Then the Shaykh took us into the mosque—impressive in its silent and reverent atmosphere. He pointed out a small alcove apart, where the Master always prayed.

Upon the wall, in an honourable place, hung a wonderful, intricately-written prayer, from the pen of the famous Mishkín Qalam; it is conspicuously signed "Mishkín Qalam, who am Bahá'í."

Other treasures were shown to us: six pen-written sacred books, presented to the mosque by 'Abbás Effendi. Some others, marvellously illustrated with pen drawings (from India). Also many precious volumes, containing some thousands of the Ḥadíths (traditional utterances of Muḥammad).

Standing about were numbers of Muslim religious students, charming-looking youths, who courteously greeted us.

Here was the large court-yard where the poor congregated every Friday to receive alms, and make their various appeals to their "Beloved Father of the Poor," 'Abbás Effendi.

Everybody said "Oh, what a loss to the world. He was Comforter, Protector, and Benefactor to all!"

'Abdu'l-Bahá lived forty years of His sanctified life in this fortress town, obeying the precepts of the following Tablet in an absolutely perfect manner.

Tablet of Bahá'u'lláh

"Be generous when thou hast possessions.

"Be thankful if all be taken from thee.

"Be just to the dependents, reward them plenteously for their work.

"Show a smiling countenance to all.

"Be a treasure to the poor.

"Give good counsel to the wealthy.

"Be careful to answer the appeal of the unhappy.

"Be not deaf to the cry of the needy.

"Fulfil thine every promise.

"Be not full of words at the gatherings together.

"Be just in thy commands.

"Be humble in thy dealings with mankind.

"Be not arrogant when in power, neither cast down when the power is no longer thine."

I am writing this on the balcony outside the room where Bahá'u'lláh lived for about five years.

This house is spoken of as the large house—the house of 'Abbúd, the Christian merchant.

Next to this house is the small house, where in one room Bahá'u'lláh lived for twelve years—eight years of which was spent without once going out, even across the street to the Bírúní!

In this house were four rooms only! For the pilgrims and for the family! (The men pilgrims who were single, and the families, were accommodated at the Khán.)

One room, the best, was always kept sacred to Bahá'u'lláh. The family, Ásíyih Khánum, the Most Exalted Leaf, their daughter, and the Master surrounded their Beloved with all the devoted care that was possible.

In one of the rooms thirteen persons, pilgrims and the ladies, sometimes slept. A shelf was there, on which an agile pilgrim would repose, and on one occasion rolled off!

This plan was for those days before the marriage of 'Abbás Effendi—when the door was opened through to a room of the larger house. This is next to the smaller house where 'Abbás Effendi brought His bride, and where all His children were born.

VARIOUS DOCUMENTS

The incident of the opening of the door has already been described in various accounts of this time.
This is the house where the Kitáb-i-Aqdas, the Most Holy Book, and many Tablets of sublime beauty were written. It was also this house which was one day surrounded with soldiers sent to arrest Bahá'u'lláh and the Master.*
I am sleeping in the room of Ásíyih Khánum. I was conscious all night of its benign atmosphere!
After visiting the mosque, we went to see the house, taken four years after the Ascension of Bahá'u'lláh, where the American pilgrims first stayed, and where all the grandchildren of 'Abdu'l-Bahá were born. In this house, guarded by Turkish sentinels, the Master was imprisoned for seven years, because of false accusations. One of the Sisters in charge spoke English: "Yes, 'Abbás Effendi was a good friend to all. He came to see me, and gave fifty pounds to this hospital. He was a kind friend to my uncle and to me." This house is now a military hospital—*British*!
2nd May:
This morning the Holy Mother and Khánum arrived, having motored over from Haifa; also Rúhangíz, sister of Shoghi Effendi, and Áqá Mírzá Hádí—rows of guests were already sitting here.
It was not very easy for us to leave, but all were anxious to visit the barracks, and the kind Captain would be expecting us. We were a party of nine ladies. Áqá Ḥusayn, the cook, who had been with Bahá'u'lláh at Baghdád, and who had determined to accompany us, came to tell us reliable details about all the places, and scenes, of the captivity.
How could I convey the impression of this visit? The Saint Sister, daughter of Bahá'u'lláh, and the Holy Mother, wife of 'Abdu'l-Bahá, as they stood looking at the little, bare rooms, where their (and our) Beloved Ones were imprisoned! One imagined in what an intimate, poignantly heart-rending flood of memories they walked, as they gazed with grief-filled eyes upon this barrack building, the home for many years of those

---
* The story of the events which culminated in this deplorable occurrence are related in another chapter, partly from a Tablet of Bahá'u'lláh written to a friend in Persia, and from a talk by 'Abdu'l-Bahá on the subject, some of the details being given by the Most Exalted Leaf.

Two—destined to be the Great Educators of the world, West as well as East, that world which is also wet with tears!

There was the little room on the ground-floor, where Bahá'u'lláh stayed for a time, when He, with His family, arrived in 'Akká. This room is being carefully preserved untouched.

Close by is the vault-like room where the rest of the family, and the seventy "Faithful Ones" who accompanied them, were shut in for those first appalling days. All fell sick with typhoid but two, 'Abbás Effendi and one man, who, therefore, was able to help Him. The Master nursed them, cooked for them, and Himself divided out the portions—seeing to it that none were neglected nor forgotten.

The Greatest Holy Leaf, her eyes charged with memories, was with us while we listened. She had been there in that terrible time, and was sick of that same fever, from the effects of which she has occasionally suffered all through her life.

* * *

A LETTER FROM MRS. THORNBURGH-CROPPER* TO
LADY BLOMFIELD SENT AS A CONTRIBUTION TO
"THE CHOSEN HIGHWAY"

Early in 1900 I received a letter from Mrs. Phœbe Hearst, my life-long friend, from California, telling me of a wonderful new religious teaching with which she had come into touch. She said that she felt that it would be of great interest to me, and that when she came to London, she would tell me all about it.

A short time later I was searching in the encyclopædia for some information about King David, about whom I had had an argument. In turning over the pages, my eye was caught by a name, "Báb." I read on after the name, and found it to be the history of a messenger of God Who had been martyred in Persia, after bringing a new interpretation of truth to the Muslims. There was something in this story of a martyr for His faith that so moved me that I went to the British Museum

---

* Mrs. Thornburgh-Cropper was the first Bahá'í in the British Isles. She passed on in 1939.—ED.

to search for further information regarding Him, and His teaching.

Later on, friends of Mrs. Hearst arrived on their way to the Turkish prison of 'Akká, near Mount Carmel. They were going in advance to make arrangements for Mrs. Hearst to visit the prison. This seemed an extraordinary voyage to make, but when I heard of the great Prisoner there, of His lifetime of martyrdom, and of the station of His Father, Bahá'u'lláh, I eagerly began arrangements to accompany Mrs. Hearst on so sacred a mission. It was then I learned that Bahá'u'lláh was the Promised One of the dispensation and teaching of the Báb. So I had been prepared.

Mrs. Hearst and I arrived in Cairo, Egypt, after a terrible storm at sea, and remained there for a few days until all had been explained to us regarding our actual journey into the prison city.

We then took a small, miserable boat to Haifa. There was a storm here also, and we were beaten about unmercifully in our all too inadequate steamer. Upon arrival we went to an hotel, where we remained until nightfall as it was too dangerous for us, and for 'Abdu'l-Bahá, Whom we were to visit, for strangers to be seen entering the city of sorrow.

We took a carriage after the night had fallen, and drove along the hard sand by "way of the sea beyond Jordan," which led us to the gates of the prison city. There our trusted driver arranged for us to enter. Once inside we found the friends who were awaiting us, and we started up the uneven stairs that led to Him. Someone went before us with a small piece of candle, which cast strange shadows on the walls of this silent place.

Suddenly the light caught a form that at first seemed a vision of mist and light. It was the Master which the candle-light had revealed to us. His white robe, and silver, flowing hair, and shining blue eyes gave the impression of a spirit, rather than of a human being. We tried to tell Him how deeply grateful we were at His receiving us. "No," He answered, "you are kind to come." This was spoken in a very careful English.

Then He smiled, and we recognized the Light which He possessed in the radiance which moved over His fine and noble face. It was an amazing experience. We four visitors from the

Western world felt that our voyage, with all its accompanying inconvenience was a small price to pay for such treasure as we received from the spirit and words of the Master, Whom we had crossed mountain and seas and nations to meet. This began our work to "spread the teaching," to "mention the Name of Bahá'u'lláh, and acquaint the world with the Message."

Mrs. Hearst went again, later in the year 1900, and took eighteen people with her to visit the Master, Who returned her visits in 1912, as He had returned ours in the previous year.

(Signed) *Maryam Thornburgh-Cropper.*

STORY OF MÍRZÁ AḤMAD (ELDEST SON OF ṢUBḤ-I-AZAL) AT THE
PILGRIM HOUSE, HAIFA, TOLD TO SITÁRIH KHÁNUM
Translated by Mírzá Aflátún

As Ṣubḥ-i-Azal (the half-brother and enemy of Bahá'u'lláh) grew older, his eldest son, Mírzá Aḥmad, left Cyprus, to take up a post in a Constantinople bank.
Two of his brothers joined him for a time. The elder of these came to 'Akká a year or two after the Passing of Bahá'u'lláh, desiring to become a Bahá'í. Soon afterwards the younger brother came to 'Akká, also wishing to become a Bahá'í. He stayed about seven months, during which time the Master was very kind to him.
Early in the year 1921 a grandson of Ṣubḥ-i-Azal, who had been employed under the British Government in the "Censor" department, wrote to 'Abdu'l-Bahá saying:
"I am very pleased to have become aware that I have so distinguished a cousin. Will you permit me to visit you?"
He came, his visit lasted some time. He told the Master that his eldest uncle, Mírzá Aḥmad, remembered Bahá'u'lláh being very kind to him as a child in Baghdád; he asked that the Master would permit him to come to visit Him.
He, himself, told the writer in Haifa in 1922 of the great joy it gave to come into the presence of the Master, after fifty-three years!
"All the bitterness of my life was turned into sweetness," said Mírzá Aḥmad.
"How glad you must be that you came in time to see the Master."
"Indeed yes, I used to wonder why the families should be separated through (as I thought) a difference in the Teaching."
"When did you become aware of the truth of the matter?"
"Not until my nephew told me."
"How did your nephew know?"
"It was in this wise: My nephew was engaged in the Censor's

office during the war. He came across many letters concerning 'Abbás Effendi, and began to realize something of His station from the reverent wording of the letters addressed to Him.

"It was with great joy that my nephew realized, in the person of this wonderful and holy Personage, the cousin of his father. When the Master's letter came, in answer to one of my nephew, he brought it to me to translate, he not being able to read the Persian language.

"By this letter I began to understand the truth and to deplore the ignorance in which I had lived for so long.

"I lived in Constantinople for fifteen years engaged in banking work.

"I did not frequent the society of Persians, for I knew they would shun me because I was the son of Ṣubḥ-i-Azal, the half-brother of Bahá'u'lláh.

"My father had the unfortunate habit of frequently marrying!"

VARIOUS DOCUMENTS

THE STORY OF SHAYKH MAḤMÚD
TOLD BY HIS GRANDDAUGHTER, NOW LIVING IN 'AKKÁ, 1922

The following story had an atmosphere of its own, spoken in Arabic, by a sweet-faced woman with a beautiful voice fraught with enthusiasm and sincerity, as she was sitting on the floor, near the feet of Munírih Khánum, the wife of 'Abdu'l-Bahá. Listening to the translation by Munavvar Khánum, as the pictures were unfolded scene by scene, that morning, at the house of the Beloved Master, the occasion was one of those experiences most deeply engraved on my mind as I wrote the following:

It was the time of Ramaḍán in the year 1850. The Shaykh and his family had fasted until sundown. Then they had their accustomed meal. When they had finished, my grandfather, then a little boy, cried out "Look! Look! The sun is risen again, the sun has come back!"

The whole family stood looking at the western sky, where a brilliant gleam was shining. It seemed to them miraculous, after the darkness which was there when they sat down to break their fast.

My great-grandfather hurried to consult an old Shaykh who was a much-revered friend. In a state of great distress he related to his friend the episode of the seeming return of the sun, being full of anxiety lest he and his family should have broken the law which requires them to fast until the setting of the sun.

The aged Shaykh made answer:

"You have not broken the law, but a terrible crime has this day been committed in a far-off city of Persia; they have murdered the Mihdí, for whom we have been waiting, who has come to herald the coming of the 'Great One' into this mortal world in fulfilment of the prophecies!

"Oh, the miserable blindness of man! How can such things be?"

On the next day the old Shaykh came to see my great-

239

grandfather. He called the young son (my grandfather, Shaykh Mahmúd) and said to him:

"Hearken unto me, my child:

"Unto this city of 'Akká will come one day the 'Great One,' He will abide in a high house with many, many steps. His sustenance will be provided by the Government (i.e., a prisoner). Now thou wilt be here, in this city, when He cometh. I and thy father will have passed from this mortal world, but mark well what I now say unto thee:

"We charge thee to deliver the salutation of our hearts' devoted worship unto Him, mine and thy father's."

My grandfather, Shaykh Mahmúd, told us that, although still a child, his father and his friend, the old Shaykh, spoke often to him, charging him to keep this, their command, ever in his mind, and to obey "when the time should have come."

Meanwhile, after many days had gone by, the terrible tidings came to us that, on the day of the episode of the return gleam of the sun, His Holiness the Báb had been shot to death in the market-place of Tabríz in Persia.

Time flowed on. The old Shaykh and my great-grandfather, Shaykh Qásim 'Arabí, died, and my grandfather, Shaykh Mahmúd, grew up into manhood, being always full of love and devotion to his religion, that of Islám.

In the year 1868, my grandfather was told that a powerful enemy of Islám had been brought to 'Akká, where he was imprisoned in a little room at the top of a high-flight of steps. My grandfather thought it was his duty to kill such an enemy of his beloved religion.

Accordingly, he armed himself with a weapon secretly hidden beneath his *'abá* (cloak).

He then requested to be permitted to speak with the Prisoner. The reply came:

"Thou hast permission to approach when thou shalt have cast away thy weapon!"

Shaykh Mahmúd was greatly astonished at the mention of the weapon, of which he had spoken to nobody.

My grandfather then said within himself, "I am a strong man, I am able to kill this enemy by the strength of my hands, without the aid of a weapon."

Again he sent his request to be received by the Prisoner. To which the reply came:

"When thou shalt have purified thy heart, then thou mayest come."

Again my grandfather more greatly marvelled.

Then a dream came. The old Shaykh and his father appeared to Shaykh Maḥmúd and thus spoke to him:

"Go to the gathering-place of the friends of this Prisoner and say unto them:

"Alláh-u-Abhá.

"They will take no heed of thee at first, then say a second time:

"Alláh-u-Abhá.

"Still they will ignore thee.

"Then cry aloud for the third time:

"Alláh-u-Abhá.

"Now one will question thee: 'What meanest thou by this word?' Then shalt thou speak of our charge unto thee, years ago, to deliver the salutations of our hearts' devoted worship."

As he heard these words, the eyes of my grandfather, Shaykh Maḥmúd, were opened, and he remembered all that the old Shaykh and his own father, Shaykh Qásim 'Arabí, had said to him of the "Great One" Who should come, even to 'Akká, and how He should abide in a tall dwelling at the top of a long flight of steps.

My grandfather sought out the gathering-together place of the friends of the Prisoner, the "Most Great Prisoner"; he was allowed to enter, and all things took place in accordance with the command given in his dream.

The one Who said to him: "What meanest thou by this word, Alláh-u-Abhá?" was our beloved Master, 'Abdu'l-Bahá, through Whom my grandfather, Shaykh Maḥmúd, was permitted to deliver the salutation of their hearts' devoted worship, the old Shaykhs' and that of my great-grandfather, Shaykh Qásim 'Arabí. And my grandfather, Shaykh Maḥmúd, believed, and all his family.

(Written down by Sitárih Khánum (Lady Blomfield), 7th January, 1922. Mansion of 'Abdu'l-Bahá, Haifa, Palestine.)

The Famous Red Robe "Tradition"*

It is related that an account is given of an Indian Muslim, a holy man of the eighth century, A.D., who, speaking of the "Great Day of God" to come, uttered these words:
"In that day the Holy One will be found abiding in a land called Karkh. He will walk beside the river, wearing the dervish turban, and wrapped in a *red robe*. He will be teaching His followers on the banks of the river. Would that I might be privileged to enter His Presence, and to shed my life-blood in His Path."

The red robe which Bahá'u'lláh wore when He was teaching His followers on the banks of the River Tigris was made of some pieces of Persian tirmih. The wife and daughter of Bahá'u'lláh fashioned this *'abá* in readiness for His return from the mountain land of Sulaymáníyyih. Karkh is the name of the district of Baghdád in which the Holy One dwelt.

---

* See page 53.

VARIOUS DOCUMENTS

NOTES ON THE BAGHDÁD PERIOD

During the sojourn of Bahá'u'lláh in the desert mountain places of Sulaymáníyyih, the Ṣúfís of those districts, with a profound reverence for Him Whom they knew as the "Nameless One, Who has magnetized the land with His love," came to Him with their problems, craving for His explanations.
Bahá'u'lláh thus speaks of the time in the wilderness retreat:
"*We took our departure . . . to deserts of solitude, and spent two years in the wilderness of isolation. Many a night we were destitute of food, and many a day the body found no rest.*
"*Notwithstanding these showering afflictions and successive calamities . . . we continued in perfect happiness and exceeding joy.*"

When He was about to depart from the neighbourhood, these mystical people were disconsolate, and begged to know when and where they should see Him again.
"I go to Baghdád," Bahá'u'lláh told them. "There you may find me."
Accordingly, later on, having discovered His abode, one of these Ṣúfís came to ask Him to describe "the journey of man towards his Creator."
Thereupon Bahá'u'lláh wrote *The Seven Valleys*.
In that remarkable work He sets forth the lands through which a pilgrim must travel before reaching his destination, which is the "Recognition of the Manifestation of God."
Hasan Balyuzi describes *The Seven Valleys* as "a gem of mystical prose, unsurpassed in its beauty, simplicity, and profundity."
Whilst in exile in Baghdád, Bahá'u'lláh unsealed *The Hidden Words*.
After His return from the mountain land of Sulaymáníyyih, walking on the bank of the river Tigris, or sheltering in the hut built by His devoted friends, clad in the red garment of

prophecy Jamál-i-Mubárak, the Blessed Beauty, spoke thus of *The Hidden Words*:

"*This is that which hath descended from the realm of glory, uttered by the tongue of power and might, and revealed unto the Prophets of old. We have taken the inner essence thereof, and clothed it in the garment of brevity, as a token of grace unto the righteous, that they may stand faithful unto the Covenant of God, may fulfil in their lives His trust, and in the realm of the spirit obtain the gem of Divine virtue.*"

In *The Hidden Words* we have the true unchangeable heart of all religion, the Voice of the Creator of all things visible and invisible, telling of the Beginning:

"*O Son of Man!*

"*Veiled in My immemorial being and in the ancient eternity of My essence, I knew My love for thee; therefore I created thee, engraved on thee Mine image, and revealed to thee My beauty.*"

Thus the Voice calls upon us:

"*I loved thy creation, hence I created thee. Wherefore, do thou love Me, that I may name thy name, and fill thy soul with the spirit of life.*"

It is Love, Love always; but we must do our part. The Voice commands:

"*Love Me, that I may love thee. If thou lovest Me not, My love can in no wise reach thee. Know this, O Servant!*"

Doing our part, our destiny is assured:

"*Thy Paradise is My love; thy heavenly home, reunion with Me. Enter therein and tarry not. This is that which hath been destined for thee in Our kingdom above, and Our exalted Dominion.*"

Beauty is our inheritance:

"*Abandon not the everlasting Beauty for a beauty that must die. . . .*"

"*O Son of Man!*

"*Rejoice in the gladness of thine heart, that thou mayest be worthy to meet Me and to mirror forth My beauty.*

"*Neglect not My commandments if thou lovest My beauty.*"

Death has no power over us:

"*I have made death a messenger of joy to thee.*

"*Wherefore dost thou grieve? I made the light to shed on thee its splendour. Why dost thou veil thyself therefrom?*

"*The gates that open on the placeless stand wide. . . .*

"*O Son of Man! Thou art My dominion, and My dominion perisheth not, wherefore fearest thou thy perishing? Thou art My light, My light* shall never be put out, why dost thou dread thine extinction? Thou art My glory, and My glory fadeth not; thou art My robe, My robe shall never be outworn. Abide therefore in thy love for Me. That thou mayest find Me in the realm of glory.

"My calamity is My providence, outwardly it is fire and vengeance, but inwardly it is light and mercy."

Our rest and peace are in God alone:

"O Son of Man!

"Wert thou to speed through the immensity of space and traverse the expanse of heaven, yet thou shouldst find no rest save in submission to Our command and humbleness before Our Face.

"O Son of Spirit!

"There is no peace for thee, save by renouncing thyself and turning unto Me; for it behoveth thee to glory in My name, not in thine own; to put thy trust in Me and not in thyself, since I desire to be loved alone and above all that is.

"O Son of Glory!

"Be swift in the path of holiness, and enter the heaven of communion with Me. Cleanse thine heart with the burnish of the spirit, and hasten to the court of the Most High."

THE "KITÁB-I-ÍQÁN"

It was during the Baghdád period that the *Kitáb-i-Íqán*, the *Book of Certitude*, was written by Bahá'u'lláh. It is one of the most important of all the Writings. In it, Bahá'u'lláh "unseals the Book" and discloses the true meaning of the symbolism and allegory of past Scriptures.

"*This servant will now share with thee a dewdrop out of the fathomless ocean of the truths treasured in these holy words, that haply discerning hearts may comprehend all the allusions and the implications of the utterances of the Manifestations of Holiness. . . .*"

The second part of the *Kitáb-i-Íqán* is an exposition of the station and nature of the Manifestation of God, that Mysterious Being Who, at various times, and under different Names, restores vigour to the dead body of religion and reveals the Truth in progressive measure to the evolving consciousness of mankind.

"*The door of the knowledge of the Ancient of Days being thus closed in the face of all beings, the Source of infinite grace . . . hath caused those luminous Gems of Holiness to appear out of the realm of the spirit, in the noble form of the human temple, and be made manifest unto all men, that they may impart unto the world the mysteries of the unchangeable Being, and tell of the subtleties of His imperishable Essence. These sanctified Mirrors, these Day-springs of ancient glory are one and all the Exponents on earth of Him Who is the central Orb of the universe, its Essence and ultimate Purpose. From Him proceed their knowledge and power; from Him is derived their sovereignty. The beauty of their countenance is but a reflection of His image, and their revelation a sign of His deathless glory. They are the Treasuries of divine knowledge, and the Repositories of celestial wisdom. Through them is transmitted a grace that is infinite, and by them is revealed the light that can never fade. Even as He hath said: "There is no distinction whatsoever between Thee and Them; except that they are Thy servants, and are created of Thee." This is the significance of the tradition: "I am He, Himself, and He is I, myself."*

We have the privilege of reading this book in the beautiful translation of the Guardian of the Bahá'í Faith, Shoghi Effendi.

VARIOUS DOCUMENTS

FROM MEMORIES OF NABÍL*

When I was transferred from the Cairo prison to that of Alexandria, the late Siyyid Ḥusayn appealed to Sharíf Páshá on my behalf, protesting that I, being an Ottoman subject, was wrongfully imprisoned by order of the Persian Consular authorities (who possessed no authority over me). I was straightway removed from the lower story of the prison to the higher floor, where there was purer air.
At the same time the Consul was questioned concerning my case.
In this prison I made the acquaintance of M. Fáris, a Christian doctor.
He tried to convert me to Christianity, and I endeavoured to make him into a Bahá'í; in this, I at length succeeded.
It came to pass that when I was in the Cairo prison, I dreamed a dream: "His Holiness Bahá'u'lláh promised me, that after eighty-one days, the hardships under which I was suffering would be at an end."
Now the very day that I was removed from the lower to the upper story of the prison was the eighty-first day after my dream.
Towards the sunset hour I went up on to the roof of the prison, where I amused myself by watching those who passed by.
To my amazement I saw, amongst those people, Áqá Muḥammad Ibráhím, who was one of the servitors of His Holiness Bahá'u'lláh.
He had landed, with an escort, to buy some necessary provisions for the continued voyage. I called out to him "Come up, come up."
He was able to persuade his guard to permit him to come up to me on the roof, the guard escort accompanying him.
Áqá Muḥammad Ibráhím told me that His Holiness Bahá'u'lláh, His family, and His attendants had been once

---
* Historian of the Bahá'í Faith; author of "The Dawnbreakers."

247

more exiled. This time their destination was the castle fortress in the city of 'Akká, and now they were on their way to that prison.

This servitor was not permitted to speak any more, but he promised me, ere he was hurried away, that on his return to the steamer, he would mention my name in the Holy Presence.

I was greatly agitated by this episode.

After a few minutes Dr. Fáris found me in a very disturbed state of mind.

I had previously related my Cairo dream to him, and he now said:

"To-day is the eighty-first day after your dream, and instead of being happy you are more miserable than ever. Why is that?"

I told him what had happened, that the Beloved of my heart was in that steamer and I had no means of gaining access to His Holy Presence!

The doctor then became as gloomy as myself.

"Had it not been that to-morrow is Friday," he said, "I should have been able to plan some means by which we both could go on board that ship and have the joy of seeing His blessed face."

Doctor Fáris said: "Write quickly what you wish to say to Him, and I will endeavour to have your letter, with mine also, taken on board early in the morning to the Blessed Beauty. I know a young man, a watchmaker, who is a Christian—he will doubtless render this service to us."

That night neither the doctor nor myself could sleep.

Early next morning we went up on to the roof to watch the ship, which was visible from our prison. After two hours we heard the whistle of the boat, and the steamer had started.

We trembled as we saw her steaming away, and were full of sorrow that Constantine had not succeeded in doing that great favour for us.

Again we saw the boat stop for a few minutes, then, alas! she started anew.

I cannot describe the turmoil of our minds and the excruciating agony of uncertainty and of expectation in those few hours until the return of Constantine, the young Christian man, who had undertaken to deliver our message to His Holiness, our Beloved.

The young man, however, came towards us with a packet in his hand.

As he handed it to us, he cried:

"By Heaven, I have seen the Father of Christ."

Doctor Fáris, in an ecstasy with tears streaming down his face, seized Constantine and kissed both his eyes, those eyes which had seen the "Beloved."

"O young man, ours was the burning desire, the longing, and the pain of separation. Yours was the bounty and the grace of entering the Presence of the Blessed Beauty."

The packet consisted of a handkerchief which contained a Tablet, written by Bahá'u'lláh's own hand, addressed to me, an epistle from the Greatest Branch, 'Abdu'l-Bahá, and a package of sweetmeats sent by the Purest Branch.

In the Tablet, which was addressed to "Nabíl," was also written the reply to the appeal of Dr. Fáris. Bahá'u'lláh assured the doctor "that he would very soon be released from the prison, in spite of the ill-wishes of his enemies."

According to the promise of Bahá'u'lláh, the doctor was set free on the third day.

He became a devout believer, and began to spread the Holy Cause among the Christians.

One of the attendants wrote a short letter to us describing how Constantine had without any difficulty succeeded in gaining admission to the Holy Presence, when he was able to present our petitions.

Immediately Bahá'u'lláh revealed the Tablet in answer to those petitions.

He sent for the messenger and, pouring forth divine loving-kindness upon him, entrusted into his hands the Tablet.

After a while I, Nabíl, was summoned to the Governor of the prison, who ordered me to begone, and to leave Alexandria, for, he said, my presence in the country created disorder and rebellion.

The Azalís in 'Akká

The high claims of Ṣubḥ-i-Azal have already been explained and their absurdity shown.

Nevertheless his mischievous intrigues continued to harass the band of exiles in 'Akká.

Ṣubḥ-i-Azal, with the few who elected to follow him, was sent to Cyprus when the exiles came to 'Akká; two or three of the Bahá'í friends were ordered to proceed to Cyprus with that party, and three Azalís were told off to live in 'Akká with the Bahá'ís. These three, Siyyid Muḥammad, Riḍá-Qulí, and Áqá-Ján, continuing the Azalí tactics, caused trouble from the first days of danger and difficulty.

The Muḥammadan population of 'Akká, being of the Sunní division of Islám, had no love for the Shí'ah world, the other chief Muslims. There was a feud between these two communities.

This dislike was seized upon by the Azalís as a great help in their intrigues against the Bahá'ís.

They, obtaining some Tablets of Bahá'u'lláh, altered some of the words, entirely perverting the meaning, thereby making it appear to support their accusation that Bahá'u'lláh was a fanatical Shí'ite and a bitter enemy of the Sunnís.

These enemies posed as devoted Sunnís, telling the already suspicious mullás that "We used to be Bábís, but now we are better informed of the truth of religion, we desire to become Sunní Muslims. We are no friends of Bahá'u'lláh, who is your deadly enemy. These Bábís are spies, and are always plotting against the true religion! The pilgrims who come from Persia are in reality fanatic Shí'ites, for ever working against the Sunnís."

They, the Azalís, being spies and full of cunning, sometimes were able to lay their hands upon Tablets revealed by Bahá'u'lláh; for this reason the names of the recipients were often omitted, as formerly in the case of the Báb, to avoid danger to the friends.

Another plan was to watch for pilgrims arriving from Persia;

they would hasten to give information to the Governor, with lists of false accusations against these innocent, devoted, and very tired Bahá'í friends, who would often be arrested, and rigorously treated.

Altogether these Azalís continued to create an atmosphere of suspicion and distrust, as harsh and uncomprehending as unwarrantable.

Several of the devoted Bahá'ís decided that these stirrers-up of mischief should be silenced.

No more should these traitors bring trouble and persecution and added hardships upon their Beloved One and the friends.

"If these spies and traitors kill us, then we shall have sacrificed our lives to protect the Holy Ones. If we kill them we shall have delivered the Bahá'ís from their most pernicious enemies. Bahá'u'lláh will excommunicate us—that is terrible! We shall then have sacrificed our souls! But this evil *shall* be destroyed! It *shall* be destroyed!"

In pursuance of their solemn determination they went to the house where the Azalís lived—called upon them to give up their wickedness. They refused.

"Then you must be killed," sternly said the Bahá'ís!

There was a fierce fight, and the three Azalís were killed.

The avengers gave themselves up to the authorities, who were full of perplexity, thinking it highly improbable that either Bahá'u'lláh or the Master would instigate such a crime.

But the people caused a great turmoil, being incited by such fanatics as were enemies of the Bahá'ís.

They were encouraged to believe that it was a case of Sunní *versus* Shí'ah, that the Shí'ites, amongst whom they counted all the exiles, from Bahá'u'lláh down to the humblest of the friends, had conspired to kill three Sunnís, because of their devotion to their religion. The tumult was violent. The people rushed towards Bahá'u'lláh's house, yelling with rage!

Bahá'u'lláh, in a letter to a friend in Persia, tells how one day, sitting in His room in the "little house," engaged in dictating Tablets to His amanuensis, sounds of a violent commotion were heard.

The Governor, a company of soldiers with drawn swords,

and a crowd of people shouting and yelling, were outside the house. The Master was in the Bírúní (reception room) on the opposite side of the street.

Hearing the turmoil, he came out. The Governor was calling to Bahá'u'lláh to come down.

With much difficulty the Master got through the crowd, which was growing denser and denser, and said to Bahá'u'lláh: "The Governor is summoning you and me to come down to him. I know not why. Something must have happened."

They were both taken to the Governor's room at the Court House.

The officials present rose respectfully and conducted them to seats of honour.

The Governor and his officials were excitedly talking together. The former came to Bahá'u'lláh and the Master, saying: "You will be more comfortable in another room whilst our consultation takes place."

They were accordingly conducted into the next room. Here they found a number of the Bahá'ís, who had also been arrested.

In this room they were detained for five hours.

During this time, a secretary tells us, the dictation of the Tablets, interrupted by the arrest, was continued.

About one o'clock in the morning the friends were taken to the horrible town prison.

At a later date I visited this prison. It is a vault-like, long, low room, very damp, with slime-covered walls and sticky mud floor. There is no light except that coming through the door when it is open, and the glimmer of a small lantern.

Across the end of the door is a stone seat; on this the jailer sat with a brutal scourge of thongs, weighted with lead, in his hand, ready for use on the slightest provocation, for instance, if a prisoner coughed too persistently, or spoke, or complained.

The prisoners, often too numerous to be able to lie down, were herded together in torturing, ghastly, unrestful misery, their chains eating into their flesh, causing excruciating agony as they and those to whom they were chained writhed in their wretchedness upon the filth of the floor—there were no beds. Sometimes a poor fellow, unable to bear his anguish any longer, would go mad and shriek out. The jailer would then stride to him, trampling on the bodies of those who were in his path, and ruthlessly beat him till he lay still, or, as often happened, he died. When he, the jailer, felt inclined, he would unchain him from those to whom he was fettered, drag the pitifully bruised and mutilated body to the door, and cast it out into the prison yard.

I cannot describe the expressions on the faces of the Greatest Holy Leaf, the dear Holy Mother, and the daughters of the Master, as they stood in this abode of horror. It was surely one of the most agonizing landmarks of all their memories of the miseries heaped year after year upon their Beloved Ones, Who were spending their lives for that humanity which, unworthy as it was, despised and tortured and scorned Them, and whom these Great Ones loved in spite of all, praying without ceasing for their pardon.

The old man, Áqá Ḥusayn-i-Áshchí, who went with us when we visited this prison, was one of those Bahá'ís who had been imprisoned here at the time of the Azalí affair; he was, therefore, well qualified to describe the conditions of the time and place.

Into this evil dungeon the Master was cast, whilst Bahá'u'lláh was confined in a room on the upper floor.

The next night a telegram arrived from the chief Válí (Governor) of Syria who was in Damascus, ordering that Bahá'u'lláh should be removed from the prison to an upper room, where He remained for thirty-eight hours.

The Master, all this time, was kept in the horror of the prison in chains!

On the third day Bahá'u'lláh was again taken to the Court House to be interrogated.

When He came into the assembly, He said:

"You obey your own law, and disregard the Law of God. Why have you not understood?"

The Governor said:

"Will you excuse me if I ask you some questions? We are compelled to do so. Otherwise we should be ourselves reprimanded. What is your name, and from what country do you come?"

Bahá'u'lláh replied:

"You will find my description in your records. Read them and you will know who I am."

"Nay, but we wish that you should tell us your name, and from what country you come."

"My name is Bahá'u'lláh, and my country is Núr."

"Why are you gathered together? If it be your wish to find occasion against me whereby to take my life, my desire is as your desire. When I pass a tree, I say 'Would that thou wert a cross, Oh, tree! and that I were nailed upon thee.' If only you could understand, I would make you hear the melody of the nightingale, who is chanting on a branch of the tree of the Lord, then would it become manifest to you that Servitude is the Essence of Worship."

The Governor said:

"Now we know that the accusation is false, therefore thou shalt be set free to return to thine own house."

"I should prefer to go back to my prison and abide with my friends until the time of their release."

"We cannot set them free," said the Governor, "because of the turmoil of the people; they must remain yet a few more days."

Bahá'u'lláh therefore returned to His house.

But the Master was left in the prison!

To Him, officials came demanding keys, saying:

"We must search the house for weapons."

The Master said:

"There are ladies there alone; you must take me with you."

They did not object, but took Him through the streets with chains on His neck and on His feet.

He held His '*abá* close, as He went into His mother's room, that she might not see the chains, but they could not be hidden from her loving eyes; she saw them and wept bitterly.

When no weapons were found, the Master explained to the officials how the tragic occurrence came to take place, and, when they understood, the Master was set free.

The men who had been concerned in the affray were tried by the court and sentenced to varying periods of imprisonment.

After a short time further investigations were made; the authorities found out what disturbers of the peace those men, the Azalís, were, and what great provocation the prisoners had endured; therefore because of these extenuating circumstances, the length of the sentences was shortened.

Such was the end of the malicious plotting of the Azalís at 'Akká.

(In another part of her manuscript, Lady Blomfield has the following account of this incident, with the notation: "Told by Ṭúbá Khánum"; evidently when she visited this prison in company with the ladies of the Family.—ED.)

When the Master was told, whilst here in this terrible place, that His house was to be searched, He said:

"I will go with you. You may search freely, but I go with you, that the ladies be not frightened."

The officials seemed too astonished by the authority in His voice to make any objection.

So our Beloved came to us, bearing still those heavy chains. He walked, thus manacled, through the streets of 'Akká.

When He came to His mother's room, He hid the chains under His 'abá, but she and I saw them, and our hearts were so sore that, weeping bitterly, we felt that we could bear no more.

He cheered us, telling us that He would very soon be with us again. He left us, and this is the place to which He returned. His very heart was wounded as He saw the intolerable sufferings of the prisoners. These poor, ignorant children of God! Not a word of His own sufferings, but: "Oh, the prisoners! Surely of all the sorrowful sons of men, the most unhappy, the most hopeless!"

* * *

How often, in the years that were to come, did the Master intercede for prisoners, obtaining at least some amelioration of their condition; again, as frequently happened, He instituted enquiries which resulted in release or shortening of the sentence, according to the facts elicited by the investigations set on foot by Him. The Master spared Himself no trouble, and rested not day nor night whilst any hope remained for these pitifully helpless victims, as they sometimes proved to be, of ill-organized law administration or of a harsh and ruthless officialdom.

SOME UTTERANCES OF 'ABDU'L-BAHÁ CONCERNING
BAHÁ'U'LLÁH

(Table talk at Abú-Sinán during the sojourn in the war days.)

One day in Baghdád He called all His friends together and spoke to them of God. Then He departed from them alone. Nobody knew just where He was. Even we were not informed. Two years passed.

Some of the time He dwelt in the mountains, again He sheltered in grottoes, and part of the time He abode in the city of Sulaymáníyyih.

Though solitary and alone, and nobody knew Him, yet all through Kurdistán it was spread abroad in the ears of all men that "This unnamed person is the most remarkable personage in the land.

"He is exceedingly well learned.

"He is possessed of a great power.

"He has a colossal, powerful attraction, and all Kurdistán is magnetized by His Love."

But Bahá'u'lláh passed all this time in poverty, even His robes and clothes were of the poor. He ate the poor food of the indigent.

The radiance of Majesty, compelling reverence, was manifested from Him as from the sun at noonday, therefore He was so greatly reverenced in this life.

Then He left Kurdistán and arrived at home in Baghdád.

The Kurds came from Sulaymáníyyih to visit Him, and found Him in great comfort, and they were astonished at the appointments, and all they saw of His surroundings, after coming from the seclusion and poverty of His life in Kurdistán.

They were exceedingly amazed at the difference of condition.

In short, the Government of Persia thought and hoped that the banishment of Bahá'u'lláh, the Blessed Perfection, from the kingdom of Persia would be the means of exterminating the Cause in the land.

Then they perceived that the Cause spread more and more rapidly. The fame became more widely circulated. The Teachings of the Blessed Perfection became more pronounced. Then the Chief of Persia determined to expel Bahá'u'lláh from Baghdád.

He arrived in Constantinople.

Whilst in Constantinople He was regardless of any custom. He paid no attention to the ministers nor to the clergy.

Then the Persian ministers succeeded in having Him banished from Constantinople—desiring to have Him kept at a great distance from Persia.

So His giving out of His Teaching had to be in secret.

In spite of all, the Cause still spread.

Then they said:

"We, indeed, are endeavouring to banish Bahá'u'lláh from place to place, but each time the Cause is more spread abroad, and His proclamation is more widely circulated through the lands, and day by day His Lamp is shining with a brighter Light. The potency of His Cause is waxing more and more strong. The reason of this daily increasing power and knowledge of the Cause is that He has been sent to cities of so large a population; therefore it would be better to send Him to a' penal colony, so that He may be considered as a suspect; so that all people may know that He is amongst criminals; that He is in the prison of murderers, of robbers, and other law-breakers; so that in a short time He and His followers may perish."

Therefore the Sháh of Persia persuaded 'Abdu'l-'Azíz to have Him banished to the prison of 'Akká.

When Bahá'u'lláh arrived at the prison of 'Akká, through the power of God, He was enabled to hoist His banner. It was at first a star.

It became a mighty sun.

The fame of the Cause of the Blessed Perfection went far and wide, into distant lands of the East and of the West.

From this prison, from within its walls, He wrote epistles to all the kings. He summoned them to arbitration and the Most Great Peace.

Some of the sovereigns received this summons with haughty pride. One of these was the Ottoman King, another the French

Emperor; the latter sent no reply; then another epistle was addressed to Napoleon III stating: "I have already sent you an epistle, summoning you to the Cause, but you heeded it not. You once proclaimed that you were the defender of the oppressed, now it became evident that this is no true claim. You are not a protector of your own distressed and oppressed people. You are devoted to your own interests; and this pride of yours, which is supported by your commands, must be overthrown.

"Because of this arrogance of yours, therefore, in a short time God will destroy your sovereignty.

"France will fall away from you, and will be vanquished by a great conquest.

"[On] the banks of its rivers will be places of lamentation and mourning.

"The women of France will weep and bemoan the loss of their sons."

Such was the arraignment which was sent, and it has been published and spread abroad.

Were you to read that epistle, you would perceive what an arraignment it is!

Now consider:

One prisoner, single and solitary, with no assistant, neither protector, moreover a foreigner, a stranger, imprisoned in the fortress of 'Akká, writing such epistles to kings! Writing such an epistle to the Sultán of Turkey, whilst He was a prisoner in 'Akká!

Bahá'u'lláh hoisted His banner within the walls of that prison.

Refer to all history. It has no parallel! No such event has ever taken place before. That a stranger, alone and a prisoner, has succeeded in advancing His Cause, and been enabled to spread broadcast His Teachings, so that, eventually, He was powerful enough to conquer the very king who banished Him.

His Cause continued to spread.

The Blessed Perfection was for twenty-five years in that prison. During all this time He was subjected to the persecutions of the people. He underwent the sorrow of the atrocities and banishments of the people of Persia.

You may learn how they pillaged His property in Persia. How they chained Him in prison. How they banished Him from Persia to Baghdád. How a second time He was banished from Baghdád to Constantinople. A third banishment was from Constantinople to Roumelia (Adrianople).

A fourth time was He banished, from Roumelia to the Most Great Prison.

During all His lifetime He had no moment's rest! He did not pass one night in restful sleep for His body!

He bore all these ordeals and catastrophes and difficulties in order that, in the world of humanity, a selflessness might become apparent.

In order that the Most Great Peace might become a reality in the world of humanity.

In order that waiting souls might become manifest as the very angels of Heaven.

In order that Heavenly miracles might become perfected among men.

In order that the faith of humanity might become adequate.

In order that the priceless, precious bestowal of God in the human temple, the Mind of humanity, might develop to its fullest capacity.

In order that infants may be (in truth) likenesses of God, even as it has been written in the Bible:

"We shall create men in Our Own Image."

Bahá'u'lláh bore all these ordeals and catastrophes for this:

That our hearts might be illumined.

That our spirits might become glad.

That our imperfections might be replaced by virtues.

That our ignorance might be transformed into knowledge.

In order that we might acquire the fruits of humanity and obtain Heavenly graces.

Although we are now on earth, let us walk [travel] in the Kingdom.

Although we are needy, let us plead for Heavenly treasure.

For these bounties to us has the Blessed Perfection borne so great difficulties.

Trust all to God.
The Light of God is resplendent.
The Blessed Epistles are spreading.

You will shortly see that the Heavenly Teachings have begun, that the Oneness of the World of Humanity is becoming a glorious Reality!

The Blessed Teachings are being spread in the East and in the West.

The Banner of the Most Great Peace has been unfurled, and the great Community of the Kingdom of God is at hand.

THE WORLD RELIGION

*A Summary of Its Aims, Teachings, and History
Written in answer to an inquirer*

by

SHOGHI EFFENDI

Guardian of the Bahá'í Faith

THE Revelation proclaimed by Bahá'u'lláh, His followers believe, is divine in origin, all-embracing in scope, broad in its outlook, scientific in its method, humanitarian in its principles, and dynamic in the influence it exerts on the hearts and minds of men. The mission of the Founder of their Faith, they conceive it to be to proclaim that religious truth is not absolute but relative, that Divine Revelation is continuous and progressive, that the Founders of all past religions, though different in the non-essential aspects of their teachings, "abide in the same Tabernacle, soar in the same heaven, are seated upon the same throne, utter the same speech, and proclaim the same Faith." His Cause, they have already demonstrated, stands identified with, and revolves around, the principle of the organic unity of mankind as representing the consummation of the whole process of human evolution. This final stage in this stupendous evolution, they assert, is not only necessary but inevitable, that it is gradually approaching, and that nothing short of the celestial potency with which a divinely ordained Message can claim to be endowed can succeed in establishing it.

The Bahá'í Faith recognizes the unity of God and of His Prophets, upholds the principle of an unfettered search after truth, condemns all forms of superstition and prejudice, teaches that the fundamental purpose of religion is to promote concord and harmony, that it must go hand-in-hand with science, and that it constitutes the sole and ultimate basis of a peaceful, an ordered and progressive society. It inculcates the principle of equal opportunity, rights, and privileges for both sexes, advocates compulsory education, abolishes extremes of poverty and wealth, exalts work performed in the spirit of service to the rank of worship, recommends the adoption of an auxiliary international language, and provides the necessary agencies for the establishment and safeguarding of a permanent and universal peace.

Born about the middle of the nineteenth century in darkest Persia, assailed from its infancy by the forces of religious fanaticism, the Faith has, notwithstanding the martyrdom of its Forerunner, the repeated banishments of its Founder, the almost life-long imprisonment of its chief Promoter, and the cruel death of no less than twenty thousand of its devoted followers, succeeded in diffusing quietly and steadily its spirit throughout both the East and the West, has established itself in no fewer than forty countries of the world, and has recently obtained from the ecclesiastical and civil authorities in various lands written affirmations that recognize its independent religious status.

The Forerunner of the Faith was Mírzá 'Alí-Muḥammad of Shíráz, known as the Báb (The Gate) Who proclaimed on 23rd May, 1844, His twofold mission as an independent Manifestation of God and Herald of One greater than Himself, Who would inaugurate a new and unprecedented era in the religious history of mankind. On His early life, His sufferings, the heroism of His disciples, and the circumstances of His tragic martyrdom I need not dwell, as the record of His saintly life is minutely set forth in *The Dawn-Breakers: Nabíl's Narrative of the Early Days of the Bahá'í Faith*. Suffice it to say that at the early age of thirty-one the Báb was publicly martyred by a military firing squad at Tabríz, Persia, on 9th July, 1850. On the evening of that same day His mangled body was removed from the courtyard of the barracks to the edge of the moat outside the gate of the city, whence it was carried by His fervent disciples to Ṭihrán. There it remained concealed until such time as its transfer to the Holy Land was made possible. Faced by almost insuperable difficulties and facing the gravest dangers a band of His disciples, acting under the instructions of 'Abdu'l-Bahá, succeeded in transporting overland the casket containing His remains to Haifa. In 1909 'Abdu'l-Bahá, with his own hands and in the presence of the assembled representatives of various Bahá'í communities, deposited those remains within the vault of the Mausoleum he himself had erected for the Báb. Ever since that time countless followers of the Bahá'í Faith have made the pilgrimage to this sacred spot, a spot which ever since 1921 has been further sanctified by the burial of 'Abdu'l-Bahá in an adjoining vault.

The Founder of the Faith was Bahá'u'lláh (Glory of God), Whose advent the Báb had foretold. He declared His mission in 1863 while an exile in Baghdád. He subsequently formulated the principles of that new and divine civilization which by His advent He claimed to have inaugurated. He, too, was bitterly opposed, was stripped of His property and rights, was exiled to 'Iraq, to Constantinople and Adrianople, and was eventually incarcerated in the penal colony of 'Akká, where He passed away in 1892 in His seventy-fifth year. His remains are laid to rest in the Shrine at Bahjí, north of 'Akká.

The authorized Interpreter and Exemplar of Bahá'u'lláh's teachings was His eldest son 'Abdu'l-Bahá (Servant of Bahá) who was appointed by his Father as the Centre to whom all Bahá'ís should turn for instruction and guidance. 'Abdu'l-Bahá ever since his childhood was the closest companion of his Father, and shared all His sorrows and sufferings. He remained a prisoner until 1908, when the old régime in Turkey was overthrown and all religious and political prisoners throughout the empire were liberated. After that he continued to make his home in Palestine but undertook extensive teaching tours in Egypt, Europe, and America, being ceaselessly engaged in explaining and exemplifying the principles of his Father's Faith and in inspiring and directing the activities of his friends and followers throughout the world. He passed away in 1921 in Haifa, Palestine, and, as already stated, was buried in a vault contiguous to that of the Báb on Mount Carmel.

According to the provisions of His Will, I, as His eldest grandson, have been appointed as First Guardian of the Bahá'í Faith and Head of the Universal House of Justice which must, in conjunction with me co-ordinate and direct the affairs of the various Bahá'í communities in East and West in accordance with the principles enunciated by Bahá'u'lláh.

The period since 'Abdu'l-Bahá's passing has been characterized by the formation and consolidation of the Local and National Assemblies, the bedrock on which the edifice of the Universal House of Justice is to be erected. There are, according to the latest reports from Tihrán,* over five hundred Local Assemblies already constituted in Persia. Organized Bahá'í communities are to be found in every continent of the globe. National Assemblies have already been formed and are functioning in the United States and Canada, in India and Burma, in Great Britain, in Germany, 'Iráq and Egypt. Such Assemblies are in the process of formation in Persia, Caucasus, Turkestan, and Australia. Local Assemblies and groups have been already established in France, Switzerland and Italy, in the Scandinavian countries, in Austria and the Balkans, in Turkey, Syria, Albania, Abyssinia, China, Japan, Brazil, and South Africa. Christians of various denominations, Muslims of both the Sunni and Shia sects of Islam, Jews, Hindus, Sikhs, Zoroastrians, and Buddhists, have eagerly embraced its truth, have recognized the divine origin and fundamental unity underlying the teachings of all the Founders of past religions, and have unreservedly identified themselves with both the spirit and form of its evolving institutions. All these centres function as the component parts of a single organism, of an entity the spiritual and administrative centre of which lies enshrined in the twin cities of 'Akká and Haifa.

---

* 1934.